# Gender Communication Theories & Analyses

*The book presents some ongoing struggles and tensions in feminist work as researchers and theorists carve niches, expand knowledge, and strive for legitimacy in the academy. . . This is a book to which I am going to return again and again because of its remarkable synthesis of past and present feminist communication work as well as its look toward the future. The examples throughout are vivid and compelling and the primary focus on the performance lens offers much to identity, cultural, and political communication and feminist studies. It is an excellent resource or springboard for future scholarship as well as a riveting and coherent analysis of scholarship that can challenge advanced students in feminist and communication studies courses. My congratulations to Kroløkke and Scott Sørensen for authoring such an interesting and needed book.*

—Patrice M. Buzzanell, Purdue University

*Fresh, sophisticated, and rigorous, Gender Communication Theories and Analyses brings gender and communication studies into the 'third wave' of feminism and the new millennium of communication studies. Kroløkke and Scott Sørensen present an able and insightful guide to the diverse and changing ways that feminist scholars in communication, linguistics, and cultural studies have theorized and researched gender communication as dominance, identity and difference, and performance. The text's innovative format links theory to research methodologies illustrated by case studies of face-to-face and computer-mediated communication. This book offers rich possibilities as a foundational text in advanced courses on gender and communication and as a valuable resource for researchers—we have been waiting for this book.*

—Kristin M. Langellier, University of Maine

# Gender Communication Theories & Analyses

## From Silence to Performance

Charlotte Kroløkke
Anne Scott Sørensen
University of Southern Denmark

**SAGE Publications**
Thousand Oaks ■ London ■ New Delhi

*For information:*

Sage Publications, Inc.
2455 Teller Road
Thousand Oaks, California 91320
E-mail: order@sagepub.com

Sage Publications Ltd
1 Oliver's Yard
55 City Road
London EC1Y 1SP
United Kingdom

Sage Publications India Pvt. Ltd.
B-42, Panchsheel Enclave
Post Box 4109
New Delhi 110 017  India

Printed in the United States of America

**Library of Congress Cataloging-in-Publication Data**

Kroløkke, Charlotte.
Gender communication theories and analyses : from silence to performance /
Charlotte Kroløkke, Anne Scott Sørensen.
    p. cm.
Includes bibliographical references and index.
ISBN 0-7619-2917-7 (cloth) — ISBN 0-7619-2918-5 (pbk.)
    1. Communication—Sex differences. 2. Interpersonal communication.
3. Gender identity. 4. Sex role. I. Sørensen, Ann Scott. II. Title.
P96.S48K76 2006
305.3′01′4—dc22

                                                2005003074

This book is printed on acid-free paper.

05   06   07   08   09   10   9   8   7   6   5   4   3   2   1

| | |
|---|---|
| *Senior Acquisitions Editor:* | Todd R. Armstrong |
| *Senior Editorial Assistant:* | Deya Saoud |
| *Production Editor:* | Kristen Gibson |
| *Copy Editor:* | Carla Freeman |
| *Typesetter:* | C&M Digitals (P) Ltd. |
| *Cover Designer:* | Janet Foulger |

# Contents

# Introduction

L et us start with a story. The following tale illustrates the aim of this book and will raise a discussion of the particular line of argument we want to establish around the issue of gender and communication.

Fadime died in 2002 at the age of 26. She was shot by her father for bringing shame on her family and undermining their honor in the eyes of the Turkish-Muslim community in Sweden. The ensuing debate has brought up a range of difficult issues concerning the recent transformation of the previously rather homogenous Scandinavian countries into multicultural societies: a diversification of ethnicity, language, religion, and so on. What was Fadime's offense? In the eyes of the Swedish public, her only crime was falling in love with a young man, a native Swede and a non-Muslim. However, the father and the family kept reiterating that the killing was provoked not by the actual fact of Fadime's liaison with a non-Muslim, but by her transgression of two implied conventions: Given her relationship, she was "exiled," meaning that she was not to visit her family or show up in their town, nor was she to publicly expose her situation. Fadime deliberately broke both of these rules, continuously articulating herself in various Swedish media in a highly self-assertive manner.

Just 2 months before her death, Fadime was invited to the Swedish parliament to talk about young immigrant women's situation in Sweden. She was hesitant, even scared, due to her family's response to her continued public presence. But she also felt that it was vital that she continue to draw attention to the issues faced by young immigrant women. Her death spurred a debate not only in the Swedish press but also in the Muslim and Turkish communities and was followed by a range of governmental initiatives aimed at helping young women in similar situations. Some of the difficult questions raised are these: Was Fadime a victim, and if so, what of? Her gender? Her ethnicity? Her religion? Her sexuality? Her culture? All of these? Or was she the victim of something else entirely? How are we to understand her media performances and the degree of agency they exposed? Is Fadime to be considered a highly competent agent, a true multicultural heroine? More difficult still: Have we the courage to understand the killer—her father—who insisted that he was the real victim?

Fadime's story illustrates the complexities facing the field of gender communication in the 21st century. In what manner can a feminist communication scholar approach this difficult case? She might, for instance, be tempted to highlight the ways in which girls and women in Turkish-Muslim communities in Sweden are expected to maintain the honor of the family and the discriminatory implications thereof: Fadime was not permitted to engage in intimate relationships with other Swedish and non-Muslim men, while Fadime's brother openly had ethnic Swedish, non-Muslim girlfriends. Or how about the way Fadime was banned from speaking in public? These prohibitions remind us of other ways in which girls and women have been silenced. Thus, a feminist communication scholar might focus on the gender-stereotypic restrictions faced by Fadime. In this scenario, Fadime is clearly a victim. She has little power and little voice. Patriarchal conventions shaped her life and ultimately killed her.

On the other hand, we know that in order to do justice to Fadime's story, we must also address her courage and her agency. Accordingly, a feminist communication scholar could home in on Fadime's strong, eloquent voice in the media, interpreting it as evidence of assertiveness and communicative skills. Yet another way of interpreting Fadime's story could be to highlight the dilemmas inherent to the situation and the conflicting discourses she had to balance, as well as the ambiguous implications of the possible positions available to her in a given situation and context. In our view, neither interpretation is a matter of "correct" or "incorrect" feminist communication scholarship. Rather, we perceive the different analyses as consequences of different assumptions about gender, communication, and power, and we further believe that these assumptions may be discussed as scholarly sets of theories and methodologies.

The aim of this book is to outline these sets, developed within feminist communications scholarship, explaining them in terms of different approaches or "toolboxes" to guide both research and the scholarly assessment hereof. At this point, perhaps the reader has no intention of conducting feminist research. Perhaps this is your first "gender" course. You may be unfamiliar with the highly academic discourse of "theories," "methods," and so on. You may not even know whether you like the subject. Perhaps you even question feminism, not even knowing how to define it. Within the context of this book, however, it is *not* important whether you consider yourself a feminist, nor is the book intended to convert you or even encourage you to engage in your own feminist scholarship. What is important is that you gain a critical understanding of what feminist academic scholarship is or can be. We believe that when you understand the assumptions that guide feminist communication scholarship, you will become a more sophisticated critic. You may also begin to relate these issues to your own personal life: like criticizing a commercial for being sexist, discussing with friends whether a movie is gender stereotypical, interpreting the homophobic humor of one of your colleagues, or wondering about the subtle communication of a lover. In each of these instances, you are simultaneously trying to make sense of your own communication, thereby drawing on your personal, implicit assumptions (theories) about gender, communication, and power.

Just as you may find yourself faced with contradictory thoughts and opinions about gender, we argue that feminist communication scholars find themselves in the middle of an intense theoretical and methodological discussion that questions the very object of our studies. We shall describe to you how the field has shifted focus from "the muted woman" to "grrl power": a move from silence to performance. We believe this was motivated by a paradigm shift traceable to a more general theoretical shift within the social sciences and the humanities, frequently described as "poststructuralism." To the poststructuralist, it makes no sense to talk about "women"/ "men" or "femininity"/"masculinity." Not only are these categories considered to be too simplistic, they are also thought to reinforce heterosexuality as the norm and uphold a gender-dichotomous communication system. However, it does makes sense to discuss gender constitution in communication, and attention then becomes focused on the ways in which we perform gender along narrow lines in order to obtain cultural legibility. Note that the performance metaphor does not suggest that gendered performances are entirely open and free, but rather that they are embedded in sets of conventions and cultural expectations. Similarly, poststructuralists propose that no one really *has* power and no one is quite *without* power, just as there is no inherently powerful communication style. On the contrary, power is productive and negotiable, albeit also unevenly distributed along a range of social stratifications, such as gender, ethnicity/race, and sexuality and diverse intersections hereof. If we relate this turn toward performance, henceforth referred to as "the performance turn," to Fadime's case, we are obliged to develop a sophisticated understanding of how Fadime was simultaneously being positioned by others and positioning herself in different situations, relations, and contexts: the media, her family, her friends, and her partner. We may then find that in some of these encounters, she engaged quite successfully in communication agency, while struggling in others—not only with the prohibitions of a sexist community but also with the expectations of a supposedly gender-equal community.

In this book, we have chosen to distinguish between feminist structuralist communication scholarship and feminist poststructuralist communication scholarship in terms of sets of theories and methodologies, which may again be subdivided. Thus, we distinguish between the "dominance and deficit approach" as opposed to the "difference and identity approach" within feminist structuralism, as well as between the "performance approach" versus the "transversity approach" within feminist poststructuralism. These distinctions serve as useful conceptual tools, but at this point, we also wish to emphasize that the interrelations of the various strands of theory and methodology are often highly complex and that each approach is continuously revitalized within the field of feminist communication scholarship.

The fact that gender and communication is now an established academic field is an important premise of our book. There is already a vast bulk of scholarship on this topic (Cameron, 2000; Foss, Foss, & Griffin, 1999, 2004; Tannen, 1990, 1993a; Wood, 1999). Add to this the literature on gender and language (Coates, 1998; Eckert & McConnell-Ginet, 2003; Hall & Bucholtz, 1995; Holmes & Meyerhoff, 2003; Mills 1995b), on gender and discourse (Bucholtz, Liang, & Sutton, 1999; Wodak, 1997), and feminist scholarship in these sub-areas (Bergvall, Bing, & Freed, 1996; Cameron, 1998a), and the body of work seems even more overwhelming. It is, therefore, time to outline our priorities. Our emphasis is on *feminist* communication scholarship, and we have chosen to highlight scholars who discuss the ways they ground their research in theories and methodologies while taking an *interdisciplinary* stand. Furthermore, we have opted to focus on scholars who have been inspirational both to feminist communication scholarship per se and to the discipline at large, even if they do not term themselves "communication scholars."

We have been eclectic in our overviews of feminist scholarship (outlined in Figures 1.1 to 3.1) in order to strengthen our chosen line of argument; thus, we want to forewarn you at this point that the range of scholars presented is by no means an exhaustive one. What is more, we have chosen to illustrate the general theoretical and methodological tenets of feminist communication scholarship within two specific contexts: the media and organizations. We realize that this choice means the exclusion of a great deal of interesting work on gender in other contexts, such as the family and interpersonal relationships. However, this strict contextual focus allows us to document how feminist communication scholarship has developed within the structuralist and poststructuralist agendas, respectively, and we hope that it will help our readers understand the way the different approaches function as scholarly toolboxes, giving rise to quite different analyses from the same contexts.

To provide a context for our own presentation of the subject of gender and communication, we shall, in Chapter 1, introduce you to feminism. We shall do so in terms of three major waves or movements, which each represent significant interactions of theory and politics during the last centuries, mainly in the so-called modern, Western part of the world. To highlight the diversity of feminism and the ways in which feminists have communicated themselves, we have chosen to include quotations and citations that illustrate the eloquence of women's voices as articulated by first- to third-wave rhetoricians. In Chapters 2 and 3, we trace the intersections between feminism, social theory, and communication scholarship, on one hand, and feminism, methodology, and communication research, on the other. Each intersection will be outlined in a model (Figures 2.1. and 3.1), to be explained in Chapters 4 through 7. We then go on to discuss examples of structuralism in feminist communication scholarship, and two distinct approaches within this conceptual framework in Chapters 4 and 5. In Chapter 4, the focus is on what we term "muted group theory" and the "dominance and deficit approach," respectively, which we again relate to sociolinguistics and conversation analysis (CA). In Chapter 5, we examine standpoint theory and the difference and identity approach, which we situate within the framework of critical theory and critical discourse analysis (CDA). Chapters 6 and 7 focus on the conceptual framework of feminist poststructuralism. In Chapter 6, we explore the challenges of performance and positioning theory and their anchoring in poststructuralist discourse analysis (PDA). In Chapter 7, we conclude our book by summing up the discussion of these different approaches, outlining a possible future for feminist communication scholarship and suggesting possible reformulations of the research agenda. We pose questions related to transgender and cyborg theory, and to transversal theory and politics, and we further discuss digital discourse analysis as the possible forerunners of a transversity, perhaps even a transfeminist, approach.

"It's not easy bein' green," sings Kermit the Frog in the Muppet Show. Nor has it been easy for us to prioritize in this manner. However, it is our hope that in so doing, we have provided our readers with something that stands out in the now well-established scholarly field of gender and communication. This book is based on the claim that there are many different ways to approach, for instance, the case of Fadime from a gender and communication perspective. For instance, one might choose a classical communication model, highlighting the transference of text/message from sender to receiver, messenger, and so on. In fact, much feminist communication scholarship has centered around methods of developing this model into a particular feminist communication model by emphasizing the dialectics of text, situation and context (Mills, 1995a). This has not been our intention. We do not wish to pursue a feminist model or any other model, but rather to investigate the basic approaches to language and discourse that form the basis of communication models. In Fadime's case, for instance, we would focus on the ways in which communication is embedded in discourses on gender, legitimacy, and power. We shall now leave Fadime for the time being, but she will be with us throughout the book, and we shall return to her in the end.

# Acknowledgments

A project such as this one is completed only with the help and support of a number of people. We are particularly grateful to the reviewers (see list below), whose comments and suggestions were invaluable. In addition, we would like to thank the College of the Humanities at the University of Southern Denmark, who generously financed revisions of our writing, as well as the Institution San Cataldo, for a stipend and residency to help in the initial writing process. We would further like to acknowledge the secretaries and colleagues at the Center for Cultural Studies at the University of Southern Denmark, without whose backing we could not have completed the project. Not to forget our husbands, sons, other family members, and friends who have taken a lively interest in the subject and displayed great generosity. Last, we would also like to extend a very special thanks to Todd Armstrong, Deya Saoud, Kristen Gibson, and Carla Freeman from Sage for their work on this book.

We are particularly grateful to the following reviewers, whose recommendations at various stages of this book's development were invaluable.

Patrice M. Buzzanell, Purdue University
Karen A. Foss, University of New Mexico
Kristin M. Langellier, University of Maine
Karen Lovaas, San Francisco State University
Erin Sahlstein, University of Richmond
Angela Trethewey, Arizona State University

# 1

# Three Waves of Feminism

## From Suffragettes to Grrls

W e now ask our readers to join us in an exploration of the history of feminism or, rather, feminisms: How have they evolved in time and space? How have they framed feminist communication scholarship in terms of what we see as a significant interplay between theory and politics? And how have they raised questions of gender, power, and communication?

We shall focus our journey on the modern feminist waves from the 19th to the 21st century and underscore continuities as well as disruptions. Our starting point is what most feminist scholars consider the "first wave." First-wave feminism arose in the context of industrial society and liberal politics but is connected to both the liberal women's rights movement and early socialist feminism in the late 19th and early 20th century in the United States and Europe. Concerned with access and equal opportunities for women, the first wave continued to influence feminism in both Western and Eastern societies throughout the 20th century. We then move on to the second wave of feminism, which emerged in the 1960s to 1970s in postwar Western welfare societies, when other "oppressed" groups such as Blacks and homosexuals were being defined and the New Left was on the rise. Second-wave feminism is closely linked to the radical voices of women's empowerment and differential rights and, during the 1980s to 1990s, also to a crucial differentiation of second-wave feminism itself, initiated by women of color and third-world women. We end our discussion with the third feminist wave, from the mid-1990s onward, springing from the emergence of a new postcolonial and postsocialist world order, in the context of information society and neoliberal, global politics. Third-wave feminism manifests itself in "grrl" rhetoric, which seeks to overcome the theoretical question of equity or difference and the political question of evolution or revolution, while it challenges the notion of "universal womanhood" and embraces ambiguity, diversity, and multiplicity in transversal theory and politics.

> We could start much earlier. In fact, we could go as far back as antiquity and the renowned *hetaera* of Athens, or we could go even further back to prehistoric times in Mesopotamia and the Mediterranean regions and discuss goddess religions and matriarchy. Or we could examine the European Middle Ages and the mystical rhetoric of holy women like Hildegard von Bingen (1098–1179). We could also highlight the Renaissance tradition of learned women such as Leonora d'Este (1474–1539) or Enlightenment *beaux esprits* such as Madame de Rambouillet (1588–1665) or Germaine de Staël (1766–1817). Another obvious start would be the struggles of bourgeois European women for education and civic rights in the wake of the French Revolution. These were eloquently phrased by Olympes de Gouges (1748–1793), who drafted a *Declaration of the Rights of Women* (1791) analogous to *The Declaration of the Rights of Man* (1789).

## The First Feminist Wave: Votes for Women

*Germany has established "Equal, universal, secret direct franchise," the senate has denied equal universal suffrage to America. Which is more of a Democracy, Germany or America?*

— Banner carried during picketing of
the White House, October 23, 1918

Imagine: During World War I, members of the National Women's Party (NWP) protest outside the White House with confrontational banners accusing the government of undemocratic practices. Germany had already granted women suffrage, but the United States—the proponent of freedom and democracy for all—had yet to enfranchise half of its citizens. The banner created an outrage, the police received orders to arrest the picketers, and onlookers destroyed the banner (Campbell, 1989). Comparing Germany to the United States was treachery. However, the picketers did receive some sympathy—after all, well-dressed, well-educated, White, middle-class women were going to jail. This was no way to treat ladies!

The demonstrators knew what they were doing: Dressed in their Sunday best, they offered no resistance to the police and thus both appalled and appealed to the public. They personified White, middle-class femininity, while engaging in very unfeminine and less-than-bourgeois practices. The action was inspired by radical agitator Alice Paul (1885–1977), who introduced militant tactics to the NWP: parades, marches, picketing (mainly the White House) as well as watch fires to burn President Wilson's speeches (Campbell, 1989). Alice Paul's tactics were confrontational but also clever, and they were a thorn in the side of President Wilson, who much preferred the less radical tactics of the National American Women's Suffrage Association (NAWSA).

*Parliaments have stopped laughing at woman suffrage, and politicians have begun to dodge! It is the inevitable premonition of coming victory.*

— Carrie Chapman Catt (1859–1947)

The first wave of feminism in the United States was characterized by diverse forms of intervention that have continued to inspire later feminist movements. But despite the activist talents of Alice Paul, the organizational skills of Carrie Chapman Catt (1859–1947), president of NAWSA, and the splendid oratory of Anna Howard Shaw (1847–1919), also a former president of NAWSA, it was a long struggle before women won the vote in 1920 (Campbell, 1989). The struggle went as far back as the Seneca Falls Convention in New York in 1848, during which more than 300 men and women assembled for the nation's first women's rights convention. The Seneca Falls Declaration was outlined by Elizabeth Cady Stanton (1815–1902), claiming the natural equity of women and outlining the political strategy of equal access and opportunity. This declaration gave rise to the suffrage movement (see Stanton, 1948).

*I always feel the movement is a sort of mosaic. Each of us puts in one little stone, and then you get a great mosaic at the end.*

— Alice Paul (1885–1977)

In the early stages, the first wave of feminism in the United States was interwoven with other reform movements, such as abolition and temperance, and initially closely involved women of the working classes. However, it was also supported by Black women abolitionists, such as Maria Stewart (1803–1879), Sojourner Truth (1797–1883), and Frances E. W. Harper (1825–1911), who agitated for the rights of women of color. Elizabeth Cady Stanton and several others from the more radical parts of the women's rights movement appeared as delegates to the National Labor Union Convention as early as 1868, before any successful attempts to organize female labor (Firestone, 1968).

---

*Dat man ober dar say dat women needs to be helped into carriages and lifted ober ditches, and to hab de best place everywhar. Nobody eber helps me into carriages, or ober mud-puddles, or gibs me any best place! And ain't I a woman! Look at me! Look at my arm! I have ploughed, and planted and gathered into barns, and no man could head me! And ain't I a woman? I have borne thirteen children, and seem 'em mos' all sold into slavery, and when I cried out my mother's grief, none but Jesus heard me! And ain't I a woman?*

— Sojourner Truth (1797–1883)

---

When women's rights activists gradually realized that disenfranchisement severely hampered reformatory efforts, they became determined to rectify this obvious injustice. Still, for women to gain the vote was a highly controversial issue. Even well-meaning skeptics feared that it would mean a setback for men of color, who were also at that time campaigning for enfranchisement, not to mention southerners' fears that the thousands of illiterate women of color would also claim their rights. Thus, although women of color continued to participate and representatives such as Ida B. Wells (1862–1931) and Mary Church Terrell (1868–1954) also strove to show how the linkage of sexism and racism functioned as the main means of White male dominance, the first wave of feminism consisted largely of White, middle-class, well-educated women (Campbell, 1989). This tendency was only reinforced by the counterstrikes of both the abolitionist movement and the working unions to also keep women involved in these movements. Furthermore, the Civil War in the United States and, later on, both World War I and World War II meant a severe backlash for women's rights, as the focus then became demands of national unity and patriotism.

---

*Resolved, that the women of this nation in 1876, have greater cause for discontent, rebellion, and revolution than the men of 1776.*

— Susan B. Anthony (1820–1906)

---

Suffragists confronted stereotypes of women and, in particular, claims of proper female behavior and talk. First, they engaged in public persuasion, which in those days was considered most unwomanly. Campbell (1989) put it this way: "No 'true woman' could be a public persuader" (pp. 9–10). Second, their very activity challenged the "cult of domesticity," which in those days dictated that a true woman's place was in the home, meeting the needs of husband and children. Women were further required to be modest and to wield only indirect influence, and certainly not engage in public activities. So, when a woman spoke in public, she was, by definition, displaying masculine behaviors. She was even ignoring her biological weaknesses— a smaller brain and a more fragile physique—which she was supposed to protect in order to ensure her reproductive abilities. Such claims led some women's rights activists to argue that women should indeed gain the right to vote from an argument of expediency (Campbell, 1999). This argument was based on the claim that women and men are, in fact, fundamentally different and that women have a natural disposition toward maternity and domesticity. However, the argument ran that it would therefore be advantageous to society to enfranchise women, so they would then enrich politics with their "innately" female concerns. Furthermore, if women had the vote, the argument ran, they would perform their roles as mothers and housewives even better. On the other hand, we find another well-used argument: justice (Campbell, 1989). Following this argument, women and men are, at least in legal terms, equal in all respects; therefore, to deny women the vote was to deny them full citizenship (Campbell, 1989, p. 14).

*I would have girls regard themselves not as adjectives but as nouns.*

— Elizabeth Cady Stanton (1815–1902)

Some first-wave feminists pursued the argument of women's innate moral superiority, thus embracing what might be called "difference first-wave feminism." This argument was part of a sophisticated rhetoric of equity, developed simultaneously in Europe and in the United States, which shared the modern, Western political framework of enlightenment and liberalism, anchored in universalism. From this point of view, patriarchy was understood as a fiasco that was both nonrational and nonprofitable and thereby illegitimate, but nevertheless reinforced women's marginal societal status and domination and made women a cultural emblem of deficiency. Politically, this view led to the claim that women and men should be treated as equals and that women should not only be given access to the same resources and positions as men but also be acknowledged for their contributions and competencies. This concept is often called "equal-opportunities feminism" or "equity feminism," and it is characterized by the lack of distinction between sex and gender. Even though biological differences were understood to form the basis of social gender roles, they were not considered a threat to the ideal of human equity, and biological differences were therefore not accepted as theoretically or politically valid reasons for discrimination.

*No race can afford to neglect the enlightenment of its mothers.*

— Frances E. W. Harper (1825–1911)

One of the earliest manifestations of liberal first-wave feminism in Europe, Mary Wollstonecraft's *A Vindication of the Rights of Woman* (1792), was written in the wake of the French Revolution and is still read as a seminal text. Virginia Woolf's *A Room of One's Own* (1929) and Simone de Beauvoir's *The Second Sex* (1949) are central to the canon as well, even though both authors were also laying the groundwork for radical second-wave feminism. Woolf introduced the notion of female bisexuality and a unique woman's voice and writing, Beauvoir the notion of women's radical otherness or, rather, the cognitive and social process of "othering" women as the second sex in patriarchal societies. We would say that Beauvoir thereby produced an authoritative definition of patriarchy.

*The woman who strengthens her body and exercises her mind will, by managing her family and practising various virtues, become the friend, and not the humble dependent of her husband.*

— Mary Wollstonecraft (1759–1797)

Parallel to this strand of liberal first-wave feminism, a distinct socialist/ Marxist feminism developed in workers' unions in the United States, in reformist social-democratic parties in Europe, and during the rise of communism in the former Soviet Union. It was initiated by, among others, Rosa Luxemburg (1870–1919) in Germany, Alexandra Kollontai (1873–1952) in Russia, and anarchist Emma Goldman (1869–1940) in the United States. Liberal and socialist/Marxist feminism shared a basic belief in equity and equal opportunities for women and men, but the latter focused particularly on working-class women and their involvement in class struggle and socialist revolution. Socialist feminists such as Rosa Luxemburg and, in particular, Alexandra Kollontai and Emma Goldman, paved the way for second-wave feminism, fighting both politically and in their own private lives for women's right to abortion, divorce, and nonlegislative partnership—and against sexism both in bourgeois society and within the socialist movements.

---

*We will be victorious if we have not forgotten how to learn.*

— Rosa Luxemburg (1871–1919)

---

Both liberal and socialist/Marxist feminism continued to develop and maintain strong voices in 20th-century feminism, though they were soon challenged by other types of feminism, as we are going to see below. The concept of equal opportunity framed a particular type of equity research, which arose outside the academy in the first half of the 20th century, and gradually provided the basis for a growing field of research in "the women issue." Following the scientific paradigm of structuralism as a set of ways and means of knowing, equity research initially took the basic format of muted group theory (see Chapter 2). In Chapter 3, we further relate this particular body of work to the methodology of conversation analysis, and in Chapter 4, we explore its manifestation as the dominance and deficit approach in terms of communication and present you with an example of conversation analytic communication work.

---

*As a woman, I have no country. As a woman, I want no country. As a woman, my country is my world.*

— Virginia Woolf (1882–1941)

---

## The Second Feminist Wave: "The Personal Is Political"

*The revlon lady tells her to put on a mask. "be a whole new person" and "get a whole new life."*

— Protest sign carried during the 1969 Miss America Pageant

The term *second-wave feminism* refers mostly to the radical feminism of the women's liberation movement of the late 1960s and early 1970s. We start our presentation of second-wave feminism with the first harbinger of a new feminism and the most publicized event in the United States: the protests associated with the Miss America Pageants in 1968 and 1969 (Freeman, 1975). Inspired by the tactics of the more activist parts of liberal feminism, radical second-wave feminists also used performance (e.g., underground or guerilla theater) to shed light on what was now termed "women's oppression."

---

*There are very few jobs that actually require a penis or vagina. All other jobs should be open to everybody.*

— Florynce Kennedy (1916–2000)

---

The Redstockings, the New York Radical Feminists, and other significant feminist groups joined the 1969 protest to show how women in pageant competitions were paraded like cattle, highlighting the underlying assumption that the way women look is more important than what they do, what they think, or even whether they think at all (Freeman, 1975). Marching down the Atlantic City boardwalk and close to the event itself, feminists staged several types of theatrical activism: crowning a sheep Miss America and throwing "oppressive" gender artifacts, such as bras, girdles, false eyelashes, high heels, and makeup, into a trash can in front of reporters (Freeman, 1975). Carrying posters reading, "Cattle Parades Are Degrading to Human Beings," "Boring Job: Woman Wanted," and "Low Pay: Woman Wanted," feminists made their message loud and clear: Women were victims of a patriarchal, commercialized, oppressive beauty culture (Freeman, 1975). It was a perfectly staged media event. A small group of women bought tickets to the pageant show and smuggled in a banner that read "WOMEN'S LIBERATION," while shouting "Freedom for Women" and "No More Miss America," hereby exposing the public to an early second-wave feminist agenda (Freeman, 1969).

---

*A woman reading Playboy feels a little like a Jew reading a Nazi manual.*

— Gloria Steinem (1934–)

---

Radical second-wave feminism cannot, however, be discussed separately from other movements of the 1960s and 1970s. In fact, it grew out of leftist movements in postwar Western societies, among them the student protests, the anti–Vietnam War movement, the lesbian and gay movements, and, in the United States, the civil rights and Black power movements. These movements criticized "capitalism" and "imperialism" and focused on the notion and interests of "oppressed" groups: the working classes, Blacks, and in principle, also women and homosexuals. In the New Left, however, women found themselves reduced to servicing the revolution, cut off from real influence and thus, once again, exposed to sexism. This was now understood as a separate oppression experienced by women in addition to racism, "classicism," and was later renamed "heterosexism." As a consequence, they formed women-only "rap" groups or consciousness-raising groups, through which they sought to empower women both collectively and individually using techniques of sharing and contesting, explained in "The BITCH Manifesto" (Freeman, 1968) and the first second-wave publication, *Sisterhood is Powerful,* edited by Robin Morgan in 1970. This type of activity and rhetoric was typical to the second-wave movement and in particular to the Redstockings, who created their name by combining *bluestockings,* a pejorative term for educated and otherwise strong-minded women in the 18th and 19th centuries, with *red,* for social revolution. The Redstockings was one of the influential but short-lived radical feminist groups of the 1960 to 1970s and produced many of the expressions that have become household words in the United States: "Sisterhood is powerful," "consciousness raising," "The personal is political," "the politics of housework," the "pro-woman line," and so on. Key to this branch of feminism was a strong belief that women could collectively empower one other.

---

*Women are not inherently passive or peaceful. We're not inherently anything but human.*

— Robin Morgan (1941–)

---

Radical second-wave feminism was theoretically based on a combination of neo-Marxism and psychoanalysis, outlined by feminist scholars such as Juliet Mitchell in *The Subjection of Women* (1970) and Shulamith Firestone in *The Dialectic of Sex: The Case for Feminist Revolution* (1970). They claimed that patriarchy is inherent to bourgeois society and that sexual difference is more fundamental than class and race differences. They even claimed that women—due to their primary social attachment to the family and reproduction—constitute a class and economy of their own, based on the unpaid work in the home, the productivity of motherhood, and their function as a workforce reserve. The Freudian theory of women's "natural" dependency and sexual frigidity was at first denounced, then later rearticulated as a mimicry of the unholy alliance between capitalism and patriarchy that designates sexism as the particular character of women's oppression

(Mitchell, 1970). At the core of this new movement was another significant book, *Sexual Politics,* by Kate Millett (1969), in which she insisted on women's right to their own bodies and a sexuality of their "own"—a sexuality that is disconnected from the obligations of marriage and motherhood. Yet other radical feminists, such as the lesbian author Adrienne Rich and the African American lesbian author Audre Lorde (1934–1992), used poetry, speeches, and writing to link heterosexuality and women's oppression. Both great rhetoricians, they claimed that heterosexuality is a compulsory institution designed to perpetuate the social power of men across class and race. In works such as *On Lies, Secrets, and Silence* (Rich, 1980) and *Sister Outsider: Essays and Speeches* (Lorde, 1984), they explored how sexism, racism, and classicism work together by means of the heterosexual imperative. Thus, in the early phase, radical second-wave feminisms were characterized by a claim for sisterhood and solidarity, despite differences among women and a simultaneous investment in the slogans "Woman's struggle is class struggle" and "The personal is political," directing the feminist agenda to attempt to combine social, sexual, and personal struggles and to see them as inextricably linked.

---

*Life on the planet is born of woman.*

— Adrienne Rich (1929–)

*Womanist is to feminist as purple is to lavender.*

— Alice Walker (1944–)

---

Women's liberation grew out of the New Left and provided alliances with socialist/Marxist feminisms in areas such as the criticism of the dual workload for women working outside as well as inside the home, the demand of equal pay for equal work, and a breakdown of the gendered division of the educational system and the labor market. Sheila Rowbotham explored these issues in her influential book *Women, Resistance, and Revolution* (1972), and Angela Y. Davis expanded on the intersections of gender, race, and class in *Women, Race, and Class* (1981). In addressing what they saw as "the woman question," they concluded that the emancipation of women would occur only with the destruction of capitalism and the rise of socialism, when women would be freed from dependency on men and the family and be involved in "productive" labor. In areas such as the criticism of "sex roles" and "the beauty myth," however, women's liberation was closer to liberal feminism, which still had a strong hold.

*Men will often admit other women are oppressed but not you.*

— Sheila Rowbotham (1943–)

Liberal feminists in all Western countries were inspired by Betty Friedan's landmark book, *The Feminine Mystique* (1963). Along with Rowbotham and Davis but from quite a different point of view, liberal feminists maintained that the discontent experienced by many middle-class women in postwar Western societies was due to their lack of social power and political influence. The solution they advocated was not necessarily paid work outside the home; indeed, one of their demands was payment for housewives— a kind of citizen's income—along with representation in public institutions, and so on. Zillah Eisenstein's work *The Radical Future of Liberal Feminism* (1981) can be said to anticipate the continuity of liberal feminism from first wave, during the second wave, and on to today's neoliberal feminism. Typical liberal feminist concerns during the second wave, however, were documenting sexism in private as well as public life and delivering a criticism of gendered patterns of socialization. In the United States, for example, the National Organization for Women (NOW) documented sexism in children's books, and parents' different responses to girls and boys were seen as examples of how deeply sexism is embedded in conventional thought and practice.

*The feminine mystique has succeeded in burying millions of American women alive.*

— Betty Friedan (1921–)

Whereas both liberal and socialist/Marxist feminists worked to access and influence the institutions of society, radical feminists were critical of these institutions and skeptical of, if not outright opposed to, the inclusion of more women in what they considered profit-driven, patriarchal institutions. The spiritual and ecofeminist parts of the movement, represented, for instance, by Mary Daly in *Gyn/Ecology* (1978) and Starhawk in *The Spiral Dance: A Rebirth of the Ancient Religion of the Great Goddess* (1979), turned to the development of separate enterprises and eventually of womanonly corporations and zones. After a few decades on the margins of feminism, this particular feminist perspective has been revived today in numerous ways: from sustainable development and simple living to corporate feminism and separatist women-only spaces, such as "SAPPHO" on the Internet.

*We've begun to raise our daughters more like our sons . . . but few have the courage to raise our sons more like our daughters.*

— Gloria Steinem (1934–)

The conflict between integration and separation signaled a basic shift from an equity approach to a difference approach. During the 1980s, this new framework grew into "difference second-wave feminism," outlined on a theoretical level by Nancy Hartsock (1983) in her paradigmatic article "The Feminist Standpoint" and a range of subsequent works. "Standpoint feminism" articulated a specifically feminist theory and practice that expanded the criticism of capitalism and patriarchy with a more complex analysis of postwar welfare societies and their consequences for women on different levels and in different situations, as we shall return to in Chapters 2 and 5. Nancy Chodorow and Carol Gilligan turned to a more woman-friendly psychoanalytic theory in order to highlight women's productive capacities in terms of motherhood and caretaking, in works such as *The Reproduction of Mothering* (Chodorow, 1978) and *In a Different Voice* (Gilligan, 1982). These competencies, neglected by both liberal and socialist feminists and derided by early radical feminists, were now reevaluated and understood as sources of knowledge, know-how, and empowerment. This particular version of difference feminism again led to the thesis of the dual spheres, gender as culture, and communication and the "genderlects" (see Chapter 5).

*Courage is the key to the revelatory power of the feminist revolution.*

— Mary Daly (1928–)

The need to address the differences among women simultaneously promoted the theory of different standpoints and the divergences between them. As a consequence, difference feminism gradually grew into what is now often referred to as "identity politics." Identity second-wave feminism was marked by a growing criticism from Black, working-class, and lesbian feminists, outlined by, among others, bell hooks in *Ain't I A Woman? Black Woman and Feminism* (1981) and Trinh T. Minh-ha in *Woman, Native, Other: Writing Postcoloniality and Feminism* (1989). In the context of the complex power relations of a postcolonial but still imperial and capitalist world, they questioned what they saw as a predominantly White, middle-class, and heterosexual feminist agenda and raised the issue of a differentiated-identity politics, based on the contingent and diversified but no less decisive intersections of gender, class, race/ethnicity, and sexuality. Identity feminism, in turn, inspired a new interest in women's lives and voices, which was at once more empirical and historical, and more mythical and spiritual. This has been known as "gyno-criticism," a method first developed by Elaine Showalter in *A Literature of Their Own* (1977), or as "womanism," in an African American context introduced by the author Alice Walker *In Search of Our Mothers' Gardens: Womanist Prose* (1983). The method signaled, on one hand, a search for authenticity and continuity in women's cultures and, on the other, an interest in understanding differences among women as constitutive. The method was further developed by Patricia Hill Collins, who argued in *Black Feminist Thought: Knowledge, Consciousness, and the Politics of Empowerment* (1990) that it is necessary to expand the analysis from merely describing the similarities and differences that distinguish the different systems of oppression according to gender, class, and race—to focusing on how they are interlocked. Assuming that each system needs the others in order to function, this discussion stimulated a distinct theoretical stance, which we shall return to in Chapters 2 and 5.

---

*Black women have not historically stood in the pulpit, but that doesn't undermine the fact that they built the churches and maintain the pulpits.*

— Maya Angelou (1928–)

---

In the United States, Black feminists voiced their concerns in organizations such as Black Women Organized for Action (BWOA) and the National Black Feminist Organization (NBFO), which both worked to bring gender and race into the national consciousness and addressed issues of poverty, health, and welfare as described by Valerie Smith in *Not Just Race, Not Just Gender: Black Feminist Readings* (1998). However, Black feminism also tended to diversify into different standpoints and identities. Women of color and third-world women, like Trinh T. Minh-ha, now spoke of themselves as the "other Others" and "inappropriated others." Gayatri Spivak's *In Other Worlds: Essays in Cultural Politics* (1987) further criticized Western feminism for speaking naively on behalf of third-world women. She elaborated on the notion of "strategic essentialism" and raised the question of the difficulty associated with translation between different groups of women, their vocabulary, and voice.

In the European context, identity feminism took an apparently different direction with what is now known as *l'écriture féminine*, articulated by authors Hélène Cixous, Luce Irigaray, and Julia Kristeva and introduced to the United States by editors Elaine Marks and Isabelle de Courtivron in *New French Feminisms* (1981). French feminists explored Western universalism and its paradoxical articulation through dualisms such as mind/body, man/woman, and White/Black and their hierarchical ordering, in which one element is not only *different from* but also *less than* the other. Developing a thesis of the "phallogocentrism" of Western thinking, they argued that it constitutes the very foundation of (Western) language(s) through a binary logic that makes the phallus the master sign and the father the origin of symbolic law. Consequently, French feminists pled for a deconstructive feminine writing and pursued the idea of the revolutionary potential of women's bodies as the productive site of multiple desires, a plenitude of *jouissance,* and thereby another semiotic logic. In her dissertation *Spéculum de l'autre femme* (1974/1985a), Irigaray took the criticism of phallogocentrism a step further and maintained that Western thinking in fact posits "man" as the "one and only" (both mind and body/matter) and "woman" not as the opposite and negative (body/matter), but rather entirely outside of civilization/language. Her point was therefore that the project for women/feminists is not and cannot be to identify with difference (such as body/matter), and she warned against the tendency to highlight an alternate desire/logic.

Irigaray's line of thought provides us with the intellectual tools necessary to grasp the dilemmas of difference feminism and identity politics. With Irigaray, we can claim that difference feminism perpetuates the dilemmas of Western universalism and its paradoxical attributions to "particularism" in terms of the implied other, which guarantees the "one and only." Gay rights activists, for example, paradoxically perpetuate the notion of heterosexuality as the norm when they attempt to secure more rights for homosexuals. Radically stated, identity politics unintentionally supports a hegemonic concept of woman (as Western, White, heterosexual, etc.). The dilemma is exacerbated, moreover, because difference feminism claims that sexual difference is universal, though in its particular manifestation as gender also historical and social and therefore both contextual and changeable. The distinction between sex and gender, emphasized by second-wave feminists, provides a sociological or cultural explanation, which at first seems to solve the dilemma between sameness and difference but does not entirely answer questions related to the sexed body, as well as differences among women. The difference argument has also tended to oscillate between positive difference as inherent in women (be it biological or sociological) and negative difference as relative (be it biological or sociological) to subordination. This line of the argument crisscrosses the sex-gender distinction and is obviously neither intellectually nor politically valid. Irigaray helps us open a door to a different kind of thought and action, in which a continued process of diversification and multiplication takes over from the frozen pairing of equity (sameness) and difference.

Second-wave feminism is not one, but many. As expressed by feminist communication scholar Julia Wood (1994), the question may not be whether you are a feminist, but which kind of feminist you are (p. 106). This question is multiplied by the emergence of third-wave feminism. But before we turn to emergent feminisms, let us conclude that second-wave feminisms have been highly theoretical and consequently have had strong affiliations with the academy. Starting in the 1970s, second-wave feminisms have generated an explosion of research and teaching on women's issues, which has now grown into a diverse disciplinary field of women's, gender, or feminist studies. While first- and second-wave academic feminisms are embedded in structuralism (Chapter 2), the concept of difference and identity feminism is rooted in standpoint theory (Chapter 2) and the methodology of critical discourse analysis (Chapter 3). Difference and identity feminism has influenced communication scholarship through the concepts of cultural feminism and gendered communication styles or "genderlects," which are explored further in Chapter 5.

## The Third Feminist Wave: Transversal Politics

*Cyber Grrls Get On-Line!*

— "Internet Tour," by Karen McNaughton (1997)

Lipstick feminism, girlie feminism, riot grrl feminism, cybergrrl feminism, transfeminism, or just grrl feminism—feminism is alive and kicking. Born with the privileges that first- and second-wave feminists fought for, third-wave feminists generally see themselves as capable, strong, and assertive social agents: "The Third Wave is buoyed by the confidence of having more opportunities and less sexism" (Baumgardner & Richards, 2000, p. 83). Young feminists now reclaim the term "girl" in a bid to attract another generation, while engaging in a new, more self-assertive—even aggressive—but also more playful and less pompous kind of feminism. They declare, in the words of Karen McNaughton (1997), "And yes that's G.r.r.l.s which is, in our case, cyber-lingo for Great-Girls. Grrl is also a young at heart thing and not limited to the under 18s."

Karen McNaughton is only one of many who have been empowered by the new grrl rhetoric, which originated among girls-only punk bands such as

Bikini Kill and Brat Mobile in the United States in the early 1990s. In their manifesto-like recording "Revolution Girl-Style Now" (1990), Bikini Kill celebrated the self-reliance and acting out of prepubescent girls and mixed the feminist strategy of empowerment with the avant-garde or punk strategy of D.I.Y.: "Do It Yourself." This message was soon absorbed by a growing number of "riot grrl" groups all over the United States and Europe and further spread by "fanzines" and net-based "e-zines." Some riot grrls made the new information technologies the primary point of departure for their activism and as cybergrrls or Netgrrls introduced them to other girls and women in books such as *The Cyberpunk Handbook* (1995), *Friendly Grrls Guide to the Internet–Introduction* (1996), and *Cybergrrl! A Woman's Guide to the World Wide Web* (1998). The movement has simultaneously criticized sexist language, appropriated derogatory terms for girls and women, and invented new self-celebrating words and forms of communication. As such, third-wave feminists have followed in the footprints of groups like Queer Nation and Niggers With Attitude by deploying a kind of linguistic jiujitsu against their enemies. Instead of condemning the stereotypes used against them, they exaggerate them, beginning with the very word *girl* (Chideya, Rossi, & Hannah, 1992).

---

*For girls to pick up guitars and scream their heads off in a totally oppressive, fucked up, male dominated culture is to seize power . . . we recognize this as a political act.*

— Tobi Vail, Bikini Kill

---

Third-wave feminists are motivated by the need to develop a feminist theory and politics that honor contradictory experiences and deconstruct categorical thinking. In *To Be Real: Telling the Truth and Changing the Face of Feminism* (1995), editor Rebecca Walker described the difficulty that younger feminists experience when forced to think in categories, which divide people into "Us" and "Them," or when forced to inhabit particular identities as women or feminists (p. xxxiii). Walker claimed that this is not because they lack knowledge of feminist history or because of the media's horrific one-sided portrayal of feminism. Quite to the contrary, younger feminists honor the work of earlier feminists while criticizing earlier feminisms, and they strive to bridge contradictions that they experience in their own lives. They embrace ambiguity rather than certainty, engage in multiple positions, and practice a strategy of inclusion and exploration (p. xxxiii). Meanwhile, they propose a different politics, one that challenges notions of universal womanhood and articulates ways in which groups of women confront complex intersections of gender, sexuality, race, class, and age-related concerns. One of the many contributors in *To Be Real*, Eisa Davis, has called for "organic laughter" and "organized confusion" that will turn all the old "isms" into sitcoms, reminding us how far feminism has come (Walker, 1995, p. 138).

---

*I am not a pretty girl, that's not what I do.*

— Ani DiFranco, musician

---

Third-wave feminism is also inspired by and bound to a generation of the new global world order characterized by the fall of communism, new threats of religious and ethnic fundamentalism, and the dual risks and promises of new info- and biotechnologies. A common American term for third-wave feminism is "grrl feminism," and in Europe it is known as "new feminism." This new "new" feminism is characterized by local, national, and transnational activism, in areas such as violence against women, trafficking, body surgery, self-mutilation, and the overall "pornofication" of the media. While concerned with new threats to women's rights in the wake of the new global world order, it criticizes earlier feminist waves for presenting universal answers or definitions of womanhood and for developing their particular interests into somewhat static identity politics.

---

*I live by my own standards. I am my own judge and jury. I refuse to look/do/say whatever it is I'm supposed to. I may burn bridges, but I don't want to go back there anyway.*

— Bilyana Vujick, DIY Feminism

---

In itself diverse and chaotic, third-wave feminism is consequently not one, but many. The common denominator is the will to redefine feminism by bringing together an interest in traditional and even stereotypically feminine issues, while remaining critical of both narratives of true femaleness, of victimization and liberation. They flaunt their femininity and seek to reclaim formerly derogatory labels such as "slut" and "bitch," while stubbornly venturing into male-dominated spaces with third-wave confidence to claim positions of power: We—the new feminists—embrace power, said new feminist Natasha Walter in *The New Feminism* (1998). Third-wave feminists want to avoid stepping into mutually oppressive static categories, and they call for acceptance of a chaotic world, while simultaneously embracing ambiguity and forming new alliances. Thus, third-wave feminisms are defined not by common theoretical and political standpoint(s), but rather by the use of performance, mimicry, and subversion as rhetorical strategies.

> *I won't stop talking. I'm a grrrl you have no control over. There is not a gag big enough to handle this mouth.*
>
> — Kathleen Hannah, Bikini Kill

Gender theorist Judith Butler signaled this paradigmatic feminist shift in her books *Gender Trouble* (1990) and *Bodies That Matter* (1993). She fueled new emergent movements such as queer and transgender politics, which take an interest in the intersections of gender and sexuality and helped articulate "performance third-wave feminism" as a theoretical framework of the politics of transgression. Central to this perspective is the understanding of gender as a discursive practice that is both a hegemonic, social matrix and a "performative gesture" with the power to disturb the chain of social repetition and open up new realities. Focus rests on the sustained tension between structure and agency, spelled out as a tension between performance and performativity, in order to overcome the split between society and subject and to situate the possibilities and means of agency and change. The possibilities for change are found in the "fissures" of deferral and displacement that destabilize claims not only of identity but also of truth and "the real" (Butler, 1990). Of immense importance to feminism, however, is that the approach further destabilizes the distinction between the social and the material, discourse and body, and, not least, sex and gender. These conceptual pairs are now seen as inextricably linked discursive practices, anchored in the heterosexual matrix, which is now being challenged (Butler, 1993; to be developed in Chapters 2 and 6).

Another significant perspective that has contributed to third-wave feminism is Donna Haraway's (1987/1991) "cyborg," which has also inspired the development of cyberfeminism. What makes this perspective unique is Haraway's appropriation of technology and her posthuman acknowledgment of the interaction between humans and nonhumans, which blurs the distinctions between humans, animals, and machines. Moreover, like Butler, Haraway does not operate with an essential division between society and subject, structure and agency, materiality and sociality, or flesh and soul.

In keeping with poststructuralist thought (Chapter 2), she has underscored the arbitrariness of such classifications and the continuous flow between supposedly "natural" categories, locations, and positions. The potential for feminism, in Haraway's thinking, is great and is still being explored by a range of feminist thinkers, to whom we shall return to in Chapters 2 and 6.

*Yr a big grrrl now; you've got NO REASON NOT TO FIGHT!!!*

— Bikini Kill

Third-wave feminism is tied up with the effects of globalization and the complex redistribution of power, which challenge feminist theory and politics. It also mirrors the diversification of women's interests and perspectives and the breakdown of master stories of oppression and liberation. For example, postcolonial, third-wave feminism is concerned with establishing a new critical global perspective and creating alliances between Black, diasporic, and subaltern feminisms, whereas queer theory and politics create a platform for what has now split into the lesbian, gay, bi-, and transsexual and transgender movements. Queer and transgender feminists attack what they see as the crux of the problem: heteronormativity. They call for recognition of queers: not only gays and lesbians but also drag queens, drag kings, transsexuals, masculine women, and feminine men (Halberstam, 1998). Emi Koyama (2003) summarized some of these concerns in "The Transfeminist Manifesto." Here, the primary principles of transfeminism are defined as the right (a) to define one's own identity and to expect society to respect it and (b) to make decisions regarding one's own body (Koyama, 2003, pp. 245–247). Transfeminists believe that individuals should be given the freedom to construct their own gender identities as they see fit and that neither the medical establishment nor cultural institutions at large should intervene. Finally, they resist essentialist notions of identity in particular.

*Do women have to be naked to get into the Met. Museum? Less than 5% of the artists in the Modern Art sections are women, but 85% of the nudes are female.*

— Guerrilla Girls

According to the postsocialist scholar Nancy Fraser (1997), the challenges to third-wave feminism are great. She has argued that in order to avoid the pitfalls of identity politics, it is necessary to introduce a concept of justice that simultaneously acknowledges and counters the claims of difference. Thus, Fraser has suggested that claims of difference should be treated partly as a question of recognition within the context of civic society and partly as a matter of redistribution within the framework of the state and the public sphere. Her aim is to reframe universalism in order to promote a new combination of, on one hand, local (singular and situated) social claims, and, on the other, the will and ability to expose universalism to a "global" democracy. She thus has delivered an alternative to the "old" universalism, which sanctioned the particularism inherent in identity politics, claiming that in the new democracy, everyone must acknowledge the particularity of the position from which they speak, instead of claiming rights as absolute and given.

---

*It's possible to have a push-up bra and a brain at the same time.*

— Pinkfloor

---

An interesting and important contribution to third-wave feminist thinking is the notion of "transversal politics." Nira Yuval-Davis, the author of *Gender and Nation* (1997), who is herself a British Jew, launched this notion, which is based on the possibility of dialogue between women across national, ethnic, and religious boundaries. Theoretically, her work has been inspired by Gayatri Spivak's theory of strategic essentialism and Patricia Hill Collins's theory of the partiality of standpoints and of situated and unfinished knowledge. Yuval-Davis has also been inspired by the politics of feminist activist groups such as the London-based Women Against Fundamentalism (WAF), which includes Christians Jews, Muslims, Sikhs, Hindus, and others, and the Bologna feminists, who work with women from groups in conflict, such as Serbs and Croats or Palestinian and Israeli Jewish women. What defines transversal politics is not only the fact that differences in nationality, ethnicity, or religion—and hence in agenda—are recognized but also that a commitment to listen and participate in a dialogue is required. Yuval-Davis has qualified these methods as "pivotal," because they encourage participants to participate in a process of "rooting" and "shifting" and thus to explore different positions, engage in different negotiations, and eventually join different alliances.

> The idea is that each participant in the dialogue brings with her a rooting in her own membership and identity, but at the same time tries to shift in order to engage in exchange with women who have different membership and identity. (Yuval-Davis, 1997, pp. 130–131)

Participants are encouraged to position themselves as women with particular national, ethnic, or religious roots, while also shifting to other ways of thinking, being, and practicing in order to realize the partiality of their own positions and to identify possible common stands and interests.

Aligning herself with Bolognese feminists, Yuval-Davis (1997) called this form of dialogue "transversalism," as opposed to both universalism and particularism, which are inherent in liberal and radical feminism, and also to the political naïveté of the rainbow coalitions of the 1980s or the "Million Man March" to Washington, D.C., in the 1990s. It is crucial here that the boundaries of the groupings are determined not by a notion of essential difference, which leads to a particular standpoint, but by a political reality of partiality, which provides for diverse and provisional alliances (Yuval-Davis, 1997, p. 129).

*When it's being used as an insult, "bitch" is most often hurled at women who speak their minds, who have opinions and don't shy away from expressing them. If being an outspoken woman means being a bitch, we'll take that as a compliment, thanks.*

— Bitch Magazine

In combination, third-wave feminism constitutes a significant move in both theory and politics toward the "performance turn" we introduced earlier. The performance turn marks a move away from thinking and acting in terms of systems, structures, fixed power relations, and thereby also "suppression"— toward highlighting the complexities, contingencies, and challenges of power and the diverse means and goals of agency. Embedded in the scientific paradigm shift from structuralism to poststructuralism, the performance turn is connected to a broader intellectual transformation. In this context, we shall introduce you to performance, cyborg, and transfeminist theory (Chapter 2), to the methodology of poststructuralist and transversal discourse analysis (Chapter 3), and to examples of performance (Chapter 6) and transversity perspectives (Chapter 7). After this description, it is time for us to sum up and present you with a model of different feminisms and our own situatedness.

## Our Own Situatedness: Transversity

Each of the feminisms discussed in this chapter has played a crucial role in 20th- and 21st-century feminist theory and politics, and together they constitute a source of inspiration for future scenarios. We have described the basic exchange between feminism and Western philosophy that runs through these feminisms, and now we will sketch a cognitive map to be used for navigation in the chapters to come. It is both possible and useful to position them along the lines of "x," Equity and Difference, and "y," Universalism and Particularism.

As already stated, we do not wish to suggest that third-wave feminism returns to the first position, thus completing the circular movement around the quadrant. Rather, third-wave feminisms break the system, positioning themselves for a transversal theory and politics of diversity and multiplicity, which we simply call "transversity." In this position, we see a potential for breaking up the "cannibalistic" reasoning of Western thought, in which

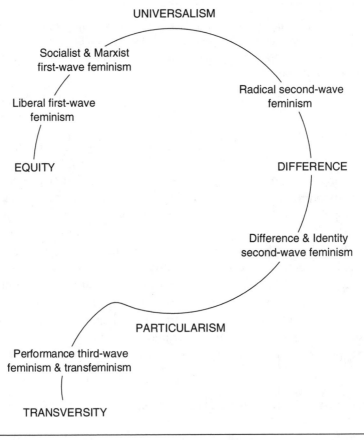

Figure 1.1    Feminist Positions: From Equity to Transversity

difference is a prerequisite of equity, particularism of universalism, and every possible stand is thus "consumed" by the "one and only."

In continuation hereof, it would be appropriate to make our own positions clear: We are in awe of both first- and second-wave feminism. At the same time, we share an enthusiasm for the feminist concept of transversal politics that we call "transversity," and we are inspired by third-wave feminists' attempts to juggle complexity and ambiguity. To us, the concept of transversity presents feminists with a theoretical and practical means by which we, as differently situated women, can simultaneously acknowledge our diverse positions and work across national, ethnic, racial, and gender lines. Transversity commands respect for the diversity of both women and men, while simultaneously presenting us with a sophisticated theoretical framework within which to understand both the fragility of the ways gender is inscribed on bodies and the ways in which power is expressed, negotiated, and ever present in gendered practices. We are inspired by young women's expressions of feminism, which, on one hand, seem to repeat gender stereotypes and, on the other, mock them through mimicry and subversion. We share the desire to reclaim laughter in order to unfold, acknowledge, and appreciate differences and remind us that we are both different and similar. We believe that there is no position outside the social or outside power from which to approach questions of gender and communication. We all continuously take part in powerful constructions of gender when we perform in social life, and we cannot avoid the pitfalls of equity and difference. This logic is often broken with contrastive arguments of equality and difference, mixing the oppositional terms of equity/difference and equality/inequality. The consequence of such circular argumentation is that if you want equality, you cannot have difference. In this way, you cannot have a valid discussion of how the double pairings relate to each other. It demands constant effort to confront the powerful discourses that force us to prioritize the aims and means of our struggle. This struggle is hampered only by invalid argumentation, such as the above-mentioned pairing of equality and difference.

Finally, we wish to emphasize the fact that we are ourselves situated in Scandinavia, at a Danish university department in the Humanities, in the field of cultural and communication studies. One of us has spent more than 10 years in the United States; the other has only occasionally visited the United States and different parts of Europe. It is our hope that although we have chosen our references and examples from an Anglo-American context, our status as outsiders can provide an English-speaking public with new perspectives on gender and communication. Thus, we will direct attention to our own situatedness only where and when it seems productive.

# 2

# Feminist Communication Theories

D o women and men communicate differently? If we believe that gender
differences in communication do exist, what are the terms underlying
this thesis? How do we validate it? Or perhaps the question is whether gender is in fact an effect of communication, and in what way.

How may we discuss this? In either case, how do we propose and assess
statements relating to gender and communication? To argue consistently or
engage in critical evaluation of research on the issue, we must have some
insight into the theory and methodology of communication studies and feminist appropriations hereof. Therefore, having introduced our readers to the
broader feminist waves of theory and politics, we now turn to the conver-
gences of feminism, theory, and communication scholarship.

## Structuralism and Feminist Communication Theories

In this chapter, we elaborate on a fundamental change in both communication and feminist studies, the performance turn, and relate it to a more general paradigmatic shift from structuralism to poststructuralism within both
the humanities and the social sciences. We caution our readers that the following reflects our choices and priorities. It is our hope that it will provide
you with an intellectual map and some guidelines to refer to when negotiat-
ing this highly diverse field. We propose that you consider structuralism
and poststructuralism to be scientific paradigms that function as guides to
our views on gender and communication by providing a set of basic beliefs

(ontology) and basic ways of knowing (epistemology). It is highly debatable when and where to define the watershed between the two paradigms. Some scholars are very concise in terms of time and space, while others refer to a continued and distributed process. We sympathize with the latter approach, which we expand on in the following. Toward the end of the chapter, we provide an overview of the two paradigms.

## The Structuralist Paradigm

To explain the structuralist paradigm, we need to revisit influential thinkers such as Karl Marx, Louis Althusser, Antonio Gramsci, Ferdinand Saussure, Ernest Laclau, Chantal Mouffe, and Jacques Lacan. Providing an overview of such an immense body of work and choosing some representatives to others is no easy task. However, we consider it important due to the influence of this tradition on feminist communication scholarship.

We begin by introducing you to Marx and Marxist thought. Known for his criticism of the political economy (capitalism), Karl Marx (1818–1883) argued that bourgeois society is built on private ownership and the division of labor. Society is split into two main classes: the capitalists, who own the production machinery, and the working classes, who are forced to sell their manual labor. This dichotomy is emphasized in the split between *private* and *public,* which leaves both production and reproduction a private matter *and* a matter of division of labor between the sexes. According to classical Marxist theory, the role of the state is to provide adequate conditions for private production, while securing an adequate supply of labor through reproduction. This is managed through the institution of the patriarchal family, by which man is made the slave of contract work but the master of women and children.

Feminist adaptations and criticisms of classical Marxist theory focus on the implied status of reproduction as both nonsimultaneous and nonproductive and the business of women and children. Feminist Marxists such as Shulamith Firestone and Sheila Rowbotham (see Chapter 1) or Nancy Hartsock (mentioned later in this chapter) claim that labor in the home is highly productive, unpaid work and that working-class women in particular not only carry a double workload but also function as a workforce reserve to be drawn in and out of capitalist production. Whereas classical Marxists put aside "the women question" to be resolved after the revolution, Marxist feminists simultaneously claim the necessity of fighting patriarchy here and now as well as the way it influences Marxist theory and the socialist movement itself. According to them, both capitalism and socialism subscribe to feudal patriarchal structures and ideas.

Another important premise of classical Marxism is the dichotomy between the basis of production and the superstructure of ideology and the deterministic relationship between the two. Thus, the means of production supposedly determines both the specific form of society and the way it is reproduced through ideology and communication. This point has been challenged by what have come to be known as "neo-Marxist" theorists, such as members of the Frankfurt school in Germany or the Althusser school in France. Louis Althusser (1918–1990), for example, introduced the concept of *overdetermination,* which denotes both the dialectics of basis and superstructure and the relative autonomy of the latter—to be challenged only by particularly determining forces. Antonio Gramsci (1891–1937) developed this point further by introducing the concept of *hegemony.* Hegemony is a powerful albeit often antagonistic web of material, social, and ideological structures, which is upheld not by, but across classes in blocks, forming levels of collective consciousness in and through complex communication patterns.

This line of thought in neo-Marxism grew into what is now known as "critical theory" and was further diversified into social semiotics, critical linguistics, critical discourse analysis, and so on (see Chapter 3). In particular, Ernesto Laclau and Chantal Mouffe have further elaborated the concept of hegemony, providing a series of analyses of the processes through which ideology interacts with both material structures and social practices to produce so-called master discourses. These are articulated by alternate and often preliminary but nevertheless dominant alliances (Laclau & Mouffe, 1985/2001). This process is not entirely unproblematic, and neither master discourses nor dominances are consistently successful or homogeneous. Hegemony is the often subtle and contingent process that takes place when a set of discourses and practices come together, are articulated, and subsequently diffused throughout society. Chantal Mouffe has applied this new framework specifically to gender theory, focusing on the structural divisions along the lines of gender, which come together to produce a systematic *gender effect.* Albeit not in any homogeneous way, these different discourses and practices that produce "woman" then reinforce each other and come together to form structured sets of social forces and articulations (Mouffe, 1983).

Critical theory has had an immense impact on second-wave feminism. First, it fused with radical feminism into muted group theory and later with difference and identity feminism into standpoint theory (to be explored below). But this fusion was also influenced by other sources. Here, we turn to Ferdinand de Saussure (1857–1913), the founder of structural linguistics and semiology (the study of signs and symbols). He considered language to be the most sophisticated sign system, constructing his theory of signs around this idea. He also considered language a self-contained sign system and distinguished between the abstract system of language, *langue,* and the actual use of language, *parole.* Furthermore, he understood *langue* as both conventional and relational. Thus, linguistic signs were supposedly composed of two elements, the *signifier* and the *signified,* the meaning of which stems from a combination of the relation between them and the relative position of the particular sign in the overall sign system. For example, it is only by convention that the signifier, that is, the combination of letters or sounds into w-o-m-a-n, denotes a human being with female bodily attributes (the signified), and the signifier is made stable only by the relative position of the woman sign within the overall system along the lines of *sameness/difference* and *closeness/distance.* The meaning of woman, then, is determined by its relative position vis-à-vis man, girl, boy, and so on. What makes the sign-"woman" meaningful is that it is not "man" or "girl" or "boy" but is still relatively closer to them than say, to "ape," although the system also implies, as described below, that woman is closer to the category of animal than man. According to the theory, the language system is organized, first, in binary pairs, such as human and animal, man and woman, White and Black, child and adult and, second, around a hierarchy of these binaries that determines their relative ordering. Woman for instance, is closer to animal or child, by virtue of the relative closeness of the term to nature/body/matter. Saussure considered these principles to be almost universal, although he also acknowledged that they were to a certain degree cultural, bound to Western thinking since antiquity. At the same time, he was not very explicit about the degree of universalism or the level of generalization possible in his theory (Bucholtz, 2003; Cameron, 1992).

We saw in Chapter 1 that French feminists have criticized the close affinity between Western philosophy and linguistics and their mutual ground in patriarchal assumptions. This criticism was particularly linked to the work of Jacques Lacan (1900–1981), who turned psychoanalysis into a theory of language, often referred to as "psycho-semiotics." To feminist scholars, Lacan has become notorious for having said, "The woman does not exist," meaning that woman occupies no indexical place in language but, on the contrary, is continuously excluded or marked as deviant. This phrase was appropriated and revised by French feminist Julia Kristeva (1974/1981), who stated that "Woman can never be defined," meaning that woman is something that cannot be represented because it belongs to realms beyond any given nomenclature.

According to Lacan, we become members of society in terms of "the Symbolic" and through language. The premise of membership is our ability to overcome our primary condition of separation and leave behind the semiotic dynamics of the "Mother/Body" (desire/the imaginary) in order to enter the symbolic dynamics of "the Father/Language" (reason/the symbolic). Both genders are forced to do so, and the effect of this dilemma on girls and women is heightened by the fact that the phallus functions as a prime symbol of the law (and thereby of both reason and desire), although it must also be understood as symbolically, not biologically, masculine. So in psycho-semiotics, patriarchy is considered an effect *in* and *of* language. Whereas to Lacan, this is a sine qua non both ontologically and epistemologically, to French feminists such as Hélène Cixous, Luce Irigaray, and Julia Kristeva, it is a question of articulating against "phallogocentrism" through a feminine communication practice (see Chapter 1). Taking its point of departure in women's supposedly nondisciplined, multiple desires and experiences at the margins of culture, "feminine writing" seeks to destabilize the law, explore what is excluded and devalued (for instance, the "Motherbody"), and create alternate visions (Marks & de Courtivron, 1981).

As illustrated in the above description of thinkers, the structuralist paradigm is itself a richly diverse field of study. Whereas, for example, Marx and Gramsci criticized capitalist society and the way it embeds language and communication in ideology, Saussure was engaged in critically examining language as a conventional and thereby arbitrary, if not "innocent," system. He nevertheless came to rather similar conclusions as to the systematic gender effects to be observed and assessed by feminist communication theorists. Feminist communication scholars have appropriated structuralism in their research in various ways. Muted group theory, for example, is constructed around the negative consequences of the Marxist argument, referring women to the margins of society and thereby condemning them to a lack of progress. Standpoint theory has, on the contrary, taken as its point of departure the potentially positive sides of the same argument, where women can be claimed to escape capitalist dynamics and thereby represent a unique, more authentic culture. We see these two feminist appropriations as fundamental to understanding what is frequently described as the "dominance and deficit approach" (see Chapter 4, muted group theory) or the "difference and identity" approach (see Chapter 5, standpoint theory), and therefore, we elaborate on these two feminist theories.

## Muted Group Theory

Muted group theory is based on the work of anthropologist Shirley Ardener (1975). It posits that women and men within patriarchal, capitalist societies tend to form two distinct circles of experience and interpretation, one overlapping the other. The masculine circle converges with the norms of society, providing a masculine signature and overriding the feminine circle. Thus, the female circle is neither visible nor acknowledged—eventually, only a small part or, rather, reflections of it are exposed. Consequently, women's experiences are felt only as "black holes" or reminiscences in society. Women's own perspectives are restricted by this enforced tunnel vision, and their voices are not publicly articulated. Women, then, are left with two choices. They can attempt to translate their point of view into a masculine mode or try to detach alternate models of communication. Both options are problematic. For one, the translation process can give rise to communication difficulties and an ensuing lack of communication satisfaction, a point pursued by Spivak (1987) concerning third-world women. There are also structural barriers to the development of alternate communication modes, as men, whether consciously or not, will perpetuate their power by preventing other voices from being heard and acknowledged, a point pursued by Spender (1980). As a result, women's expression is muted.

Note, however, that muting is not the same as silencing and that muting is successful only when the nondominant group (in this case, women) ceases to find and develop alternative communication styles to express their experiences and code their messages. When this happens, only traces are left of the original, a kind of palimpsest. But note also that muted group theory takes its inspiration from a particular view of language derived from the work of linguistic anthropologists Edward Sapir (1884–1939) and Benjamin Lee Whorf (1897–1941). They took their point of departure in the tradition of functional linguistics (see Chapter 3) and understood language as a culture-specific means of defining and creating reality. From this, they developed the so-called Sapir-Whorf hypothesis: the idea that native tongue has a crucial impact on how one perceives the world. It has later given rise to two different outlines: a stronger (deterministic) view and a weaker (relativistic) one: (a) the deterministic view holds that the structure of particular languages (i.e., grammar and semantics) *determines* the way speakers of that language see the world/reality; and (b) conversely, the relativistic view does not suppose language to determine our perceptions, but to *predispose* us toward certain views of reality. According to this hypothesis, vocabulary does not function as an indicator of the values, beliefs, and power structures of a given society, but rather shapes them. Sapir and Whorf, however, owed much of their work to a structuralist paradigm insofar as they focused on the functional, rule-based, and generative aspects of language use. In so doing, they shared the structuralist tendency to underestimate both agency and dynamics in communication.

Feminist communication scholars such as Dale Spender, Cheris Kramarae, and Julia Penelope have documented the ways in which "masculine" language both inhibits and infects women's forms of expression and how women are forced to double-code their messages through different rhetorical means. We take a closer look at their most significant research from a muted group perspective in Chapter 4. According to this theory, women face a dilemma arising from the fact that their experiences and means of communication are restricted by their marginalization in society and their relative isolation within the private sphere—deemed not only irrelevant to public discourse but also less effective than paid labor and consequently less valuable. An example comes from Cheris Kramarae and Paula Treichler (1990), who have pointed to dictionaries as instances of cultural authority; dictionaries instate and perpetuate the belief system of their almost exclusively male writers, as they persist in excluding the words, definitions, and thoughts of women and "render . . . [women] invisible, reduced to stereotypes" (p. 155). Kramarae and Treichler have clarifed early efforts to change language, such as the work of Mary Wollstonecraft in the late 1700s or Charlotte Carmichael Stopes in the early 1900s. Today, this task falls to Deborah Cameron, who addressed sexism in language in *Verbal Hygiene* (1995b) and promoted "good practice" through more sophisticated and inclusive communicative styles in *Good to Talk? Living and Working in a Communication Culture* (2000).

Muted group theory provides a rather generalized perspective on women's oppression: (All) women are muted, and (all) men mute. As such, it replaces Marxist class-related concerns with gender-related concerns, and although this perspective puts gender at the focus of analysis, the category of sex—women as a group and men as a group—is maintained. Women are left with two options. Either they can refine the ambiguous art of coding and translating, aspiring to be bilingual, or they can go backward, delving into layers of communication competencies previously acquired and abandoned. However, muted group theory is also relevant to other marginalized groups, and it may be applied to the multiple layers and intersections of muting according to class, race/ethnicity, and sexuality. As mentioned previously, postcolonial theorist Gayatri C. Spivak (1987) has focused on third-world women. She has also renewed the theoretical concept of translation, issues of bilingualism, and the complex mixture of gendered, ethnic, and linguistic identities with modes of expression (Spivak, 1988). At this point, however, we turn to another theory inspired by structuralist thinkers that presents us with a somewhat different perspective.

## Standpoint Theory

Nancy Hartsock's article from 1983 is, as mentioned in Chapter 1, often described as the locus classicus of feminist standpoint theory (Hallstein, 2000). During the 1970s and 1980s, Hartsock opened up the field, assisted by contributions from other scholars, among them Sandra Harding (1986) and Patricia Hills Collins (1986). Standpoint theorists have maintained their commitment to theorizing the standpoint occupied by women in the context of capitalism: the sexual division of labor, unpaid work in the home, reproductive responsibilities, the lack of power in society, and so on. Compared with muted group theory, women's shared experiences in standpoint theory constitute a privileged vantage point from which to maintain the dual vision of being simultaneously inside and outside the "malestream" of society. This is the starting point from which standpoint theorists criticize male dominance, patriarchal institutions, and ideology.

Standpoint theory is first and foremost a theory of the interrelationships between power and knowledge. It took its inspiration from G. W. F. Hegel's (1770–1831) theory of slavery, according to which the different positions of master and slave make them perceive slavery quite differently, rendering each perspective limited and partial. However, standpoint theory maintains that some perspectives are more partial than others. Thus, the dominant perspectives tend to be more biased, since they at once maintain the status quo and obscure the standpoint of the less powerful. Conversely, the perspective of the less powerful provides us with an individual, more objective perspective. According to this way of thinking, marginalized groups are not only forced to develop their own standpoints from a less privileged position but are also required to understand the standpoints of the more powerful. They become, as Patricia Hill Collins (1986) has said, "outsiders within": The slave must understand the master's standpoint to survive whereas the reverse cannot be said to be true. Although standpoint theorists find that women generally uphold such bifurcated or double vision, Collins, in particular, refers to women of color. She has also persistently recognized differences among women along the lines of class, race/ethnicity, sexuality, and so on, offering the theory of intersectionality as a means of analyzing both the particularity of sexism, classism, and racism and the ways in which they work together. According to Collins, one cannot be understood without the other. Sexism, for instance, cannot work alone; it articulates other types of oppression in order to again subdivide women along other lines, and vice versa. It is also important to note that bifurcation is achieved only through permanent struggle, social mediation, and a continuous interplay of theory and practice (Hallstein, 2000).

Another application of standpoint theory is the work conducted by feminist communication scholar Marsha Houston (1992), who has documented African American women's production of knowledge and their communication practices. In her work, as in the work of Patricia Hill Collins, it is evident that women of color inhabit several standpoints: They are women, and they are women of color. Houston also claims that it is significant that Black women are at once united and divided by complex circumstances; they have multilayered experiences and must therefore develop multiple tiers of consciousness. According to Houston and the African American tradition, this has turned into a particular communication method of shared knowledge called "signifying," explicated by Henry Louis Gates in *The Signifying Monkey: A Theory of African-American Criticism* (1988). Signifying, usually performed by Black people in less powerful positions, is language play that aims at tricking other—usually more powerful—people. According to Gates, the signifying monkey is a trickster who aims to subvert dominant speech for its own purposes. A rich example of signifying can be seen in Black film producer Spike Lee's work (such as *Do the Right Thing*), as well as in hip-hop or rap.

The distinction between sex and gender is essential to standpoint theory. Whereas sex is to some degree considered a given ontological premise, shared by women, gender is considered a contextual and changeable phenomenon that also divides women, even if they do experience patriarchy and sexism as almost as given as their sexual bodies. Feminist standpoint theorists have thus tended to underscore the commonality of women, ascribing to them a position at once both suppressed and privileged in societal terms of knowledge and communication, even while simultaneously insisting that gender is simply a social construct and a diversified one at that. This inherent contradiction has weakened standpoint theory from an academic point of view. However, the field has been revitalized throughout the 1990s by demonstrating the complexity of women's experiences and the differentiation of standpoints. It has also been brought into dialogue with poststructuralist feminism through the work of Hartsock (1998), Harding (1997a, 1997b), Collins (1997), and Heckman (1997). Due attention has been paid to the unique methodology of researching and acknowledging women's own experiences and points of view on the basis of the epistemological claim that truth is found in women's lived experiences and may be nourished by a feminist methodology of mutual respect and shared standpoints (Hallstein, 2000).

Let us take, for example, a form of scholarship inspired by standpoint theory. Psychologist Carol Gilligan has presented us with a slightly different version of standpoint theory in her now classic study on gender and moral reasoning. She concluded that women, in their moral reasoning, demonstrate an ethic of care and equity, thereby contrasting with the masculine ethic of justice and equal opportunity (Gilligan, 1982). Along the same line, rhetoricians Sonja Foss and Cindy Griffin (1995) have suggested departing from the patriarchal notion of using persuasion to effect change and begin appreciating "invitational rhetoric," which invites the audience to enter the world of the speaker. Grounded in the belief that women by virtue of their position in society have a different standpoint (than men), these feminist rhetoricians propose a particular feminine model resting on new communication concepts. But to explore these ideas, we would have to digress into the fields that are considered significant from a standpoint perspective and provide our readers with examples of difference and identity approaches to be explored further in Chapter 5. Let us, therefore, leave these areas for now, and turn to poststructuralism and the feminist appropriations hereof.

# Poststructuralism and Feminist Communication Theories

Poststructuralism marks a paradigmatic shift within a range of disciplines and schools of thought in the second half of the 20th century. It fundamentally challenged the notions that had hitherto been upheld: an understanding of subject, language, and society as unified, stable, and separate entities, as well as the interaction of systems and structures in dialectic exchange, and definitive explanations and determinations.

The perspectives inherent in poststructuralism highlight the interplay of subject, language, and society and emphasize agency, complexity, and contingencies in the exercise of power. Poststructuralism marks a *performance turn,* that is, a turn toward performance as an embodied communicative practice.

## The Poststructuralist Paradigm

The work of scholars Michel Foucault, Jacques Derrida, Jacques Lacan, and Judith Butler is fundamental to the poststructuralist paradigm and has been a major source of inspiration to communication scholarship.

Philosopher and historian Michel Foucault (1926–1984) has been a dominant force in poststructuralism. In a series of works from the 1970s to 1980s, Foucault criticized Marxism and psychoanalysis, arguing that our current ideas, institutions, and behavior patterns are to be understood as discursive regimes. These regimes structure our existence as a series of historically and culturally situated interpretations of what it is to be human, which we simultaneously live and become by choosing and inhabiting the embedded subject positions. Foucault referred to this as a "simultaneous process of subjectification and embodiment," in which discourses become both subjective and material. Another of his key points is that truth and systems of power are linked in a complex relationship, which both induces and extends itself, and that power is considered to be both complex and contingent—and productive as well as destructive. Consequently, truth and power are not monolithic institutions or structures, but rather the names given to a complicated strategic situation in a given society. In his own research, Foucault concentrated on how (groups of) individuals have been classified and constructed as either mad, sick, criminal, or sexually deviant and how these groups have been marginalized, pathologized, and put forth as legitimate targets of medical, legal, and governmental intervention.

Another source of poststructuralist thinking has been philosopher and linguist Jacques Derrida (1930–2004). Derrida delivered a basic critique of what he called the Western metaphysics of essence and presence. He claimed that identity always bears a trace of what is not there—of absence and difference. He drew on Saussure's theory that a sign obtains meaning from what it is not, from its difference from other signs, and from its place within the overall system of signs. But Derrida went one step further by deconstructing the distinction between language as a system and language in use and the notion of a one-to-one-relationship between signifier and signified. Instead, he unfolded a theory stating that language is heterogeneous, in constant flux, and has no stable center to generate and bind the relation between sign and meaning. Meaning springs, he maintained, from the empty spaces that continuously emerge in the endless interplay of signs. Derrida thereby introduced the renowned notion of *différance,* in which he combined the noun *différence* (difference) and the verb *différer* (defer) in its present principle, *différant.* He thereby suggested a simultaneous move in space and time in order to signify the ongoing play of signs between signifier and signified, sign and meaning. Différance denotes that there is no absolute difference and thereby no absolute identity, only an ongoing process of diversification. Derrida also criticized the notion that language mirrors an outside reality. Instead, he suggested that origin is in itself an imitation, or rather imitation is as real as the original: The world is one big "text" that continuously reproduces itself through intertextuality. Derrida has been much disparaged for this particular claim, as critics felt he was introducing a radical social constructionism that denies any form of reality or materiality. We do not go into detail here; suffice it to mention that this has also been said of Foucault (and Butler, as we shall see) and that they have countered the criticism in very different ways.

Of particular importance to feminism is Derrida's criticism of the combination of opposition and dominance in Western philosophy, as made manifest in "phallogocentrism" and its hegemonic arrest of language play in a frozen, hierarchic binary. Inherent in phallogocentrism is the assumption that the sexual difference is the primary one, with the phallus as the prime signifier of both reason and desire, which again stages the feminine both in opposition to and lesser than the masculine. Throughout his work, Derrida suggested counteracting phallogocentrism by focusing on the workings of displacement and exclusion in language and what he called the return of the marginalized and devalued in order to establish a deliberate strategy of destabilization and subversion.

Derrida's work evolved in a dialogue with Jacques Lacan, whom we have already introduced within the structuralist paradigm. Lacan has been influential to both feminist structuralist and poststructuralist scholars, and we therefore return to his work, particularly his ideas on the evolution of identity. He proposed that the subject is always constituted through the violence of separation and the substitution in and by language, a situation preceded by the "mirror phase," in which the subject learns to know itself as a reflection in the eyes of the (m)other. According to Lacan, the constitution of a subject takes place through its own imaginary identifications, on one hand, and the different symbolic positions offered by language, on the other. Accordingly, subjects can never be self-identical, and "the Real" can exist only in the intersection between "the Imaginary" and "the Symbolic." French feminists such as Hélène Cixous, Luce Irigaray, and Julia Kristeva have further developed this notion of the split, never self-identical subject, thus paving the way for feminist poststructuralism. However, a fully developed new paradigm emerged only with the work of feminist philosopher and rhetorician Judith Butler, who has combined the impulses from Foucault, Derrida, and Lacan.

In her paradigmatic works from the early 1990s, Butler promoted an understanding of gender, along with other significant social markers such as sexuality and ethnicity, as discursive practices that produce the very effects they presume to name, always intricately imbued by power and inflected by each other but simultaneously unstable and prone to displacement (Butler 1990, 1993). Inspired by Anglo-American pragmatics and particularly by the speech act theory of John L. Austin (1911–1966) as well as Foucault, Derrida, and Lacan, Butler advanced the idea that language and communication neither merely reflects nor affects gender. Gender is *effected* through language and communication. Consequently, we now turn toward a description of feminist appropriations of poststructuralist communication theory in performance and positioning theory, respectively.

## Performance and Positioning Theory

Performance and positioning theories rest on the criticism of structuralism and critical theory. They represent quite a diverse research field, originating from the intersections of some of the main sources of poststructuralist thought discussed above. At the same time, they are closely connected to queer politics and theory, which we explore further in Chapter 6. Performance and positioning theories have from their very outset been closely related to feminist theory as theories of social categorization, identification, and agency. They have been promoted not the least by the work of Judith Butler.

Because Butler has combined many of the poststructuralist strands of thought into an integrated theory, we have chosen to focus specifically on her approach. In our view, Butler's work is exceptional in its clarification of the delicate interplay between subject, society, and communication (understood as speech acts) and in the approach to discourse as an entity of mind, body, and articulation. The strength of Butler's approach still lies in the way it widens the scope of different, discursive subject positions and the possible ways not only of moving between them but also of displacing them, thereby opening up new horizons to inhabit. At the core of her theory is the concept of performance as a display of powerful discourses in a "stylized citational practice," which in the very act of stylization and citation almost inevitably pushes that which is cited out of its regular framework, thereby causing a leak or a fissure to be occupied (Butler, 1990, p. 5). According to Butler (1993), gender is a "regulatory social practice" that conditions the way sex is materialized and that is installed on the body as a repeated stylization, as "bio-power" (p. 6); however, as such, it is also subjected to continued de- and reconstructive moves.

Inspired by Foucault's concept of the heterosexual matrix, Butler has criticized second-wave feminist scholarship for distinguishing between "sex" and "gender," focusing on the latter (Butler, 1990). According to Butler, "sex" and "gender" are one and, as such, a question of discursive practices to be continuously generated from the heterosexual matrix, which requires two supplementary genders. Pointing out the close affinity between sex, gender, and sexuality, Butler argues that the heterosexual matrix reinstates itself through the "installation" of regulatory, normative gender practices, on one hand, and the outlining of the perversions (homosexuality, for example), on the other. Although the heterosexual matrix may be destabilized (example: a male child care worker), it also constantly reinforces itself (example: the male child care worker being simultaneously heterosexual and married). So, although the matrix is continually challenged, it is reinstated by adjusting gender and sexual practices.

To qualify her ideas and balance the deterministic trend in Foucault's theory of gender and sexuality as installed by master discourses, Butler took further inspiration from speech act theory and particularly from Austin's theory of the performative. According to Austin, *the performative* is a verb that acts in the very moment of speaking—for instance in naming, hailing, and cursing—deriving its illocutionary force from the embodied enactment of a particular ritual. From this, Butler (1997) developed the core thesis of the performative "nature" of gender as a discursive practice, which tends to bring about that which it names insofar as it embodies established social rituals. Thus, "girling" can be said to be an embodied social practice that produces girls—starting with the midwife's announcement "It's a girl" (Livia & Hall, 1997).

To make her thesis even more dynamic, Butler found inspiration in Derrida and his critique of Austin's "true" performative. Whereas Austin claimed that the illocutionary power of the performative is determined by a combination of the proper context (example: holding a christening in a church) and the right procedure (the clerical proceedings and ceremonial liturgy of a baptism), Derrida claimed that the power of the performative springs from the fact that it is iterable and free of context: For instance, you can have a baptism taking place in several places at the same time, or vice versa. Like signatures, Derrida maintained, performatives generate their authority from their iterability as signs and their continued use over time and place—though this is also what exposes them to displacement and eventual destruction. To this end, Butler (1997) has added her own claim: the significance of the body. Because of the potential gap between the spoken word, the speaking body, and that which is spoken of, the performative, in order to work, must rely on the correlation of sign, body, and social setting. Thereby, it is also rendered fragile and susceptible to any "weak links in the chain." On the basis of these complications, Butler (1997) maintained that the performative is always exposed to and operating within what she calls the "queering effect." Thus, the performative must always be reinstated by the (bodily) authority of the speaker; but once the performance is there, it has a material life of its own—be it verbal, textual, or visual, it is simply *there*. This is the basis of what Butler called "performative agency," which we are going to explore further in Chapter 3 and again in Chapter 6.

Butler has herself been criticized for reducing agency to the freedom to mime powerful discourses in terms of gender conventions. However, our claim is that the sophistication of her theory is often overlooked. In *Bodies That Matter* (1993), she emphasized the distinction between performance and performativity, inherent in Austin's position, thereby anticipating the discussion regarding the difference between performance and performativity perspectives (to be explored in the following section). She also encountered the criticism of radical social constructionists in explicating the importance of the body: Bodies do matter as matter, according to Butler, in an intricate interplay with the title of her book. In similar ways, she has brought up the topic of understanding this matter in terms of desire, which is where she brings in Lacan. She may not have definitively resolved the discussion about the relations between bodies, desires, and discourses, but she has brought the problem to light.

Let us at this point make the connection to positioning theory. Positioning theory may be said to be embedded in Butler's theory of the discursive "nature" of gender, which provides a range of subject positions to inhabit, thereby transforming them. However, it has also emerged as a separate theory at the contact point between discourse theory in the Foucauldian tradition: current trends within psychology such as "psycho-socio-linguistics" and recent reformulations of, for instance, speech act theory (Baxter, 2003b). Social psychologists Jonathan Potter and Margaret Wetherell, psychologists Rom Harré and Bronwyn Davies, and sociologist Luk van Langenhove are often perceived as the founders of positioning theory, representing a distinct tradition and body of work. Their common factor is a poststructural approach to identity and society, which has mobilized a criticism of psychological ego and role theory, as well as Freudian psychoanalysis. Positioning theory, much like performance theory, operates with terms such as *discourse, subjectivity,* and *positioning* in order to analyze the dynamic aspects of social encounters. In other words, focus is on discursive practices and the ways in which people are positioned by, and position themselves as, agents through those practices, thereby generating their own subjectivity (Potter & Wetherell, 2001).

Positioning theory outlines the relationship between subject, discourse, practice, and positioning (Davies & Harré, 1990/2001). Discourses are here understood to provide subjects with positions to inhabit in practice. Having assumed a particular position, a person inevitably sees the world from the vantage point of that position in terms of certain images, metaphors, story lines, and concepts, also known as "interpretative repertoires." The possibility of choice, then, stems from the existence of many discourses and (the intake of diverse), maybe even conflicting positions in different relations, situations, and contexts. Furthermore, according to Davies and Harré, positioning is displayed simultaneously on different levels of discourse, from the microlevel of grammar and sentence building; to the mesolevel of conversation, storytelling, and social interaction; and on to the macrolevel of aesthetic schemata, discursive repertoires, idioms, and so on. Within the framework of positioning theory and analysis, the main object of investigation is the mesolevel (i.e., interactional level), and the focus, therefore, is on conversation understood as "a structured set of speech acts, that is, as sayings and doings of types defined by reference to their social [illocutionary] force" (Davies & Harré, 1990/2001, p. 263).

Even if the fields of performance and positioning theory designate two distinctive theoretical frameworks, we have chosen to present them as related versions of feminist poststructuralism, to be further explored in Chapter 6 in terms of significant feminist communication scholarship and the contexts of media and organization. We also discuss their methodological implications, under the heading of "feminist poststructuralist discourse analysis," in Chapter 3 (to be exemplified in Chapter 6).

## Transgender and Cyborg Theory

We now turn to the latest developments within the field of feminist poststructural theory, namely, the notion that viewing gender as "performance" does not necessarily lead to a deconstruction of gender. We here direct our attention once again to Judith Butler, this time complemented by performance and communication scholar Kristin Langellier and the work on developments in transgender and cyborg theory by Sandy Stone and Edward Davies.

We now focus on the theoretical tension between *performance* and *performativity*. Performances can be thought of as embodied enactments distinguishing certain events, for example, a group of boys playing hopscotch on a playground during a school lunch break or young women at home after school transforming into "Net-grrls" in a chat room. Such performances are first and foremost about the mastery of form and the display of competencies in doing so in relation to a given situation and context. Performativity, however, can be thought of as the embodied enactments that are tied to and comment on the powerful discourses and institutionalized frameworks that constitute them. In the above case, the performance of the young boys and girls would be performative insofar as they comment on their own performance, for instance, by pointing out their performances as astereotypically gendered. According to Langellier (1999, 2001), it is in fact quite difficult to distinguish between these two levels, but what interests communication scholars is exactly how communication acts are situated in discourses and distributed according to power. With Langellier, you might say that performativity articulates the struggle for agency, while simultaneously reflecting the forces of discourse and the institutionalized networks of power: school, the media, family, and so on (Langellier, 1999, p. 129). Feminist communication scholars, then, wish to explore how gender performativity emerges from the tension between agency and the underlying norms, which are frequently unconscious and appear natural, thus preceding the subject. Note that these norms are constituted in discourse and thus do not preexist outside communication, although they are not fabricated by the communicators themselves.

To sum up: The performativity perspective situates performances in specific contexts and histories, critically exploring the tension between the act and that which is acted upon, both in terms of the agents involved and the spectator/researcher. Performances that reflexively explore the slippage between the act and that which is acted upon are of particular interest to the performativity perspective. Whereas Butler (1990) has exemplified this through the drag-queen figure and the drag show (see Chapter 6), Langellier (2001) has used the narratives of, for instance, women with breast cancer (see Chapter 7).

Transgender theorists suggest engaging in the delicate interplay of performances and performativity by naming and legitimizing a plethora of gender possibilities, thereby avoiding the pitfalls of a two-gendered system (Davies, 2004; Halberstam, 1998). Judith Halberstam (1998), for example, put the spotlight on female masculinity, as such extending Butler's analysis of the drag show. Whereas queer and transgender theory has tended to focus on male-to-female performances, the drag queen, and gay male culture, Halberstam has encouraged us to see the performances of drag kings and masculine women as a challenge to the idea that masculinity is inherent only to males. In fact, these performances demonstrate how masculinity is constructed, subsequently moving it out of the realms of the nonperformative. Edward Davies (2004) has suggested that we may even discuss gender in the shape of "gender mobility," "gender migration," or "gender transgression," in which "new" gendered and sexual categories are named and legitimated. He has further suggested a four-step process along the lines of evolution, revolution, involution, and evolution: imagining sexual identity (evolution), outing sexual identity (revolution), establishing sexual identity (involution), and reviewing sexual identity (evolution) (Davies, 2004, p. 114). Sandy (Alluquere Roseanne) Stone (1991) is another vocal proponent of transgender theory, and she situates the notion of transgender in what she calls the "gender borderlands." To Stone, gender/sexual identity is not fixed, nor is it a temporary stage that individuals outgrow, but rather a "real" and "meaningful" experience. Putting *trans* into *gender* thus facilitates a move beyond conventional manifestations of gender and sexuality. To transgender theorists, it is vital to also engage in the politics of naming, to assure recognition and acceptance: "A positive politics of naming will require the silent and secret discourses to be replaced by reflexive articulation and openness about one's sexual location and allegiances" (Davies, 2004, p. 114).

Feminist scientist Donna Haraway has taken another radical step in deconstructing the boundaries between the human and the nonhuman animal or machine. In her famous "Cyborg Manifesto" (1987/1991), she delivered a criticism of Western humanism for privileging humans over both other living beings and nonorganic materials or machines. According to Haraway, Western techno-science has gradually undermined the relevance of the distinction between human and machine, and she sees the potential for feminists (and others) in the making of "cyborgs." Cyborgs transcend not only the categories of gender but also other "natural" boundaries, such as race and sexuality. For example, the category "woman of color" is a hybrid identity that the "cyborg" can embody: a kind of "postmodernist identity out of otherness, difference, and specificity" (Haraway, 1987/1991, p. 155). In the making of new classificatory types, there is a great urge to reinstall gender, but now, according to Haraway, we have the chance to do it differently. Cyborg politics is a feminist politics that does not rely on the "logic of appropriation, incorporation, and taxonomic identification" (p. 157). That does not mean, however, that Haraway is an idealist. On the contrary, she stresses materiality, the importance of situating oneself as a scientist or a feminist in a specific situation, place, or body, and she suggests the critical position of embodied "she-cyborgs." Furthermore, according to Haraway, all knowledge is situated, and new knowledge can be generated only from this outset.

Feminist philosopher Rosi Braidotti has supported Haraway and reintroduced women's bodies as particular "body sites" (Braidotti, 1996). Braidotti has argued in favor of what she calls a "perverse-productive" alliance between technology and body and between technology, politics, and art. She has encouraged the development of new techno-cultures, promoted in and by cyberspace, that draw on parody, irony, and playful performance, and she sees feminist groups like the Guerrilla Girls and Riot Grrls as particularly important sites of feminist resistance. Braidotti has further considered successive repetition, mimetic strategy, and strategic juxtaposition to be forms and a means of feminist agency.

Transgender theory and cyborg theory have come together to articulate new theoretical frameworks that deconstruct the two-tiered gender system and provide a plethora of gender possibilities, thereby also challenging the idea of distinct feminisms and opening up the possibility of transfeminism. Transfeminism denotes not only the diversity and possible mixture of different types of feminisms but also the very possibility of a new reflexive framework that cuts across feminisms and even challenges the idea of particular feminist concerns, grounded in the notion of gender. Because many of the "gender migrations" or examples of "gender borderlands" have occurred in the interface of computer-mediated communication (CMC), we return to CMC in our final considerations (see Chapter 7).

# Conclusion

Like feminist structuralism, feminist poststructuralism addresses the workings of power through discourse, although it is conceptualized differently. Within the structuralist paradigm, discourse is assumed to work dialectically insofar as it continuously reshapes and is shaped by "reality." Within the poststructuralist model, there is no opposition between discourse and reality; on the contrary, social and even material phenomena are considered to be discursively produced. Discursive practices systematically shape the subjects as well as the objects of which they speak. Furthermore, power is now conceptualized as being fluid, complex, and contingent, and attention centers mainly on the power of agency and the empowerment of groups and individuals. However, while it is important to be aware of this paradigmatic shift, it is also important to distinguish between the early manifestations of poststructuralism in performance and positioning theory and the later focus on performativity, transgender/cyborg, and even transfeminist theory.

We compare and contrast feminist structuralism and poststructuralism, both in methodological terms (in Chapter 3) and in research terms (in Chapters 4 to 7). But first, let us introduce Table 2.1, which presents our mapping of the theoretical framework of feminist communication scholarship. We wish to stress, again, that this chronological device is provisional and that dates refer to the time at which each paradigm was initially articulated, as they were, and indeed continue to be, constantly rephrased and applied in new contexts.

**Table 2.1** Feminist Communication Theories

| Positions | Feminist Communication Scholarship | Theory | Characteristics: Premises and Perspectives |
|---|---|---|---|
| Chapter 4 1960s–1970s First- to second-wave feminism | **Dominance and Deficit Communication Scholarship** | **Structuralist Theory:** | 1. One-culture model in which women (as a group) are dominated by men (as a group). |
| | | | 2. Women's voices are muted and rendered deficient in heteropatriarchy. Women are bound to "translate" their experiences into "man-made language." |
| | Exemplified by: Robin Lakoff, Dale Spender, Julia Penelope, Cheris Kramarae, Shirley Ardener, Susan Herring | Muted Group Theory | 3. Language is sexed and treats women differently than men—woman is the marked sex. |
| Chapter 5 1980s–1990s Second-wave feminism | **Difference and Identity Communication Scholarship** | **Structuralist Theory:** | 1. Two-culture model: Due to women's different social standpoint and socialization, women develop (a) a double vision and a more privileged point of view and (b) feminine communication mode as opposed to masculine mode (genderlects). |
| | Exemplified by: Carol Gilligan, Deborah Tannen, Jennifer Coates, Deborah Cameron, bell hooks, Trinh Minh-ha, Patricia Hill Collins, Marsha Houston | Standpoint Theory | 2. Women's style of communication is seen as a valid alternative, which leads to a reevaluation of certain forms of communication (e.g., gossip). |
| | | | 3. Differences among women are highlighted. Feminist communication scholars of color stress intersections of gender and race and develop "womanism" as an alternate communicative framework. |

| Positions | Feminist Communication Scholarship | Theory | Characteristics: Premises and Perspectives |
| --- | --- | --- | --- |
| Chapter 6 1990s to Present Third-wave feminism | **Performance Communication Scholarship** <br><br> Exemplified by: Don Zimmerman and Candace West, Judith Butler, Mary Bucholtz, Kira Hall, Don Kulick, Karen Lovaas | **Poststructuralist Theory:** <br><br> Performance and Positioning Theory | 1. Gender is no longer a source of identity and language but rather a consequence hereof—a doing or an effect of semiotic practices. <br> 2. Gender is "a performative gesture" with queering effects, by which we both adapt and negotiate discursive subject positions. <br> 3. We participate in gender performance by a rhetoric of mimicry and subversion. <br> 4. Notions of "gendering" intersect with those of race, class, sexuality, ethnicity, and nationality. |
| Chapter 7 Future visions | **Transversity Perspectives** <br><br> Exemplified by: Kristin Langellier, Judith Halberstam, Sandy Stone, Donna Haraway, Nira Yuval-Davis | **Poststructuralist Theory:** <br><br> Transgender and Cyborg Theory | 1. Cyberfeminists position themselves as new pioneers and posthuman she-cyborgs transgressing earlier divisions and positions. <br> 2. Transgenderism further denotes attempts to pass through the looking glass of gender and develop new gender options. <br> 3. Sex and gender, body and language are intertwined as "material-semiotic" practices and effects. <br> 4. Opening toward transfeminism. |

# 3

# Feminist Communication
# Methodology

There is no such thing as *the* feminist communication method. So far, feminist communication scholars have simply not agreed that any single method is fundamentally feminist. Nor is there any single method that feminists agree is fundamentally antifeminist. Rather, feminist communication scholars engage in a range of methods. We have chosen to celebrate the diversity of methods that feminist communication scholars draw upon in their work. None of these methods is "inherently" feminist, yet each, in its own way, helps recover women's voices and uncover the gender issues at stake in communication.

Below and in each of the chapters to come, we highlight three different methodological approaches and loosely sketch a fourth. Our choices reflect the thesis that each feminist methodology in question *has been* and *can be* related to the feminist communication theories outlined in the previous chapter, on one hand, and to more specific methodological frameworks, on the other—again, divided along the line of structuralism and poststructuralism. We claim that methodology can be thought of as "packages," and we again suggest a tentative mapping, this time to outline the relationship between methodologies and feminist appropriations hereof.

## Structuralism and Methodology

The structuralist paradigm makes itself felt in different methodological "packages" that to some extent correspond to the theories discussed in

Chapter 2. To illustrate the workings of the structuralist paradigm in communication methods, we have chosen to describe two distinctive methodological frameworks: (a) sociolinguistics and conversation analysis and (b) critical semiotics and critical discourse analysis. Both of these methodological packages consist of the larger methodological framework (sociolinguistics and critical theory) and a method (conversation analysis and critical discourse analysis). Both have also been used and appropriated by feminist communication scholars, and examples of this work will be briefly mentioned below and more discussed in detail in Chapters 4 to 5.

## Conversation Analysis (CA)

Sociolinguists study language in use and the occurrence of conventional patterns in speech. During the 1960s, this was viewed as a paradigmatic shift away from formal linguistics in the tradition of, for example, Noam Chomsky and the view of language-as-a-system exemplified by Ferdinand Saussure (see Chapter 2). Sociolinguistics inspired a range of methodological considerations and developments, such as ethnography of communication, ethnomethodology, and conversation analysis (CA).

Sociolinguistics was initially concerned with determining the relationship between the use of particular vocabularies, grammatical features, and pronunciation patterns, on one hand, and, on the other, certain social stratifications such as sex, class, race, and sexuality. The field gradually expanded to study the correlations between language in use and the social world. William Labov and John Gumperz (1972), for example, found that pronunciation and language use vary not only with the social strata of the speaker but also relative to the situation in which the speaker finds himself or herself. Gumperz (1982) further developed this notion and talked about a codelike relationship not only between language and the social but also between different types of language use among particular groups or speech communities.

Scholars focused on the numerous ways in which speakers change their language depending on social circumstances: for example, speaking standard English in some situations and a vernacular form of English in others. Of particular interest was language use in heterogeneous, multicultural societies and how language is used across linguistic and cultural groups in various kinds of interethnic communication, not least in cases understood as miscommunication. What started as a rather simple study of variation patterns in language use, reflecting a given social stratification, was now distinguished by the investigation of the complex patterns of social, cultural, and linguistic contact and developed into interactional sociolinguistics.

Ethnography of communication was another field in which sociolinguistics was applied. The goal of ethnography of communication is to study particular ways of communicating that occur within specific speech communities in order to highlight "native" communication practices. Ethnographic methods such as interviews, observations, and tape and video recordings are used to study spoken discourse, always from the perspective of the members of the group studied and in terms of their own cultural framing. Ethnographers of communication observe contextual patterns of communication within a given community and understand them in terms of culture.

Dell Hymes, an influential figure in the field, distinguished between three interacting layers of communication: (a) the speech act, which is embedded in (b) the speech event, which again is embedded in (c) the speech situation, for example, a joke made during a conversation at a party (Fitch, 2001). Hymes further proposed that studying communication from the perspective of a given community should include the "SPEAKING" grid. The grid is made up of the different components of communication: "S" stands for the setting, "P" for the participants (speaker, sender, audience), "E" for the ends (purposes and goals), "A" for the act (message), "K" for the key (tone and manner), "I" for instrumentalities (channel-verbal, nonverbal, mediated), "N" for norms of interaction, and "G" for genre (Schiffrin, 1994). According to tradition, speakers are aware of the ways they use the SPEAKING grid, and contextualize it in terms of a "native" speaking and as a means of creating local speech communities. Moreover, Hymes borrowed the phrase "linguistic competence" from Noam Chomsky and reframed it as a "creative communication competency" to denote the awareness of and ability to use the grid in community building.

Erving Goffman broadened the framework by hypothesizing that communication is a performance that follows particular generic formats and types of embodiment, much the same way as in ritual and drama. Goffman's central insight was that interactions follow certain procedures that again constitute a distinctive syntax, a socio-logic of interaction that provides for the framing, the sequential ordering of acts, and the relative positioning, called "footing," of participants (Heritage, 2001). Of further importance is the concept of front- and backstage performances (the norms of public and private) and of maintenance of "face" (keeping one's self-respect and the mutual respect of communicators), that is, the moral laws behind interaction, directing the rights and obligations of communication in different contexts. On the basis of these insights, Goffman (1959) generated the hypothesis that communicative conventions are linked to social institutions and even to the matrix of societies.

We now turn to the method of CA. To conversation analysts, talk is a joint enterprise, and the primary methodological focus is on talk-as-action (Kitzinger, 2002). It is posited that interlocutors actively (though often unwittingly) create and attend to conversational order and that it is what people *do* with talk that is of interest. Conversation analysts want to understand how conversations are structured and what makes them successful (see, for instance, the work of Harvey Sacks, Emanuel Schegloff, and Gail Jefferson). This includes, for example, turn-taking organization, turn allocation techniques, sequence organization, repair work (in terms of face-keeping), and turn-constructional units (Heritage, 2001). Conversation analysts argue that we rely on conversational rules in our everyday language use: One person speaks at a time, each speaker gives way to other speakers so that no one monopolizes the floor, silence takes place only in a limited way, and simultaneous speech is kept at a minimum. We even develop rules as to when it is time to "jump" into a conversation. Intonation, stress, and pausing remind us that a "turn transition point" is at hand. Current speakers may also select the next speaker (through eye contact, directional questions, etc.), the next speaker may self-select (voluntarily contribute), or the current speaker may continue speaking (Cameron, 2001). Within each conversational "unit," exchanges must relate to a previous exchange in such a manner that a greeting follows a greeting and a question is followed by an answer. This relative ordering, also known as "adjacency pairs," is a powerful way of organizing utterances (Cameron, 2001; Kitzinger, 2002).

CA emerged not only within the general framework of sociolinguistics, but more specifically within the context of ethnomethodology, and it was strongly inspired by the work of Harold Garfinkel. To ethnomethodologists, and Garfinkel in particular, it is important to note that constructs such as power and oppression are *accomplishments*. They are not preexisting, objective, or coherent phenomena. Rather, they are processes that are continually created, sustained, and resisted through talk and interaction (Kitzinger, 2002). An ethnomethodological perspective commits us to understanding people as active agents who engage in the reinstatement of and resistance to the social world (Kitzinger, 2002). Ethnomethodology, therefore, constitutes a provocative turn away from not only formal structural linguistics but also structural sociolinguistics, preparing the ground for poststructuralism and the performance turn. Not surprisingly, CA has been an inspiration to both structuralist and poststructuralist feminist communication scholarship, and it will be discussed further in Chapters 4 to 7. However, ethnomethodology has also been criticized for being preoccupied with the systematic formatting of talk-in-action, and frequently, because of its rather general statements about rules for talking, it has been seen to reinforce a universal Western position. As we shall see, these claims have been reflected in feminist communication studies and met on different terms, according to the particular theoretical framing.

CA focuses on naturally occurring materials of interaction and on people's own orientation to talk. Consequently, CA practitioners tend to avoid predetermined research agendas, and power is understood as something enacted in communication itself. Thus, questions of gender and power are considered relevant in the analysis only if the participants themselves do so. Nevertheless, as discussed above, feminist CA practitioners such as Susan Herring (1996) have insisted that this aspect, although central to ethnomethodology, can be redefined in feminist-inspired CA work (see Chapter 4 for further discussion). Herring is an example of a feminist researcher who has stayed with CA throughout the different theoretical and empirical orientations of feminist communication research. She has continuously renewed the framework and applied it to new contexts, such as computer-mediated communication. However, we claim that sociolinguistics, and in particular the feminist appropriations of CA, are most closely connected to early second-wave feminism, muted group theory, and the dominance and deficit approach (see Chapter 4).

## Critical Discourse Analysis (CDA)

During the 1970s to 1980s, critical theory met with linguistics and the now expanding field of semiotics concerned with different types and uses of signs. From this scientific contact grew new approaches to communication, such as critical linguistics and social semiotics. Let us first take a look at some of the more pertinent examples of critical theory in order to then introduce you to critical discourse analysis (CDA).

Robert Hodge and Gunther Kress (2001) provided communication scholars with a critical theory approach grounded in linguistics, semiotics, and communication research and developed a methodological approach under the headline of critical linguistics or social semiotics. Building on sociolinguistics, they were interested in a socially relevant linguistics in the guise of the correlative perspective mentioned above and of the slightly different perspective of choice and intention in the tradition of, among others, Michael Halliday (Kress, 2001). This new approach gave rise to the study of differences in language use or, rather, how the social is manifested in the utterance, text, or communication practice in question, for Kress (2001) argued that the social is *in* the sign. Moreover, in a plausible social view of language, sign makers transform the resources available to them in their social environments and in relation to the power of the imagined audience/recipients of the sign-as-message: "Yet emphasis on 'interest' ensures that there is a real agency, transformative action, *work*" (Kress 2001, p. 37; italics in original). Thus, social semiotics critiqued the relation between power and communication manifest in communication itself. The intent of the researcher is to study and address the social challenges experienced by subordinated groups, and thus the emergence of this field marks a turn toward a critical view of the use of signs as a means of communication invested with power (Kress, 2001).

Another take on critical theory can be found in the work of Ernesto Laclau and Chantal Mouffe (see Chapter 2). Laclau and Mouffe (1985/2001) built on Gramsci's definition of hegemony as a strategic situation in which political alliances arise around particular issues, transcending classes and the historical division of (economic) basis and (ideological) superstructure in powerful discourses. They redefined hegemony as a set of discourses on the antagonistic oppositions of society, which involve not only class interests but also racial, ethnic, gender, and other conflicts. Together, these discourses comprise vast argumentative webs or orders, which people both inhabit and transform through articulation. Though bound to given discourses, individuals, or rather groups of individuals, continuously strive to establish new orderings by creating what Laclau and Mouffe have called "chains of equivalence," "nodal points" or "master signifiers." They may eventually disturb the orders of discourse and thus contribute to revising them. Although Laclau and Mouffe developed critical theory into a distinct methodological approach in a range of significant studies on political and social subjects, Norman Fairclough, Lilie Chouliaraki, and Ruth Wodak have contributed most consistently to CDA.

In a series of works published during the 1980s to 1990s, Norman Fairclough elaborated on the link between critical theory as a theory of discourse and critical linguistics as a methodology of discourse analysis (Fairclough, 1995a, 1995b). One may say that Fairclough combined discourse theory with sociolinguistics and created CDA. To establish a connection between the different traditions, Fairclough (1995a) suggested that discourse is to be understood as the use of language in a particular form of social practice, thus underscoring the suturing of communication and social agency (p. 7). He further suggested that discourses are, on one hand, distinct from nondiscursive practices and, on the other, from "pure" grammar. However, to implement CDA, both grammar and nondiscursive practices must be considered. Thus, CDA must not only focus on a given "text" (be it written or spoken, mediated or unmediated), it must also consider the discursive practices of text production and consumption as well as their embeddedness in larger social practices. Whereas the microlevel includes phonology, grammar, vocabulary, structure, meaning, and so on, the mesolevel includes generic types, media formats, and the particular forms and conditions of both production and consumption, and the macrolevel includes the wider discourses and social practices of groups, institutions, and so on. Of particular interest, however, is the *intertextuality* on all levels, in both time and space, which is explicit in terms of citations and references and implicit in that they draw on the same discourse orders. The focus on intertextuality also expresses the methodological interest of CDA in investigating how "webs" of rhetoric and argumentation are created, spread, and challenged.

Ruth Wodak, Teun van Dijk, and Michael Billig have also contributed to the development of the link between critical theory and CDA. According to van Dijk, critical discourse analysts take an explicit sociopolitical stance and spell out their points of view, perspectives, principles, and aims both within their discipline and within society at large. Their work is openly political, and their ambition is to instigate change through critical understanding. They believe in the possibility of identifying global and local power structures and elites, as well as social inequality and injustice (van Dijk, 2001).

Van Dijk has worked extensively with discrimination and racism and provided a significant example of CDA in action in his analysis of a speech given in the British House of Commons in 1985 by conservative representative and Member of Parliament (MP) Mr. Marcus Fox (van Dijk, 2001). The speech is occasioned by a case from Bradford, England, where the mostly Asian students, their parents, and the city council accused the principal of a local secondary school, Mr. Honeyford, of racist speech and writings; he blamed certain groups of students for schooling problems. Fox argued that Honeyford had merely delivered an original and deserved critique of multicultural education and that his opponents were personally harassing him and thus posed a threat to free speech. Fox associated the opposition with totalitarian communism, known to be against freedom and democracy, and tried to discredit it. Fox's claim was that by attacking Honeyford, his opponents were limiting freedom of speech and attacking democracy itself (van Dijk, 2001, p. 311). Van Dijk demonstrated how Fox's speech was built on an argumentative shortcut; it had a thesis, but no support. He also showed how Fox used his position and power to promote his argument and give it legitimacy—but in so doing also misused the formal speech genre of the House of Commons and his position as an MP. Thus, the speech supported the system of ethnic-racial dominance, both directly and indirectly.

Wodak, who is also a prolific writer on the topics of feminist discourse theory and analysis, has worked along the same lines and contributed extensively to the elaboration of the methodology of CDA. She has suggested the following definition: "Critical Discourse Analysis sees discourse—the use of language in speech and writing—as a form of social practice" (Wodak, 1996, p. 17). She has further defined the methodological issue in the following way: "Describing discourse as social practice implies a dialectical relationship between a particular discursive event and the situation, institution, and social structure that frame it: the discursive event is shaped by them, but it also shapes them" (Wodak, 1996, p. 17). Thus, Wodak has accepted the idea of a basic dialectic between the social and the discursive, but she has argued that discourse combines the two as social practice. In line with Fairclough, she has adapted Foucault's concept of "orders of discourse" and applied it to ordered sets of discursive practices associated with particular social domains, institutions, and settings. These range from private, informal conversations to ritualized genres like medical counseling or educational lectures. Such discursive practices may, in turn, be strongly or weakly demarcated, may be used more or less consciously, may serve to express approval or protest, and so on. Thus, boundaries between and within orders of discourse are constantly shifting. Wodak has elaborated on the methodology of CDA, paving the way for a renewal of the method, inspired by poststructuralism and the performance turn (Weiss & Wodak, 2003; Wodak & Meyer, 2001). We return to her work in Chapter 5.

Despite such complexities, the basic interest of CDA has been, and still is, power: the organization and articulation of social power through discourse and as dominance but also as modes of challenge and "counterpower" in identity work and oppositional discursive practices. In our case study in Chapter 5, we present an example from Wodak's (2003) study of European politicians' discourses in the context of the European Union (EU).

# Poststructuralism and Methodology

The theoretical development of poststructuralism is also made manifest in new constellations of theories and methodologies, which are, in turn, challenged and adapted by feminist communication scholars. Poststructuralism first comes to expression in a critique of structuralism and then transcends it to reveal new theoretical and methodological horizons. In this context, we have chosen to outline performance theory and positioning theory in poststructuralist discourse analysis and take a brief look at methodological transversity in continuation of transgender and cyborg perspectives.

## Poststructuralist Discourse Analysis (PDA)

The poststructural turn to discourse and performance has led to a general interest in communication and agency. We now see a revival of rhetorical studies and also a new feminist rhetoric, and we experience a revival of speech act theory and performance studies and the point of contact between the two. Therefore, Judith Butler's work is again of particular interest. Taking her point of departure in Foucault and discourse theory and inspired by John L. Austin's speech act theory, Pierre Bourdieu's critical communication theory, and Jacques Derrida's semiotics, Butler (1997) has presented us with a rhetorical perspective that bridges these different traditions. Or rather, she has rearticulated the former in terms of the latter and created a highly influential framework for PDA. To follow her reflections on speech acts, however, we need a short introduction to speech act theory.

John Austin's *How to Do Things with Words* (1962) is considered the seminal text of speech act theory. Austin distinguished between different types of speech acts: constatives, which are evaluated in terms of truth or falsity, and performatives, which are evaluated in terms of success or failure. Examples of constatives are (a) "the Queen of Denmark smokes," a statement that is true, or (b) "the Queen of England is 50 years old," a statement that is false. Examples of performatives are (a) "I do" (take this woman to be my lawful wedded wife), which is felicitous in the course of a marriage ceremony, or (b) "I name this child Jonathan William Turner," which is also felicitous in the course of a christening ceremony. Austin further dissolved performatives into three dimensions, which also constitute different types: the locutionary act (the utterance of an act—the sounds, the words, or the very act of saying something), the illocutionary act (the act performed in saying the locution), and the perlocutionary act (the consequential effects). The above-mentioned speech acts are first and foremost illocutionary compared to, for instance, "I will become angry, if . . ."

Austin later on claimed that all speech acts are somehow performatives and that two qualities need to be present in order for a performative to work: text and context. For example, the use of the performative verb "I do" is an illocutionary act only in that exact wording and in a particular setup, in this case a wedding ceremony; "I name" is an illocutionary performative when performed correctly during a christening ceremony. It is only by maintaining the conventional scripts that the "doing" and "naming" perform a "real" act, in this case marriage and baptism. Consequently, a speech act can fail to perform the act due to an incorrect script or the absence of the right setup, and thus, there is always the possibility that a performative may misfire. What happens, for example, when the statement "I pronounce you man and wife" is made to two same-sex individuals?

Butler has reinterpreted Austin and placed the performative at the center of a North American discussion of hate speech. Butler (1997) claimed (with Althusser, see Chapter 2) that it is in and by language that we are instantiated as social beings and that our social existence can therefore be threatened in and by hate speech. However, opposing legislation and prohibition of, for instance, sexist or racist statements, she has also claimed that the speech act is still not equal to acting directly on the body. The words create a slippage between the doer and the deed and also between the deed and the one acted upon, which not only leaves room for agency but also is somehow already an acknowledgment of the right of the acted upon to speak up or talk back. The point is that in naming each other, whether we hail or curse, we acknowledge each other as social agents. Nevertheless, an injury still occurs when the performative gains illocutionary force by calling upon a strong social convention. For example, the use of the words *slut* or *nigger* still calls upon a history of sexism and racism that precede the subjects involved.

Significantly, Butler (1997) has reinterpreted Austin's concept of "sovereign autonomy in speech," widening the criteria for the illocutionary force of the performative as both socially and bodily embedded. For an illocutionary performative to work, it has to be supported both by the social context and by the bodily authority of the speaker (see also Chapter 2). If not, there is a possibility of back-talking, in the moment, and of resignification, over time. The word *nigger,* for example, can be counteracted by appropriating and subverting the expression. Thereby, the hate speech is displaced and a space left open for resignification. Butler's success criteria for hate speech or back-talking, however, still depend on whether the performance is both embodied and socially embedded.

In her elaboration of these criteria, Butler (1997) drew partly on French sociologist Pierre Bourdieu, who emphasized social legitimacy and status, and partly on Derrida, who claimed that the quality of the sign itself is important. Butler has focused, however, on the embodiment of the speech act in terms of a coherence of word and body and the anchoring of the words in the social relation in question. Her prime example is a parable, taken from the African American author Toni Morrison's 1993 Nobel Lecture in Literature, in which language is conceptualized as a living thing itself. In the story, young children play a cruel joke and ask a blind woman to guess whether the bird in their hands is living or dead. She responds by displacing the question: "I don't know . . . but what I do know is that it is in your hands" (Butler, 1997, p. 6). The old woman thereby forces the youngsters to take responsibility themselves—not only for the bird but also for the way they speak and interact. She furthermore displaces the implied conventions about age, ability, and gender. What gives her performative agency in the situation is neither convention, nor context and social power, nor her forceful wording; it is the way she embodies her speaking in the situation and in the relation between the persons involved. Thus, she turns the theme of life and death into the *form* of their exchange.

An example of a long-term intervention is the successful resignification of the word *queer*. Queer has been used to condemn a group of people, but it is now being cited against its original purpose, thus breaking "the ritual chain" and remaking the semantic contents (Butler, 1997, p. 14). Queer has become a word that in certain contexts at least, signifies pride and strength.

To Butler, the speaking body is the ultimate criterion of the illocutionary performative. It is because of the correlation between the word/saying, the speaking body, and the thing spoken about that it works, but it is also in the slippages hereof that the possibility of change exists. This is Butler's special contribution to speech act theory and methodology, comparable to the implication of the proper context (Austin), the social power (Bourdieu) or the iterability/history, and the break from context by the graphemic mark itself (Derrida).

Another trend within PDA stems from the point of contact between discursive psychology and psycholinguistics: what Bronwyn Davies and Rom Harré (1990/2001), Jonathan Potter and Margaret Wetherell (2001), and Kenneth J. Gergen (2002) have referred to as "positioning analysis." Davies and Harré (see Chapter 2) have argued that discursive practices provide subject positions that include both a conceptual repertoire and a location. Having assumed a particular position, a person inevitably sees and acts on the world from the vantage point of that position and in terms of certain images, metaphors, story lines, and concepts known as "interpretative repertoires." The possibility of choice stems from the existence of many, often contradictory, discursive practices. It follows that positioning is displayed at different levels of discourse: at the microlevel of grammar and sentence building; at the mesolevel of conversation, storytelling, and social interaction; and at the macrolevel of aesthetic schemata, discursive repertoires, idioms, and so on (see also Chapter 2). However, within the framework of PDA, the main object of investigation is the mesolevel, and focus is on conversation understood as "a structured set of speech acts, that is, as sayings and doings of types defined by reference to their social [illocutionary] force" (Davies & Harré, 1990/2001, p. 263).

Davies and Harré (1990/2001) gave an example, taken from one of their own conversations during a conference stay abroad, in which one (the woman, a feminist) falls ill and the other (her male colleague) darts hastily into a range of shops to ask for medicine. At a certain point, he stops and states, "I'm sorry to have dragged you all this way when you're not well." She promptly replies, "You didn't drag me, I chose to come" (p. 263). This exchange sets off a chain of (anxious, angry, etc.) responses, directed by the positioning effects of the first exchange of statements, intended or not. The woman feels that she is being positioned as disempowered and paternalized, whereas the man maintains that he did not intend to position anyone with his excuse and thus feels misunderstood, or positioned by a political (feminist) project.

This little interaction reveals a whole range of mechanisms to be identified and described within positioning theory and analysis (van Langenhove & Harré, 1999). One of these mechanisms is first- and second-order positioning: Whereas the first one is reflective, the latter is reflexive. Thus the woman's response, "You didn't drag me, I chose to come," can be considered not merely a reflection of the first positioning but also reflexive in terms of commenting on their relationship and the very act of positioning each other. From this distinction follows several others: between performative (immediate) and accountive (metacommunicative) positioning, between personal and professional communication, intentional and nonintentional communication, and so on. However, the main focus is on the mechanism of self- and other positioning that takes place in most utterances: "Whenever somebody positions him/herself, this discursive act always implies a positioning of the one to whom it is addressed. And similarly, when somebody positions somebody else, that always implies a positioning of the person him/herself" (van Langenhove & Harré, 1999, p. 22). This is certainly the case in the example given above, in the two opening remarks of the conversation. The double positioning and the subtle effects hereof initiate a chain of reactions and becomes an issue in itself.

To find a way to analyze the process of positioning and being positioned, both Davies and Harré (1990/2001) and Wetherell (2001) have used the concept of interpretative repertoires: a way of balancing between, on one hand, the ideological effects and, on the other hand, the possible subject positions embedded in the (conflicting) discourses available. Thus, interpretative repertoires function as a kind of conflict management; however, they can also themselves be in conflict, and conversations or "talk-in-action" are accordingly approached as "battlegrounds," where opposing ideological stands and subject positions are negotiated (Wetherell, 2001). Therefore, another variation of PDA is narrative positioning, in which the possibility of positioning oneself is attached, on one hand, to the narrative perspective or point of view and event construction, and, on the other hand, to a performance-based approach to oral and conversational narration (Bamberg, 2000, 2004; Gergen 2002).

Judith Baxter, who has a background in linguistics and CA, has taken her point of departure in poststructuralist discourse theory (2003a). She has persistently developed poststructuralist discourse theory into a concise method and has furthermore outlined it in terms of a specifically feminist PDA (2003b). She has also discussed the intersections of CA, CDA, and PDA and inspired us by indicating similarities as well as differences (Baxter, 2002). Her definition of the feminist poststructuralist approach runs like this: "I highlight a central concern of the FPDA approach: namely to examine the ways in which speakers negotiate their identities, relationships and positions in the world according to the ways in which they are *multiply* located by different discourses" (Baxter 2003b, p. 10). Compared to, for instance, Davis and Harré or Wetherell, she thus underscores not only the complex and contingent web of discourses and positions for subjects to navigate between but also that subjects are located and locate themselves in and by different discourses. We therefore return to Baxter in our case study in Chapter 6.

## Transversal Discourse Analysis (TDA)

*Transversal discourse analysis* (TDA) is a term we have coined for the future directions of feminist communication methodology, which breaks with established methods. At its outset feminist, TDA draws its inspiration from third-wave feminist transversal politics (see Chapter 1) and the performance and performativity turns (see Chapter 2). TDA focuses on crossing disciplinary boundaries, and its strength lies in recombining conventional methodological packages. In the process, new conceptualizations, connections, alliances, and webs of understanding seem to develop. Whereas the method is not yet clearly articulated, we find examples of it in performance and performativity scholarship (Langellier), computer-mediated communication and cyberfeminism (Stone), and transgender discourse (Halberstam). In crossing boundaries and recombining of tools and concepts, TDA also signals the emergence of a transfeminism. Let us first, however, look at the points of inspiration.

TDA is inspired by feminist transversal politics, in particular the work of feminist scholar Nira Yuval-Davis (see Chapter 1). It involves a constant pivoting of the center of analysis: what Yuval-Davies (1997) referred to as the process of "rooting" and "shifting." She used this method in the context of conflict management and the process of building feminist solidarity that does not fall prey to homogenizing the "other," but we believe that her guidelines can serve as methodological tools as well. Transversal feminists seek to avoid essentialist identity groupings and instead engage in the critical interrogation of essentialist terms such as *feminine, masculine, female, male, butch, femme,* and so on. To engage in sophisticated shifting, however, is to engage in *strategic essentialism,* a term borrowed from Gayatri Spivak and a form of role play that helps the researcher understand how communication unfolds without also falling victim to easy identity categories. A communication scholar may, for example, be critical of the description of a transgendered person as "a woman trapped inside of a man's body" *or* see it as a form of strategic essentialism that engages in essentialist categories to gain visibility and acceptance in a heteronormative culture that would rather see transgendered people as "biological errors" than challenge the two-tiered sex and gender category systems (Koyama, 2003).

Gender theorist Judith Halberstam (1998) has employed TDA through a range of methodologies that she collectively calls a "queer methodology" (p. 10): textual criticism, ethnography, historical surveys, archival research, and the production of taxonomies. Halberstam could have remained methodologically "faithful" to one type of criticism but has deliberately refused to fit her project into any one conventional methodological category and has instead engaged in a range of methods that help spotlight various locations of female masculinity, from the Hershe Bar Drag King Contests in 1995–1996 to Queen Latifah's performance as the butch character "Cleo" in *Set It Off,* from 1997. Engaging in multiple methodologies not only opens up to various locations of female masculinity but also provides both the scholar and the reader with a historical context in which examples of female masculinity can be critically interrogated. Halberstam (1998) has referred to it as a "scavenger methodology" (p. 13), which is particularly useful when we wish to study individuals who have traditionally been excluded from studies of human communication.

The methodological challenges that computer-mediated communication pose to communication scholars have also contributed to our idea of a TDA. How do we study communication when the body of the speaker is unknown? When bodies are only textual? When speech is interactive? Or when communication is constantly changing and always unfinished? We believe that TDA and the methodological tools of "rooting" and "shifting" may help understand the gender implications of CMC. Whereas communication scholars have tended to read online bodies as true representations of offline identities, a pivoting of the center will help uncover the ways in which gender and other identity markers are textually managed, always in flux, and constantly challenged. We discuss this further in Chapter 7.

# Conclusion

Methodological approaches tend, in general, to have become established without feminist involvement and are consequently often criticized for being sexist (Kitzinger, 2002). The notion that "the master's tools will never demolish the master's house" has led some feminist communication scholars to search for their own methodological approaches, whereas others have continued their work within particular communication subdisciplines and have found imaginative ways to include feminist concerns and thereby revise scholarly agendas (Kitzinger, 2002). One of these scholars is Celia Kitzinger, who has worked with feminist-inspired CA. During the 1990s, she debated the relevance of gender and social identity to CA with Emanuel Schegloff, in many ways the standard-bearer of the methodology (Kitzinger, 2002). Ruth Wodak (1996, 2003) has also contributed to the development of CDA in cooperation with Norman Fairclough, and she has taken gender perspectives to the core of the methodological debates.

Moreover, Judith Baxter has developed PDA as a methodological framework and has initiated a debate on feminist poststructuralist methodology that embeds both performance and positioning approaches. Although scholars have debated whether CA, CDA, and PDA are mutually exclusive or mutually supportive (Baxter, 2002; West, 2002), we wish only to note that the initial formulations of each of these methods were inspired by theories (sociolinguistics, critical theory, and performance theory) to articulate a distinct methodological focus. What these scholars share, however, is an insistence on putting gender issues at the forefront of their work and, as a result, they have made important contributions to the field of communication.

In Chapters 4 to 7, we argue that feminist conversation analysis (FCA) is related to the difference and dominance position through the generic enterprise of explicating how dominance is carried out in communication. Consequently, early second-wave feminist scholars are more likely to have engaged in FCA as a method. Feminist critical discourse analysis (FCDA) may be related to the difference and identity position of second-wave feminist scholarship, and feminist poststructuralist analysis (FPDA) to the performance and positioning position inspired by third-wave feminist scholarship. It should be noted, however, that these approaches are subject to continual reassessment and renewal. We therefore caution our readers that none of the methods described "belong" to any particular feminist communication perspective. For example, whereas CA was used in classic feminist communication dominance work in the 1970s and 1980s, in its current form, it is just as, if not more, valid within poststructuralist feminist communication work, and it is continually reclaimed for feminist purposes today. Just as feminist communication perspectives have changed, so have the feminist applications of these methods, and as we have seen, we now seem to be in the midst of a deliberate recombination of methods and a turn to a TDA.

We hope that by including a discussion of feminist communication methods, we give our readers an opportunity to see theory and method in mutual interaction, thus not only paving the road for future feminist scholarship but also equipping our readers with critical lenses through which to make their own educated evaluations of feminist communication scholarship (see Table 3.1).

**Table 3.1**    Feminist Communication Methodology

| Method | Methodology | Feminist Communication Studies |
|---|---|---|
| Chapter 4 Conversation Analysis (CA) | Sociolinguistics: Ethnomethodology & Ethnography of Communication | Feminist Conversation Analysis (FCA) |
| Harvey Sacks, Emanuel Schegloff and Gail Jefferson, David Silverman | Harold Garfinkel, Erving Goffman, John Gumperz, Dell Hymes, William Labov | Celia Kitzinger, Pamela Fishman, Janet Holmes, Susan Herring, Candace West and Don Zimmerman |
| Chapter 5 Critical Discourse Analysis (CDA) | Critical Theory: Critical Linguistics & Social Semiotics | Feminist Critical Discourse Analysis (FCDA) |
| Norman Fairclough, Lilie Chouliaraki, Michael Billig, Teun van Dijk, Ruth Wodak | Ernesto Laclau and Chantal Mouffe, Robert Hodge and Gunther Kress, Norman Fairclough, Teun van Dijk, Michael Billig, Ruth Wodak | Deborah Cameron, Jennifer Coates, Marsha Houston, Mary Talbot, Sara Mills, Ruth Wodak, Penelope Eckert and Sally McConnell-Ginet |
| Chapter 6 Poststructuralist Discourse Analysis (PDA) | Discourse Theory: Performance and Positioning Theory | Feminist Poststructural Discourse Analysis (FPDA) |
| Michael Bamberg, Margaret Wetherell, Bronwyn Davies and Rom Harré, Judith Baxter | Jonathan Potter and Margaret Wetherell, Rom Harré, Luk van Langenhove, Bronwyn Davies, Judith Butler | Don Kulick, Deborah Cameron, Bronwyn Davies, Judith Baxter, Kira Hall, Mary Bucholtz, Kristin Langellier |
| Chapter 7 Transversal Discourse Analysis (TDA) | Transversity Perspectives: Performativity, Transgenderism, and Cyberfeminism | Feminist Transversal Discourse Analysis (FTDA) |
| Kira Hall, Donna Haraway, Nira Yuval-Davis, Edward Davies, Judith Halberstam | Kira Hall, Donna Haraway, Nira Yuval-Davis, Edward Davies, Judith Halberstam | Brenda Danet, Shannon McRae, Sandy Stone, Kristin Langellier |

# 4

# Sexist Discourse, Deficit and Dominance

I t is often claimed that women are more conventional communicators than men. How are we to make sense of such a statement? In this chapter, we focus specifically on feminist dominance communication scholars who through their work exemplify the influence of structuralism and muted group theory. First, however, we shall describe early deficit scholarship, especially the work of one of the most ardent chauvinist writers, Otto Jespersen, and the first feminist responses elicited by his writings, which came about in the wake of second-wave feminism. Whereas the deficit perspective found its proponents mostly among nonfeminist scholars, it also infiltrated early dominance work and is, as we shall see, still discussed within the field of feminist scholarship. We conclude the chapter with a case study illustrating the continued influence of dominance communication scholarship and linking it with conversation analysis methodology.

## From Deficit to Dominance

The deficit model is well represented in the work of Danish linguist Otto Jespersen. In his book *Language: Its Nature, Development, and Origin*, from 1922, he declared women's speech to be trivial and thereby deficient and inferior to that of men. Even when research conducted by his (male) contemporaries demonstrated that women were linguistically quicker than men, Jespersen and his allies maintained that women's superior answering skills are in fact caused by their intellectual inferiority: "With the quick reader it is as though every statement were admitted immediately and without introspection to fill the vacant chambers of the mind, while with the slow reader every statement undergoes an instinctive process of cross-examination" (Ellis, in Jespersen, 1922, p. 252). The argument runs that since men's minds are evidently so full of words and ideas, they will hesitate upon the choice of words, whereas women, with little else to occupy their minds, could naturally answer more quickly. Jespersen attributed many, though not all, of these conventional communication differences to women's lack of education and the roles that women occupied in society, such as mothering, which was understood to require little deep thought (Jespersen, 1922, p. 254). At the time of his work, male speech was unquestionably the norm, and since he provided no scholarly evidence for his claims, it is unsurprising that it encountered harsh criticism from second-wave feminists. However, his work is not entirely without importance today, as feminist communication scholars take his stereotyped preconceptions of female and male speech styles as their point of departure. So let us now consider the early beginnings of gender communication studies.

## A Dominance Perspective in the Making

*Language and Woman's Place*, by linguist Robin Lakoff (1975), was one of the first works to put gender communication on the feminist agenda. Although Lakoff echoed highly stereotypical notions of women's speech, she wrote from a feminist perspective, making an important contribution to this emerging field. Largely circumstantial and based on introspection, intuition, and anecdotes, the book is not a typical scholarly work. Nonetheless, Lakoff contended that most of her claims would hold for the majority of speakers of English (p. 5). Her main thesis was that women experience linguistic discrimination in two ways: the way that women are taught to use language and the ways in which language is used to describe women (p. 4). Because she tended to ascribe linguistic discrimination to women's lack of cultural and political power, Lakoff's text is an early example of what later came to be known as the "dominance approach" (Cameron, 1990).

Lakoff (1975) maintained that cultural forces oblige women to speak differently than men: Men, for example, use camaraderie, backslapping, joke telling, nicknaming, slang, and so forth, while women have no comparable strategies (p. 79). Conversely, women use empty adjectives (such as "divine," "charming"), question intonation (such as tag questions, e.g., "It's a nice day today, isn't it?"), italics, and hedges (such as well, "y'know," "kinda") (pp. 53–56). Women's speech is hesitant and filled with tag questions that are used for a variety of reasons: to be polite, to leave a decision open, and to avoid imposing themselves on others—all strategies that reinforce women's lack of social power (p. 16). Furthermore, Lakoff maintained that women have few linguistic options open to them and are, in fact, stuck in a double bind. To avoid ostracism, women must learn to speak in a feminine manner: "If she doesn't learn to speak women's language she's dead: she is ostracized as unfeminine by both men and women" (p. 61). According to Lakoff, the price that a woman pays for *not* speaking in a feminine manner is her femininity, but if she *does* speak in a feminine way, her lack of power is reinforced every time she opens up her mouth.

To Lakoff (1975), women's lack of choices in communication was intimately connected to their lack of social value and power. For instance, the reason that women distinguish between "lavender" and "purple," Lakoff theorized, is because what women say or do matters very little. Noncrucial decisions, such as distinguishing nuances of color, are relegated to women. Furthermore, women are assigned relational roles, both linguistically and culturally, such as "Mrs.," "mother," "wife," or "housewife." In contrast, men are assigned roles that emphasize their educations, careers, and professional accomplishments. Call a man a "professional" and he will be seen in terms of his career, but call a woman a "professional," and she will be seen as a prostitute, so there is no parallelism of terms, and this informs us of the ways in which women and men are conventionally viewed differently (p. 28). Women are defined in terms of their relationships with and to men, whereas men are defined in terms of what they do. Women are, however, also considered to be able to move beyond gendered communication, because gendered speech is learned: "If we are aware of what we're doing, why we're doing it, and the effects our actions have on ourselves and everyone else, we will have the power to change" (p. 83).

Other scholars also concluded that gender communication differences exist and that these differences are largely due to gendered power differentials. Let us highlight here the early conversation analyses conducted by Pamela Fishman on communication between intimates and the work done by Don Zimmerman and Candace West on interruptions: In "Interaction: The Work Women Do," Pamela Fishman (1983) examined the ways in which conversations are initiated and maintained among romantic couples. Her study showed that on average, women initiated 47 conversations and men 29. Of the 47 topics raised by women, 17 succeeded (i.e., developed into conversations), while 28 of the 29 topics that were raised by men succeeded. In short, women raised 62% of the topics, but only 38% of these evolved into conversations (p. 97). Overall, women were more engaged in ensuring interaction: They asked more questions, used more attention beginnings, did more support work, active maintenance work, and so on. Because conversations centered on topics raised by males, Fishman concluded that women are the "shitworkers of conversation." They do all the maintenance work but receive none of the credit.

Sociolinguists Candace West and Don Zimmerman (1983) arrived at similar conclusions in their work on interruptions in cross-gender conversations. They compared earlier research on cross-gender interactions with new research between previously unacquainted persons in laboratory settings. Interruptions, West and Zimmerman concluded, basically violate the current speaker's right to speak. Repeated interruptions become a way of establishing status differentials and thus a means of "doing" power. When these interruptions are applied to men interrupting women, they are also a way of "doing" gender (p. 111). When we consider interruptions in light of women's lack of social power, they become "constant reminders of women's subordinate status" (p. 110).

At the time, feminist reactions to Lakoff's work were mixed. Her argument that women's speech was tentative and uncertain continued an all-too-familiar tradition of comparing women's speech with men's and consequently viewing it as inferior and deficient. To the feminist critic, a series of questions remained: What is tentative speech? Does speaking tentatively always mean speaking powerlessly, regardless of the circumstances? Tentative speech in courtroom settings may be associated with lacking credibility, but is this also the case in other settings? What if a person with power—for instance, the judge—uses tentative speech? Will it then also be associated with lack of power? And what if women in fact use gendered speech only to signal recognition and acceptance, what Julia Penelope (1990) called a "cosmetic universe of discourse" (CUD). Because Lakoff echoed the conclusions of earlier work, such as Jespersen's, her feminist argument that women's tentative speech stems from a lack of cultural power became less perceptible. In fact, she reinforced and maintained male speech patterns as the norm, although this was perhaps unintentional. It was all too easy to concur with the idea that if women's subordinate status is confirmed whenever they speak, what women need to do is change their way of speaking.

It is no surprise, then, that Lakoff's distinction between powerful and powerless speech became an axiom for nonscholarly assertiveness-training programs. Assertiveness training did not originate as a feminist practice, nor was it originally aimed at women (Cameron, 1995b, p. 177). Assertiveness now became a way for women (if they were smart and ambitious) to linguistically sidestep their oppressed, gendered speech patterns and practice what was conventionally seen as powerful speech (Cameron, 1995b).

Included in the list of elements to avoid were tentative speech and the use of tag questions. Precisely because the assertiveness strategy did not have its roots in a political feminist movement, it was compatible with mainstream aims that partially recognized societal discrepancies in power but believed the solution to lie in training women to become more powerful (i.e., more like men). Cameron (1995b) referred to this as the "verbal equivalent of power-dressing" (p. 184). The underlying assumption was that if women were to talk more like men, they would gain more positions of leadership. However, since institutional power structures and male speech patterns remained intact, this feminist perspective implied that there was no need for men to change.

Popular books such as Bloom, Coburn, and Pearlman's *The New Assertive Woman* (1975) and Anne Dickson's *A Woman in Your Own Right* (1982) popularized the notion that women's lack of social power was, in large part, due to women's inability to communicate assertively. Embedded in this popular claim was also the unexamined notion that some speech styles are inherently more powerful than others (Cameron, 1995b). Radical feminists opposed this strategy, however, and considered assertiveness training a dead end for women. As feminist linguist Dale Spender pointed out, "Women will still be judged as women no matter how they speak, and no amount of talking the same as men will make them men, and subject to the same judgments" (Spender, 1985, p. 79). Now, we shall turn to the tenets of radical feminist scholarship, the foundation of feminist dominance communication scholarship.

## Marked and Muted

*Sticks and stones may break my bones, but words can never hurt me.*

Feminist linguist Julia Penelope began her thought-provoking book *Speaking Freely: Unlearning the Lies of the Fathers' Tongues* with the ditty quoted above. Penelope (1990) demonstrated that this is a "primary dogma" of what she referred to as the "patriarchal unit of discourse" (PUD) (p. xiii). PUD is, according to Penelope, a dangerous "consensus reality" in which patriarchal communication practices are automatically considered the norm (p. 37). Those who accept PUD assume that it accurately reflects reality, but in fact PUD reflects a monodimensional, male-imposed reality. In PUD, language is conceptualized as a "gendered container": Women and language form a container (uterus), and men insert their ideas (penises) into women and language (p. 31). Thus, the world is strictly divided into two unequal, stereotypical spheres—one female, the other male—and in this world, the female/language is a passive recipient and the male an active creator of both (p. 38). Moreover, words such as *feminine* and *masculine* are made to perpetuate a heterosexist patriarchal reality within which the feminine is always valued as "less than" the masculine. Penelope referred to this reality as "negative semantic space" and claimed that within it, women are denied a voice (p. 52). Inherent to PUD are a number of ways in which the female and the feminine are marked as being "opposed to" and "lesser than" the male and the masculine. This again influences women's conceptualization of themselves and the way they approach language and communication.

Penelope's idea of PUD provided a framework for feminist research to conceptualize the ways in which language is used to discriminate women. Her work is very much in accordance with muted group theory. In this type of research, "marking" is a central aspect of patriarchal linguistic classification. Lakoff (2000) correctly traced the concept of "marking" to Ferdinand de Saussure (see Chapter 2), claiming that unmarked forms are semantically and morphologically simpler than their marked counterparts. Gender is a category, subject to marking; thus, the feminine and the female are marked, leaving the male and the masculine unmarked. Let us consider a couple of examples: *woman physician* functions to highlight and mark a woman who practices in a profession dominated by men. Likewise, a *male nurse* is a man working in a woman-dominated sphere. Here, the marking signals that job functions are conventionally seen as female (nurse) or male (doctor). Another example: The "lioness," the female part of the species is marked, yet the "lion" is unmarked. Marking is therefore not exclusively a product of numbers of women or men (as in the case of the physician or nurse); it is very much a product of power. Feminist dominance communication scholars argue that because physicians, for example, hold higher cultural status than nurses, they are classified as male. The animal "kingdom" (notice again the male-oriented language) also reveals a similar linguistic classification system. With power comes the ability to name and label oneself "unmarked."

Patriarchal language is literally, not figuratively, man-made (Spender, 1985). In *Man Made Language*, from 1985, Spender argued that men are seen as the superior gender, and because men hold more social power, maleness and/or masculinity becomes the norm. Male supremacy is projected to such an extent that a male-enforced reality comes about, creating two fundamental categories that Spender called "males" and "minus males" (p. 23). To be linked to the masculine, Spender said, is to be linked to everything good. Absence of masculine qualities can only lead to inferiority, and women become "minus males" (p. 23). Consequently, words for women are loaded with negative and frequently sexual overtones. In one study, Julia Penelope (formerly Stanley, 1977) found 220 terms for sexually permissive women and only 22 terms for sexually promiscuous men. In man-made language, anything female or feminine is trivialized or used as insults to other men (such as "sissy" and "girly"). Feminist dominance communication scholars have argued that the consequences of this are severe, since man-made language mutes women.

Language is a battle for the ability to define and create a large part of reality. As noted in our description of muted group theory, the Sapir-Whorf hypothesis has been influential in shaping early feminist communication work (see Chapter 2). Whereas Lakoff, for example, takes a relativistic view of the influence of language on thought and action, Penelope's and Spender's angle is more deterministic (see Chapter 2). Feminist communication scholars generally believe that language is crucial to the creation of gendered realities, while the more radical faction of dominance communication scholarship takes a more deterministic stance. To them, linguistic classification is never impartial, but marks women as sex objects and the property of men. Cameron (1990) provided a very illuminating example of this agenda, taking as her point of departure a rape case reported in the newspapers. While Cameron cannot be classified entirely as adhering to a dominance approach, these examples still serve to demonstrate the prevalence and persistence with which a male-dominated reality is perpetuated in print:

> A man suffered head injuries when attacked by two men who broke into his home in Beckenham, Kent, early yesterday, he was pinned down on the bed by intruders who took it in turns to rape his wife. (*Daily Telegraph*, in Cameron, 1990, p. 17)

> A terrified 19-stone husband was forced to lie next to his wife as two men raped her yesterday. (*The Sun*, in Cameron 1990, p. 17)

In her analysis of the two accounts quoted above, Cameron cited that the crime of rape was being presented as though it were perpetrated against the man. In the *Daily Telegraph* example, the intruders broke into "his" home and raped "his" wife. In the *Sun* story, a man was "forced" to lie next to his wife, while she was raped (Cameron, 1990, p. 17). In both examples, the rape was presented as a crime against the man/husband, whereas the woman was out of sight and her experience accordingly erased: She was, in short, muted (pp. 17–18).

To dominance communication scholars, language is literally both man-made and used by men as a means of domination. This claim is inspired by John Austin's speech act theory (see Chapter 3), which conceptualized sexist speech as "linguistic misbehavior" (Lakoff, 2000, p. 105). Let us briefly consider how the performative works in the context of feminist dominance communication work. Language such as "I pronounce you man and wife" performs an action, that of marriage, and to dominance communication scholars, it is critical to note that in this performative, the man maintains his independent status (he is "the man"), whereas the woman loses her status as an individual (she becomes "the wife"). Feminist dominance scholars understand sexist speech as hate speech that reinstates years of discrimination and physical injury to women. Attention has been paid to sexist speech, for instance, on U.S. campuses, which were among the first to put speech act theory to work in making out campus speech codes, which also anticipated the demands of politically correct speech. Here, like before, we see a difference in the estimation of the range of such speech acts. Lakoff (2000) preferred to distinguish between verbal and physical acts: If given the choice between a punch on the nose or a battle of words, most would choose the latter (p. 107). Spender (1985), on her part, pointed to the wide-ranging consequences, for instance, in terms of persuasive speaking, which society deems a superior norm and is for this precise reason used as a means of perpetuating dominance. When confronted with persuasive speech, women, according to Spender, tend to withdraw, thereby conforming to the norm. When women do break these rules, they are felt to be talking too much, maybe not compared with men, but compared with one of the norms for women: *silence* (Spender, 1985, p. 42).

To early feminist communication scholars, speech act theory therefore addressed the physical and psychological traumas inflicted by sexist and racist speech. Dominance scholars pointed to the wide-ranging consequences of the "male-as-norm" standards, for example, in the field of communication studies. These standards contaminate everything from the elements included in a basic communication model (where focus is on the speaker, not the listener) to what is considered persuasive speaking. Thus, speech follows a male/female dichotomy: Speaking is associated with power (men are good speakers), while listening is associated with passivity (women are good listeners) (Spender, 1985). This pattern of male superiority also functions inversely, so that women's communication choices are always considered less valid than men's. If women use tag questions in their speech, they appear hesitant, noncommittal, uncertain, and powerless. When men use tag questions, they are likely, as illustrated in Jespersen's work, to be understood as thoughtful and full of sophisticated ideas. Women are considered "talkers" and "chatterers"—they simply won't shut up! But as has already been pointed out, feminist dominance communication scholars see this as a set of conventionally based sexist expectations.

Feminist dominance communication scholars suggest that it is necessary to develop a quite-new language. Such a language might replace masculine definitions with feminist ones, or it might, as in the example of "Láadan," incorporate women's experiences into new words and phrases. Láadan, the subject of Suzette Haden Elgin's science fiction novel *Native Tongue*, is a language that more accurately mirrors the lives of women (Elgin, 1984, 1990). It has a very limited vocabulary but presents an example of how women's realities may be expressed. Feminist dominance communication scholars argue that there is no point in repeating patriarchal hierarchies. Liberal feminist scholarship, as manifested in books with titles such as *The Great Women of History* or *Great Women Public Speakers,* is considered to lack vision and zest, because it fails to realize that the standards for "greatness" are male defined. Similarly, rhetorician and writer Sally Miller Gearheart (1979) has argued that the definition of rhetoric as persuasion, the ability to change people, must be challenged, as it is based on a "conquest model" of human interaction, which does not fit a female perspective or female experiences (p. 196). Contemporary rhetoricians Sonja Foss and Cindy Griffin agree that there is a dire need for new perspectives derived from women. They have suggested the use of "invitational rhetoric" to challenge the notion that control and hierarchy must be elements of "persuasion":

> Most traditional rhetorical theories reflect a patriarchal bias in the positive value they accord to changing and thus dominating others. In this essay, an alternative rhetoric—invitational rhetoric—is proposed, one grounded in the feminist principles of equality, immanent value, and self-determination. Its purpose is to offer an invitation to understanding, and its communicative modes are the offering of perspectives and the creation of the external conditions of safety, value, and freedom. (Foss & Griffin, 1995, p. 2)

They further articulate the ambition of developing a feminist rhetoric to challenge "the ideology of domination that permeates Western culture" (Foss, Griffin, & Foss, 1997, p. 129). Invitational rhetoric invites the audience to enter the communicator's world and see it from this angle, using a nonhierarchical, nonjudgmental framework.

Within the dominance perspective, focus has gradually shifted from women as receivers of communication to women as communicators, and the inclusion and validation of women's topics and modes. It has thereby gradually moved into the difference and identity perspective that we shall explore in detail in Chapter 5. So now, we turn to another hallmark of dominance communication scholars: the challenge to sexist language and the call for communication reform.

## Pronoun Envy: The Battle Over Words

*A woman, without her man, is nothing*

*A woman, without her, man is nothing*

From the perspective of dominance theory, language grants us the ability to name and define. Thus, language mutes women, but at the same time it offers possibilities for naming and renaming. Even something as apparently mundane as a definition is not as neutral as one might think; Lakoff (2000) encouraged us to consider words such as *fetus, rape, marriage,* and *sexual harassment,* which have been at the center of battles of definition. When does the embryo become a fetus? What constitutes rape? What is marriage, and who is it for? How is sexual harassment defined? According to dominance communication scholars, the fact that sexual harassment has only recently become a term to be reckoned with shows that naming has formerly been the domain of men. These definitions, and many more like them, are hotly debated. To the pro-lifers, life begins at conception. The pro-choice group disagrees (consequently renaming pro-life individuals "anti-choice"). Is rape an action performed only by men, or can women rape? Is rape defined strictly as penetration, or does it also comprise other sexually aggressive acts? In a Western and Christian context, marriage most often refers to heterosexual couples, but most gay and lesbian activists would argue that the right to marry should be extended to all. Each group seizes the power to name, and thereby the power to. exist and act. This is a theme that linguistic anthropologist Don Kulick (2000) has argued runs through much of the early gay and lesbian work as well, that is, the notion that naming confers existence; conversely, the lack of naming denies existence. In this section of the book, we shall provide an overview of some of the most pertinent feminist dominance communication scholarship available on the subject of naming.

To linguist Muriel R. Schultz (1990), women's linguistic derogation may be traced historically. In her article, "The Semantic Derogation of Woman," she provided a long list of examples. Female kinship terms such as *wife* used to be euphemisms for "mistress"; *aunt* used to mean "old woman," and then later "prostitute" (p. 137). Even *sister* described a "disguised whore" in the 17th century, and *hussy* derived from Old English "housewife" and at one point meant "the female head of the house" (p. 137). *Doll* referred to a small-scale human figure, but now also refers to young women (p. 137); *peach* is now used for an attractive young woman, but used to refer to a "promiscuous woman"; and *broad* used to refer to a young woman but is now more frequently used in reference to a prostitute (p. 138). Women are also frequently equated with food ("peach," "cookie," "hot tomato," and "honey pie"), animals ("cat," "bitch," "chick," and "fox") and possessions ("his wife" and "my girl"). According to Schultz, feminine terms have been subject to semantic derogation, but masculine terms have largely been left untouched (consider words such as *father, brother, uncle,* and *nephew*). Schultz further demonstrated this by pointing to the semantic differences between the words *cat* and *dog*. Cat is more often associated with something stereotypically "female" and is considered spiteful and untrustworthy (p. 141). Dog, on the other hand, is usually used in reference to men in a half-joking, half-admiring fashion, such as "He's a sly dog" or "Oh, you're a clever dog" (p. 141).

Schultz is by no means alone. Susanne Langer (1979), an influential philosopher of language, has suggested that language is a "vehicle for the conceptions of objects" (p. 60). Language stereotypes *and* polarizes women and men: Men are classified as rational and physically strong, whereas women are classified as emotional and weak (both physically and, because of the stereotype of women's emotional "nature," also psychologically). Stereotypes serve to simplify reality, and they are most often polarized pre-conceptions: Women are feminine, men are masculine, and thus a woman who uses assertive speech is engaging in a masculine mode of communica-tion (she is most likely a tough/unfeminine, unwomanly woman), whereas a man who uses emotional speech is feminized and most likely gay. In other words, woman is what man is not, and man is what woman is not. To dom-inance communication scholars, language is never neutral despite pretences to the contrary.

The concept of "generic language" provides us with one of the best exam-ples of the nonneutrality of language. Writer Tillie Olsen (1990) called generic language "inherited language," as generic language is the perpetua-tion of ancient patriarchal practices: "male rule; male ownership; our sec-ondariness, our *exclusion*" (p. 164). Generic language desensitizes speakers and writers to the gendered nature of language. Because generic terms are so widely accepted as "professional titles," the maleness they represent conve-niently goes unnoticed. Feminist dominance communication scholars have helped us understand that what to the speaker or listener may be generic lan-guage is often exclusively male focused. Most empirical research suggests that when people hear "he" or "congressman," they automatically think of a man. When a group of children were asked by researchers to select pho-tographs for a textbook with the chapter titles "Urban Man" and "Man in Politics," they unsurprisingly nearly always chose photographs of males. When non-gender-specific chapter titles were given, such as "Urban Life" and "Political Behavior," children were more likely to choose a variety of photos (Schneider & Hacker, 1973). Sociologist Wendy Martyna (1978) argued that language shapes reality to such an extent that female students take longer to process male generic pronouns (he, him) than inclusive pronouns (she or he, they). The ambiguity with which the male generic pronoun has to be understood ("Does this imply men only?") puts female students at a distinct disadvantage (Martyna, 1978). Female students have to spend more cognitive energy trying to figure out the "correct" interpretation. If generic language is left unquestioned, maleness becomes the norm. Dominance communication scholars conclude that maleness is more visible and more dominant, as though men literally outnumbered women. Male generic language reduces women's visibility, creating the notion that women are exceptions to the rule. The ungrammatical "they" may seem awkward, and the "she and he" cumbersome, but inclusive communication is more precise and therefore more direct.

In her thought-provoking article "Androcentrism in Prescriptive Grammar: Singular 'They,' Sex-Indefinite 'He,' and 'He or She'," Ann Bodine (1990) persuasively challenged the notion that there is no sex-indefinite pronoun for the third-person singular in the English language. She pointed out that "they" has been used as a grammatically correct third-person singular, a tradition that was vigorously challenged by grammarians (p. 170). The condemnation of third-person singular "they" or "he/she" and "she/he" is based on the convention that men are more important than women. This, of course, is not readily admitted; rather, the argument runs, "he" is grammatically correct. Bodine described these grammarians as individuals failing to confront their own androcentric biases (p. 177). A thought-provoking transgression of this norm is found in computer-mediated environments such as multi-user domains (MUDs). In these environments, participants can mark their identities in a manner that breaks the "she/he" pronoun dilemma. Computer-mediated communication scholar Brenda Danet (1998) pointed to the potential of these environments when listing the various pronoun options: female (she), male (he), neuter (it), either (s/he), spivak (E), splat (*e), plural (they), egotistical (I), royal (We), 2nd (You), person (per) (see Chapter 6). In this manner, feminist dominance communication scholars have sensitized us to the nonneutrality of language and called into question the absolute authority of male-imposed communication practices.

In *Verbal Hygiene,* Cameron (1995b) sketched a history of attempts to improve language, motivated by moral concerns distinguishing between "liberal verbal hygiene" and "radical verbal hygiene" (p. 155). Feminist dominance communication scholarship reflects both of these perspectives, but radical verbal hygiene is more closely aligned with the radical faction of feminist dominance communication scholarship. Here, gender-neutral terms such as *humankind* and the use of plural pronouns or he/she does not draw

Table 4.1    Communication Hygiene

| Generic Language | Liberal Solution | Radical Solution |
|---|---|---|
| Congressman | Congressperson | Congresswomyn |
| Mankind | Humankind | Womynkind |
| Chairman | Chairperson | Chairwomyn |
| Girl | Woman | Womyn |
| God | Spiritual entity | Goddess |
| History | History | Herstory |
| Freshman | First-year student | First-year student |
| The doctor . . . he | The doctors . . . they | The doctor . . . she |
| | The doctor . . . he or she | The doctor . . . she or he |

sufficient attention to women. Radical verbal hygienists pose a solution in which femaleness must be highlighted. The sentence "the doctor-he" would read, "the doctor-she" or at a minimum, "the doctor-she or he" (notice that "she" occurs prior to "he"). Most feminists agree that the generic masculine does not work, but they differ in their proposed linguistic solutions. Radical verbal hygiene is based on the notion that a more radical solution brings attention to the ways in which language constructs a gendered reality. Calling attention to the female ("doctor-she") provokes a reconsideration of the role of language in shaping reality. A few examples of this difference are shown in Table 4.1.

Attempts at linguistic reform have encountered their share of criticism. Concerns about what has been called "McCarthyism," "the feminist word police," or "feminazis" (Cameron, 1995b; Lakoff, 2000) are examples of a backlash against what opponents have frequently portrayed as the work of humor-deprived feminists with little else to do. Nonfeminists ask why they don't turn their attention to really important matters. The attention that inclusive language, also known as "political correctness" (PC), has elicited not only reveals different opinions on the importance of language in constructing reality but also highlights the sensitivity with which changes in language must be implemented and, hence, the importance of language itself.

Ridicule seems to be opponents' standard response to PC: Words such as "physically challenged" appear alongside "follically challenged" (bald), "vertically challenged" (short) and "morally challenged" (corrupt) (Lakoff, 2000, p. 100). The ridicule continues: "Black coffee" is renamed "coffee without milk," and "person" is renamed "perdaughter." As funny as these examples may seem, linguistic inventiveness is, in this case, an attempt to minimize the importance of language. This is rather interesting, because opponents postulate that the matter is entirely trivial and laughable, while simultaneously demanding that feminists focus on the "real" stuff, such as equal pay for equal work. Yet those who ridicule attempts at linguistic reforms also spend a great deal of linguistic energy opposing these changes. As Cameron asks, one can only wonder why opponents of PC expend so much energy on something so evidently trivial. How can intervening in language be both a trivial diversion from politics and a threat to our most fundamental liberties? How can such intervention both constitute useless, superficial tinkering, the only appropriate response to which is laughter, and at the same time be an attack on language and communication so serious it has "got to be challenged"? The two charges are incompatible (Cameron, 1995b, p. 140).

From a feminist dominance communication point of view, the point of challenging conventional ways of speaking is indeed to call into question conventional hierarchies in which adult, professional women are referred to as "girls" or "gals" and all of humanity is referred to as "mankind." As for the concern that "person" will soon become "perdaughter," Cameron (1995b) called it a hoax; a cover-up for the fact that words like *policeman* are gender-marked morphemes, while *perdaughter* is not (p. 131). Opponents considered suggestions of linguistic reform a serious attack on the First Amendment. Any mention of the First Amendment immediately makes an issue newsworthy, as freedom of speech is a tenet of American democracy. If, for example, freedom of speech is limited through speech codes, opponents argue that American democracy can no longer flourish. The First Amendment argument draws a definite line between speech and action: Words do not injure; actions do. The argument is somewhat similar to other so-called entitlements of American society, for example, "Guns don't hurt people; people with guns hurt people."

Cameron and Penelope do see dangers in some kinds of linguistic reform, however. Consider, for example, the term "differently-abled" as a euphemism for persons with a "disability." Certainly, most persons with disability would prefer this to the denomination "crippled," but the euphemism suggests, according to Penelope (1990), that the individual simply has different abilities. Cameron (1995b) pointed to another potential glossing-over of power differentials occurring with the use of the term *sex worker* (to replace the word *prostitute*). The term sex worker fails to highlight differential power relationships that often, if not always, exist in the gendered sex hierarchy between (mostly) women selling sex and their clients and potential pimps, who are (mostly) men. Euphemisms help us avoid uncomfortable topics, but according to Penelope and Cameron, they can also prevent us from telling the truth.

Whether women's communication styles are attributable to the socialization that women undergo, as Lakoff has theorized, or to muting, as Spender has proposed, the dominance communication approach still plays a central part in feminist communication studies. In the eyes of the critic, however, the dominance communication approach presents a monolithic view of communication and power. According to linguist Mary Talbot (1998), power becomes an almost biologically acquired characteristic: "It is assumed that all men are in a position to dominate all women," and male dominance becomes pan-contextual (p. 49). Some of the pitfalls of dominance communication research, then, include its failure to critically examine "men" and "women" as groups. If all men have power, then all women lack power—an axiom of the most stringent forms of feminist dominance communication research. More contemporary feminist communication research, such as the work done by standpoint theorist and communication scholar Marsha Houston (1992), has emphasized the importance of recognizing the diversity inherent in the category of "women." Differences of ethnicity, race, sexuality, and class must be reckoned with. Thus, there can be no *single* female muting experience. Likewise, the category of "men" must be considered equally diverse; ethnicity, sexuality, and class are a few of the categories of analysis that elucidate the fact that not all men experience and wield power to the same extent.

Before ending this discussion of the feminist dominance communication approach, it would be helpful to mention some of the areas of communication scholarship undertaken with a dominance perspective in mind. Hence, we shall quickly review past and current research, which is either theoretically grounded in the work of early dominance communication scholars or highlights the underpinnings of muted group theory. In the process, we shall be paying particular attention to dominance communication scholarship in organizational and mediated communication before finally considering a contemporary example of feminist dominance communication scholarship.

## Situated Dominances

No survey can do justice to the amount of work done with a feminist dominance communication perspective in mind. We have chosen to present a selection of important dominance communication research carried out in organizational and media settings. These will help to clarify the dominance point of view, and it will be followed by a discussion of feminist-inspired conversation analysis and our case study.

## Media Dominances

Media research from a dominance perspective has focused on underrepresentation of women in the media, ways in which they are stereotyped, and the reinstatement of gender in dichotomous and hierarchic setups that may normalize discrimination and even abuse against women. Because the media act as gatekeepers while being powerful conveyors of information, they are said to shape our views on gender.

Sociologist Erving Goffman was one of the first to discuss the ways in which women are portrayed in advertising. In *Gender Advertisements*, from 1979, he concluded that advertisements portray gender displays as natural, although they are, in fact, staged representations: "If anything, advertisers conventionalize our conventions, stylize what is already a stylization, make frivolous use of what is already something considerably cut off from contextual controls. Their hype is hyper-ritualisation" (p. 84). According to Goffman, the gender representations we see in advertisements are meaningful to us because they are ideal gender representations, and thus they are easily read. Gender displays tend to be conveyed and received as if they were natural, but they are, in fact, at their very best, a "symptom, not a portrait" (p. 8). Goffman therefore questioned the naturalness of gender, deriding what he considered to be the energy that goes into securing these stylized dichotomous gender expressions (p. 8). What appears natural to the viewer is, in fact, a cover-up for profoundly asymmetrical relationships (p. 8). The advertiser takes a recognizable gender scene—the helpless father, the protective husband, the seductive young woman, the physically smaller wife, the smiling and sensual woman—and although these images may appear innocent enough, to Goffman and feminists alike, they constitute ritualized forms of female subordination. In advertising, women and men act in stereotypical ways, portraying ideal female and male behavior. As such, they not only conceal how women and men really act but also function prescriptively to show how they should act.

Feminist scholar Laura Mulvey (1975) extended the feminist dominance communication perspective to film. In her groundbreaking essay "Visual Pleasure and Narrative Cinema," she applied psychoanalytic theory to movies. Because the camera is male dominated, she argued, men are portrayed as active and women as passive, but men are also made the "bearers of the gaze," whereas women are made the "object of the gaze" and identified with the image to be looked upon. In this way, the spectator and the audience, either male or female, are encouraged to identify with the male protagonist and the male gaze. Mulvey argued that movies—Hollywood-produced movies in general and Alfred Hitchcock's movies in particular—are shaped by the dominant order and serve to structure the ways the audience sees women in movies according to a patriarchal society. Thus, patriarchal spectatorship and the male gaze evolve alongside an active/passive/heterosexual set of dichotomies. In Mulvey's theory, women's ways of looking and women's cinematic gaze are nonexistent, and the spectator, female or male, is denied the possibility of critical thinking. Unsurprisingly, Mulvey was the advocate of an alternative cinema to break the complex and deeply entrenched patriarchal structures inherent in mainstream movie production.

In dominance scholarship, gendered media representations serve to illustrate hegemonic practices (see Chapter 2), and contemporary feminist media scholar Bonnie Dow (1996) has superbly demonstrated this. She has investigated hegemony as a theoretical framework in feminist media analysis and has sought to uncover the multiple ways it is reinstated in different genres. Women in the media are underrepresented (as newscasters, anchorpersons, etc.); they are stereotypically portrayed (as victims, prostitutes, wives, etc.); and are frequently exposed in pornographic ways. The stereotypical portrayals include unrealistic images that, in some cases, even serve to normalize violence against girls and women. Exposure to sexual violence in the media is moreover connected with a greater tolerance of sexual violence against women (Hansen & Hansen, 1988).

Computer-mediated environments are also found to convey a gendered reality: Cyber-anonymity encourages sexual harassment and even virtual rape. And Mulvey's crucial essay found a revival of sorts in cyber-research on computer-mediated communication (CMC) and CU-SeeMe cybercommunities. Even CMC reinforces patriarchal discourses. Linguist Susan Herring (1999) demonstrated that in asynchronous CMC (such as e-mail and discussion groups), men tend to post more messages, they receive fewer responses, and they engage in adversarial communication, while women's messages are generally shorter, and they engage in the communication styles described by Lakoff (1975). They are hesitant, making use of hedges and apologies, while also being more polite, using questions to elicit interactions, and so on. In synchronous CMC (such as chat rooms), female participants may get more responses, but since these are often harassing and sexist in nature, they serve to mute female participation and cause many women to adopt gender-neutral user names to avoid unwanted attention (Herring, 1999). Herring's main conclusions are found in Table 4.2, and we will return to Herring later, in our case analysis.

## Organizational Dominances

Feminist organizational studies reveal similar observations. In her now classic text *Men and Women of the Corporation,* Rosabeth Kanter (1977)

**Table 4.2**   Computer-Mediated Communication

| Communication | Asynchronous Communication | | Synchronous Communication | |
|---|---|---|---|---|
| | *Men* | *Women* | *Men* | *Women* |
| Participation | Longer messages<br><br>Post more messages<br><br>Receive more responses | Short messages<br><br>Post fewer messages<br><br>Receive fewer responses | May get fewer responses | May get more responses |
| Discourse styles | Strong assertions; absolute and exceptionless adverbs<br><br>Impersonal, presupposed truths<br><br>Exclusive first-person plural pronoun<br><br>Rhetorical questions<br><br>Self-promotion<br><br>Disagreement with others<br><br>Opposed orientation<br><br>Less polite | Attenuated assertions; hedges and qualifiers<br><br>Speaker's feelings and experiences<br><br>Inclusive first-person plural pronoun<br><br>Questions as a means to elicit a response<br><br>Apologies<br><br>Support and agreement with others<br><br>Aligned orientation<br><br>More polite | Use more violent verbs<br><br>More profanity<br><br>More sexual references<br><br>Evaluative judgments<br><br>Sarcasm, insults | Use more neutral and affectionate verbs<br><br>More emoticons and laughter<br><br>Attribution of self and others<br><br>Appreciation and support |

SOURCE: Herring, S. & Panyametheekul, S., Gender and Turn Allocation in a Thai Chat Room, in *Journal of Computer-Mediated Communication, 9* (1), November 2003. Reprinted with permission.

pointed to four stereotypes that women encounter in organizational settings: sex object, mother, child, and iron maiden. The "sex object" stereotype defines a woman in terms of her sexuality and her sexual appearance. The "mother" stereotype instigates a set of expectations that women (by nature or by culture) are more nurturing. This stereotype is also quite literal: Women who have children are viewed as mothers first and workers second. Stereotyping women "children" reflects a view of them as less mature, more emotional, and less competent than their male coworkers; communication, then, is more likely to be patronizing. Overall, these stereotypes contribute to women's lack of advancement and lesser pay. Women, as workers, are seen as less reliable, less capable, and less committed than their male counterparts. The "iron maiden" stereotype, however, contradicts all of the above. The iron maiden is an unwomanly woman. She is ambitious, independent (of males), competitive, and hardworking—in other words, she is as unfeminine as she can possibly be. The iron maiden is perhaps a desirable employee, but the price she pays is her femininity. Because coworkers are so entrenched in the three stereotypes mentioned above, they find it difficult to relate to her, which reduces her chances of networking with others and may ultimately lead to professional isolation.

Educational institutions are also powerful agents of gender socialization. For example, in their study of educational settings, Lee and Gropper (1974) argued that gender inequity is perpetuated by a hidden curriculum: prevalent and persistent sexism in school settings manifested through institutional organization, curricular content, and teaching styles. Educational institutions reflect the hidden curriculum by assigning leadership roles to men and less important roles to women. The prevalence of White men in positions of power leads to a lack of woman and minority role models for young women and people of color. The hidden curriculum is also reflected in the curricular content: From children's books to college texts, feminist dominance communication scholars propose that boys and men are strongly favored. In their study of curricular material, Purcell and Stewart (1990), for example, revealed that males are not only featured more frequently than females, they are also portrayed as adventurous and engage in a wider range of careers. Women, on the other hand, are often invisible and, if shown at all, are passive, dependent victims. Their role in history is minimalized, and consequently, few students know of women such as Maria Goeppert-Mayer, who won the Nobel Prize in physics in 1963, or Annie Oakley, a 19th-century entertainer and advocate for women's athletics.

Even the classroom climate is chilly for women. In a pioneering study by R. M. Hall and B. R. Sandler (1982), a range of communication behaviors were identified that all favored men: Professors were more likely to know the names of male students than female students; they were more likely to maintain eye contact with male students than female students; they gave longer and more significant verbal and nonverbal feedback to comments made by men; they called on male students more often; they devoted more time to male students than to female students; and female students' contributions were often ignored or dismissed. These gender biases in teachers' communication encourage male students and discourage female students. Regrettably, later studies have shown the same tendencies (Spender, 1990). Teaching styles also contribute to the cumulative tendency that values boys over girls; therefore, these scholars have suggested that classroom environments are masculine speech communities.

These examples reflect past as well as more contemporary feminist dominance communication research, and it convincingly indicates myriad ways by which male dominance is perpetuated and women are muted in communication. We now move on to our case study in which the author employs conversation analysis (CA) to demonstrate feminist dominance in action.

## Case Study: Feminist Conversation Analysis (FCA)

In this case study, we shall explore the theoretical and methodological connections to a feminist dominance perspective and to feminist conversation analysis (FCA) found by sociolinguist Susan Herring in her research on gender differences in CMC. First, however, it is important to note that Herring was one of the first scholars to study CMC from a gender and CA perspective. In her work, she has explored the tenets of CA to understand how communicators in computer-mediated environments actively attend to conversational order and the multiple ways in which issues of gender resurface in online communities.

As demonstrated in Chapter 3, Harvey Sacks, Emanuel Schegloff, and Gail Jefferson are key CA scholars, and Herring has used their concepts to demonstrate that CMC challenges both written and spoken discourse. In the interest of clarity, let us briefly restate one aspect of CA work, namely turn-taking, and Sacks, Schegloff, and Jefferson's three strategies: (a) The current speaker (through gaze, posture, naming, or in any other way) selects the next speaker; (b) the next speaker self-selects; and (c) the current speaker continues speaking. These strategies are in the order of (a) being preferred over (b) and (b) over (c) (Herring & Panyametheekul, 2003; Jefferson, 1995). Each turn ideally consists of a period of talk, and turns are organized in a manner that keeps overlaps and silences at a minimum (Jefferson, 1995). Herring applies this CA observation to an excerpt of Internet Relay Chat (IRC) (Herring 1999; Herring & Panyametheekul, 2003):

[1]  ashna: hello?

[2]  dave-g it was funny

[3]  how are u jatt

[4]  ssa all

[5]  kally you da woman!

[6]  ashna: do we know each other? I'm ok how are you

(Herring & Panyametheekul, 2003, pp. 2–3)

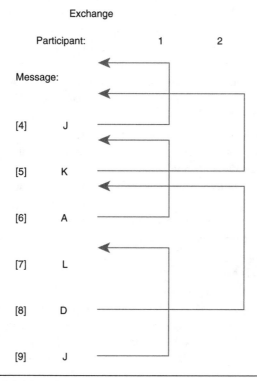

**Figure 4.1**    IRC Message Construction

SOURCE: Herring, S. & Panyametheekul, S., Gender and Turn Allocation in a Thai Chat Room, in *Journal of Computer-Mediated Communication*, 9 (1), November 2003. Reprinted with permission.

Schematically, Herring proposed the turn-taking organization shown in Figure 4.1. In IRC, participants must coordinate their turns in a creative manner. Unlike face-to-face conversations, in which participants respond to questions with answers in the form of adjacency pairs (see Chapter 3) and turns can be coordinated nonverbally, IRC presents us with an example of what at first glance appears to be disrupted, incoherent, and fragmented communication (Herring, 1999; Werry, 1996). In IRC, participants do not have eye contact, pausing, or intonation to signal that a turn must take place. But participants nevertheless apply CA rules to their conversation by, for example, addressing—and thus selecting—individual persons by their screen names ("how are you jatt"); by requesting reactions from anyone in the group ("hello?"); by self-selecting ("kally you da woman!"); or by continuing one's own turn. In IRC, more than one conversation can take place at a time, and at any given time, a response to one message occurs several messages later on the list. Thus, Herring concluded that IRC, albeit novel and unique, still relies on the classic conversational rules outlined by Sacks, Schegloff, and Jefferson.

This example of a classic CA analysis begs the question: Are the focus and aim of FCA different compared with classic CA? Let us observe an example from an IRC chat channel named "#india" (Herring, 1999). We shall make two overall observations from an FCA perspective: first, an overview of total participation (active participants, number of messages, words, and actions) and then an in-depth analysis of an excerpt from #india chat. It is worth noting here that both participants and scholars determine the gender of participants on the basis of names and other gendered information that participants disclose in the conversation. Seven participants were thus of indeterminate gender and were not included in Table 4.3. Consequently, Herring read CMC styles as reflective of "true" offline gendered identities, defending this position in various ways. Note that this is a much-debated topic among researchers in the field, but we choose to maintain that this tendency to read "online bodies" as representative of "offline bodies" is characteristic of structuralist-informed feminist communication work.

In Table 4.3, it is evident that more men than women participate in #india, and as expected within a feminist dominance communication perspective, men are more active participants: They compose longer messages and are the only ones to employ actions (such as kicking someone out of the chat). Herring (1999) speculated that the lack of female participation may be due to women's generally more

**Table 4.3**    Participation by Gender in #india Sample

|  | M | F | Total |
|---|---|---|---|
| Total participants | 57.5% | 25% | N = 40 |
| Active participants | 58.3% | 41.7% | N = 12 |
| Messages (utterances) | 57.8% | 42.2% | N = 211 |
| Words | 61.9% | 38.1% | N = 1147 |
| Average words/messages | 5.8 | 4.9 | 5.4 |
| Actions and kicks | 100% | 0% | N = 16 |

SOURCE: Herring (1999, p. 154).

negative experiences with IRC groups (p. 154). It is consistent, she maintained, with the notion that women feel less entitled to occupy verbal space and that women's messages become shorter when they experience verbal harassment, in response to male intimidation tactics (p. 155). Let us apply FCA to an excerpt:

<rani> Vice: what the fuck is ur prob.?

rani has been kicked off channel #india by ViCe

(u bitch–lighten up)

rani has joined channel #india

<Aatank> haha

<rani> st:uhh I just got a lot on my mind . . . sorry

<Aatank> rani how would u like a lot IN u

<rani> aatank: whatever

rani has been kicked off channel #india by Aatank (quite the stupid valley girl talk)

<Aatank> quit even

rani has joined channel #india

<ViCe> haha

(Herring, 1999, p. 158)

"Aatank" and "ViCe" are both #india operators, and both men. They are the only ones in the chat who can execute "kicking," an action that disconnects a participant from the chat and forces them to log back on (if they want to return). Kicking someone off a chat interrupts the participant both symbolically and literally, and kicking thus serves as an assertion of interactional dominance (Herring, 1999, p. 155). None of the female participants use "actions" or "action descriptions," and Herring speculates that women are in fact discouraged from using actions. Rani's initial response to the harassment, "what the fuck is ur prob.?" albeit aggressive, is followed not by an action like "Action: rani punches ViCe smack in the middle of his face," but by an apology "uhh, I just got a lot on my mind . . . sorry." And when rani responds "whatever" to yet another harassment episode, she is once again kicked off the chat. The excerpt illustrates how the two operators, ViCe and Aatank, abuse their conversational power (their operator status and kicking) to intimidate the only female participant in the chat. ViCe and Aatank exercise conversational dominance over rani, and when they kick her, they very effectively silence her. This excerpt also illustrates the main claims of feminist dominance communication research: that women and men have recognizably different communication styles and men not only dominate women in online discussion groups and chat rooms, but women are frequently alienated from online communication opportunities and forced to create communities of their own. Detailed analysis of mundane CMC underpins the theory that new communication environments reinforce asymmetrical gender dynamics. Despite the linguistic inventiveness characteristic of this medium, stereotypically gendered communication continues to take place. In the words of feminist linguist Kira Hall (1996), "Cyberspace is generating goddesses and ogres, not cyborgs" (p. 167).

The use of gender as a category of analysis in CA, however, is not entirely unproblematic. In *Working with Spoken Discourse,* Cameron (2001) outlined the controversy between what she called "pure" CA and FCA. "Pure" CA poses that the issue of gender, for example, is relevant to the analysis only if participants themselves make it an issue. Thus, if gender is not explicitly an issue for the participants in their talk, the analyst should not make it an issue either (Cameron, 2001). The simple fact that a speaker is a man does not justify the analytical definition of his communication style as "masculine," and unless the participants orient themselves to his "maleness" or his "masculinity," it is an act of "theoretical imperialism" to include it (Schegloff, in Kitzinger, 2002). In his guide to CA, Paul ten Have (1999) likewise suggested that researchers bracket more permanent identities such as "woman" or "mother," including them in the analysis only insofar as they are necessary in understanding the local action (pp. 107–109). Clearly, pure CA is significantly divergent from much feminist communication scholarship. Key points of feminist critique regarding CA are the extent to which the underlying theory of ethnomethodology (see Chapter 3) is compatible with feminism; the difficulty of reconciling a CA participant orientation with the researchers' own focus on gender, race, and sexuality (to name a few); and CA's obsession and preoccupation with detailed talk (Kitzinger, 2002, p. 51). Kitzinger suggested that feminist-informed CA is not an oxymoron, however, and as illustrated by Herring, FCA does help us see the many workings of gender.

To sum up, this case leads to two main FCA lines of inquiry: How is the conversation ordered (the use of turn-taking, turn allocation, sequence organization, repair work, and turn constructional units), and how is conversational organization related to issues of gender and power? Who begins the conversation? How is conversation initiation related to gender? Who talks the most? Whose topics are chosen for further conversation? And how is this related to gender and power? We suggest the following list of items to consider when planning research from an FCA perspective:

1. What is the particular problem you want to address?

2. Which tools from CA are appropriate?

3. In what ways do conversationalists attend to, break, or reform conversational rules?

4. Does gender (and other markers of identity) affect the conversational order?

5. Where and how do you locate power in the conversation, and is gender an issue?

6. How can you illustrate a detailed analysis of talk-in-interaction?

7. How can you reconcile your focus on gender with other lived experiences, such as class, race, ability, and so forth?

By now, we have presented the main tenets of the feminist dominance communication approach, situated dominances, and an example of feminist conversation analysis in action. In the next chapter, we shall introduce feminist communication scholars who focus on difference and identity, along with examples in which standpoint theory comes into play.

# 5

# Discourses of Difference and Identity

G endered discourses, gendered stylistics, or even genderlects—the approach and body of work has many names. In this chapter, we introduce you to the interrelationships between second-wave difference and identity feminism, feminist standpoint theory, and feminist critical discourse analysis (CDA) from which this particular approach within feminist communication scholarship has emerged. The chapter will present significant empirical studies that relate to this tradition; will outline our two chosen contexts, media and organization; and will conclude with a discussion of a case study that illustrates feminist-informed CDA.

## Gender, Discourse, and Articulation

At the core of the difference and identity approach is the conviction that there is a correlation between gender and communication in terms of gendered sets of adapting and articulating discourses. Such sets consist of a gendered use of voice, vocabulary, speech genre, rhetoric, and media, often referred to as "gendered stylistics" or even "genderlects," inspired by the ethnography of speaking (see Chapter 3). This correlation may be considered relative to situation and context and the social categories of the actors, but it is nevertheless decisive. Renowned feminist communication scholar Sara Mills (1995a) has provided an overview of the field. Let us start with the question of articulation in a very concrete sense: the gendered uses of voice.

## Gender Voices

Questions of articulation and discursive practices are very important to feminist communication scholarship, and the different approaches outlined in this book offer different explanations. Within the difference and identity approach, articulation is most often considered to mirror a genuine—even if also socially formed and thereby changeable—gender identity and to do so consistently in terms of voice, style, strategy, and so on.

The use of voice has not been sufficiently researched within gender and communication scholarship and much less theorized. One of the main resources on this particular aspect is *Gender Voices,* which provides an overview of empirical research and discusses the findings from a standpoint position (Graddol & Swann, 1989). The authors have directed our attention to the fact that most people can easily tell whether a voice belongs to an (anatomical) boy/man or an (anatomical) girl/woman and that this fact seems to be reflected in popular stereotypes about men as "loud" and women as "softly spoken" (see also Baken, 1987; Lee, Hewlett, & Nairn, 1995). However, Graddol and Swann also stated that we know very little about the hows and whys of gender differences in voice. We do know that voice is produced by the use of the vocal cavities (timbre), the vocal tract (resonance/formants), and the vocal cord (pitch/frequency). These factors and their interaction are determined to a certain degree by genetics and influenced by hormones. Thus, men will tend to develop longer and thicker vocal folds, and in most cultures, boys' voices drop drastically in pitch in puberty (see also Baken, 1987; Lee et al., 1995). In a Western context, it has also been documented how women's voices are affected by menstruation and pregnancy and that women experience these changes as positive, even in the case of premenstrual "dysphony."

These differences are usually considered biologic facts, but Graddol and Swann (1989) emphasized that they can and should also be interpreted as cultural. Thus, both men and women are reported to have a broad range of voice, which they do not, however, make full use of. The pattern shown in Table 5.1 seems to be agreed upon in a Euro-American context.

**Table 5.1    Sounds of Gender**

|            | *Women* | *Men*    |
| ---------- | ------- | -------- |
| Pitch      | high    | low      |
| Timbre     | light   | dark     |
| Resonance  | easy    | forceful |
| Breath     | weak    | strong   |

This pattern is usually found to be the norm with certain standard variations. Lee et al. (1995) have documented how young girls tend to have more extremes of frequency and a greater intonation variety than boys. Such variations can also be found to be national/regional. For instance, American women have been reported to use a larger vocal range than British women, whereas American men have been reported to employ a more limited vocal range than British men (Graddol & Swann, 1989).

Vocal differences are, however, difficult to describe without a subjective dimension; indeed, voice evaluation will always somehow be interwoven with gender expectations. For example, the reporting of younger women's larger scale of voice may be due to a common understanding of greater gender flexibility in this period of life. Or the larger scale supposedly at the disposal of American women tells us more than the "factual" scale about expectations of gender flexibility for women in this local context, just as the estimated lower scale available to American men may be attributed to narrower definitions of masculinity in this particular speech community. Graddol and Swann (1989) therefore went on to ask whether it is possible to identify a common logic in the reported findings, be they more objective or more subjective, and conclude by suggesting a model (p. 33), which we have elaborated on (see Figure 5.1).

In this very structuralist-inspired model, the extremes are represented by the sex-typed male/female (masculine male/feminine female), juxtaposed with the opposite terms (feminine male/masculine female). In between are the nexus of male/female (undifferentiated male/female) and the not yet opposite (androgynous male/female). The point is that the positions in question are differently appraised. While the female spectrum often connotes weakness, insecurity, and loss of authority, the male spectrum connotes strength, self-assurance, and authority. Both are associated with sexual attractiveness when coupled with the "right" gender, as we see in relation to studies of "sweet talk" in Chapter 6.

According to Graddol and Swann (1989), this is probably why radio and TV in most Western countries feature men in news programs and hosting documentaries and other "serious" programs. Woman speakers partner in news "couples" or do voice-overs in certain programs, for example, those targeting a female audience. On the other hand, women aspiring to higher positions in society adapt to the male norm and deliberately change their voices. For example, former prime minister of the United Kingdom, Margaret Thatcher, reportedly received voice training in order to be heard in her first years as prime minister in the 1980s (Graddol & Swann, 1989, p. 38).

Graddol and Swann (1989) explained gender differences in articulation in social and cultural terms, and they highlighted the complex ways in which

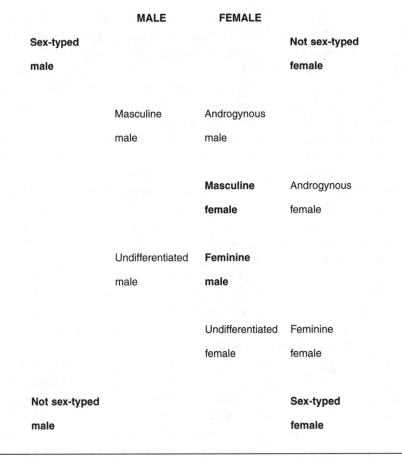

Figure 5.1    Gender and Voice

society and culture influence both the ways women and men use their voices and the ways these voices are heard and reported. One of their most illuminating examples stems from an American psychiatric case history. The parents of a young boy brought him to a clinic because they felt that his voice was pathologically feminine, and he was given hormone treatment. Meanwhile, Graddol and Swann also highlighted cross-cultural differences, and thus differences among women, and even seem to have suggested that orchestration of voice may best be understood as a stylized way of performing gender, a point highlighted in other overviews (Eckert & Mc Connell-Ginet, 2003).

Later, we discuss how these findings are related to intersections of gender, class, race/ethnicity and sexuality, for instance, when young working-class or Black women use higher pitch when code switching from standard English to vernacular English or when "signifying" (Gates, 1987). For now, we turn to research on articulation in terms of different ways and means of expression, made into sets or "styles" of communication. The body of work on this issue from a difference and identity approach is both exhaustive and sophisticated.

## Stylistic Gender Differences

American anthropologists John Maltz and Ruth Borker were the first to introduce the two-culture model in terms of gendered communication styles, designating them the "cooperative" versus the "competitive" style, respectively. In an often-cited review article, they referred to a range of studies of gendered communication that they saw as precursors to a new framework, for example, a study of children by their colleague, Marjorie Harness Goodwin (Maltz & Borker, 1982/1998, p. 420). Goodwin, with a video camera, had followed a group of African American children in a neighborhood in Philadelphia as they played (Goodwin, 1990; based on her original thesis, 1978). She found that children organized themselves differently according to gender and displayed gendered group dynamics and language strategies. The girls played in twos or threes in small, nonhierarchical groups and made joint decisions with minimal status negotiation, a high degree of cooperation, and only indirect use of directives. The boys, on the other hand, formed hierarchical teams or gangs, engaged in status negotiation and competition for leadership, and used directives as commands. On the basis of such research, Maltz and Borker concluded that girls use speech to create relationships, criticize others in acceptable ways, and interpret others' speech accurately in order to keep the group going. Boys, on the other hand, use speech to denote their position, attract and maintain an audience, and assert themselves when other speakers have the floor (Maltz & Borker, 1982/1998, pp. 424, 426). They further claimed that because of the different social contexts in which American children grow up and learn the rules of conversational interaction, boys and girls learn to use language in different ways and for different purposes at a very early age.

Due to the heated debate on her research from 1978, Goodwin (1988/1998) later emphasized that her data documented more complex patterns, for instance, that girls also compete, albeit in slightly different ways than boys. When her dissertation on the research in question, *He-Said-She-Said,* was published in 1990, she further claimed that task and situation are of great importance to understanding competition when children play. For instance, she now found that "he-said-she-said" was a specific genre of dispute among girls in which they ostracized group members but that they also engaged in playful cross-gender verbal disputes. Goodwin (1990) ended up stating that "cooperation and competition are not mutually exclusive agendas and often co-exist within the same speech activities" and moreover, with reference to Maltz and Borker, that "the specific type of joint action which is exhibited [in girls' play] does not resemble 'supportive' forms of collaboration described elsewhere as characteristic of female speech" (p. 284). In a recent study on bilingual Spanish- and English-speaking girls, primarily second-generation Mexican and Central Americans playing hop-scotch, Goodwin (1999) further nuanced her own research results, claiming that these girls participated in many supposedly male communicative features, such as legalistic language, "footing" or stance, and irony (p. 403). In yet another article on the issue, however, she raised the question of class and ethnicity in her own earlier study of young Black African Americans, and she introduced the interpretation that the assertive approach among the girls could partly be ascribed to the fact that they were working-class Blacks (Goodwin, 2003). Following other research on cross-cultural differences among children at play, she further suggested that among African Americans and Italian Americans, playful and teasing confrontational talk provides a way of displaying character, constructing social identities, cultivating friendships, and both maintaining and transforming the social order of the peer group. This is also said to be characteristic of the practice of "signify-ing" among adult African Americans, which makes it difficult for outsiders to distinguish between in-group confrontation and out-group opposition, for instance, to "Whitism" (see Chapter 6).

A range of additional studies in gendered communication styles have followed Goodwin's research. Barrie Thorne, for instance, researched children's play and communication extensively in an ethnographic study of two American schools in different neighborhoods of different class, reported in *Gender Play: Girls and Boys at School,* from 1993. Like Goodwin, Thorne reported complex patterns of gender segregation and mixed settings and also a range of nongendered activities and communica-tion strategies. Amy Sheldon (1990/1993) focused on conflict management in a communication study on "pickle fights" and disputes among pre-school American children. She found that both girls and boys engaged in conflict management, but they did so in different ways and for different purposes. The female-associated conflict style balanced signals of interest, support, and agreement, such as keeping turns short and giving the floor to others, and was accordingly referred to as "community oriented." Conversely, the male-associated conflict style manifested in signals of oppo-sition, directive speech, and even threats and physical intimidation, and

Sheldon accordingly classified it as "self-oriented" (p. 104). In other studies, Sheldon refined her thesis in accordance with standpoint theory, describing girls' conflict management as "double-voice discourse" and claiming that it is an example of communicative competencies. However, she also asserted that such competencies are displayed among boys who are close friends and can thus be ascribed as much to the quality and style of a particular group as to gender (Sheldon 1992, 1997).

The conversational styles of co-optation and competition have framed a range of studies in the 1980s and 1990s. However, as discussed above, this has also been questioned by some scholars who have called for sensitivity toward intersections of gender, class, and race/ethnicity, as well as to the contextual framing, the task or format in question, the multifunctionality and embedding of particular communicative features, and so on.

## Same-Sex Interaction

One of the main interests of feminist communication researchers in the 1980s and 1990s was to document gendered speech communities and talk in same-sex groups and to explore the thesis of dual stylistics under such circumstances. However, few of these studies are comparative, and more research has been carried out on women's in-group communication than on men's. British scholar Jennifer Coates has most consistently pursued the subject (1997a, 1997b, 1989) and has also delivered an in-depth discussion of female style in *Women Talk* (1996).

In this study, Coates's empirical data derived from tape recordings of informal, private meetings of an established group of women friends (British, White, middle-class, in their 30s–50s) over a period of 12 years (Coates, 1996). Coates focused on formal features and suggested that they formed both a coherent aesthetic and an implied ethic. Features that at first seemed very similar to the findings of the dominance and deficit approach (tag questions, hedges, minimal responses, epistemic modality, incomplete utterances, recycling of lexical terms and phrases, latching of turns, and simultaneous speech) turned out to constitute a unique format when understood as elements of a formal structure. For instance, participants were seen to use minimal responses to signal active listening and support for the current speaker or to mark recognition of different stages of topic development. They used epistemic modalities to signal that they did not "take a hard line" and to minimize conflict, secure agreement, and signal respect for other participants. Simultaneous speech was used to complete others' contributions and produce a collaborative story. According to Coates, all these phenomena constitute a conversational dynamic that allows topics to emerge and shift gradually and by mutual effort into a joint discourse, the goal of which turns out to be the continuity and flow of communication. This is particularly evident in a distinct sequential progress, which Coates illustrated in the following way:

A introduces topic,

B tells anecdote on the same theme,

C tells another anecdote on same theme, leading into general discussion,

D summarizes,

A has the last word. (Coates, 1989, p. 99)

The main point both in Coates's early reports on the study and in her 1996 monography is that women's conversational mode can be verified as a specific style in which the pattern of formal features, structure, and format creates a distinctive aesthetic, which, in turn, implies an ethic of cooperation. Thus, this conversational mode is considered to support the collective rather than the individual and to facilitate equity and collaboration. In her conclusion, however, Coates (1996) called for further research to document whether the characteristics she identified may be found in other contexts or might turn out to have other purposes, thus anticipating future criticism.

One of the most controversial discussions of same-sex communication during the 1980s and 1990s was concerned with the choice of topics. Coates's (1996) opinion was that the findings of the dominance and deficit approach concerning women's interest in the home, family, emotions, everyday life, and so forth, are valid but that they must also be refined and reinterpreted. Her own study showed how topics in an all-female group vary according to situation, context, framing, and so on and that they develop over time and according to age. Furthermore, topics tended to concentrate on issues of home and family when the women in the group were in the midst of child rearing, but they tended to diversify as the children grew up. Coates found the opposite trend in a longitudinal study of a group of teenagers who, at the age of 12, reportedly exhibited a multifaceted and almost anarchistic communication pattern. At the age of 16, however, they tended to focus on their own performance in relation to boys, friends, and each other, but they also turned out to be both self-reflexive and socially aware (Coates, 1999). Other studies, still mostly in an Anglo-American context, have shown how women's "personal talk" includes not only topics such as children, home, and intimate relationships but also work and professional relationships and, to a lesser degree, politics and religion (Johnson & Aries, 1983/1998).

In her study of the role played by talk in women's friendships, Coates (1996) paid particular attention to the subject of chatter and gossip. Disagreeing with the dominance and deficit approach, she claimed that chatter and gossip do have positive functions. Deborah Jones (1980/1990) had found that gossip is generally considered trivial, is exclusively attributed to women and scorned by men, and is therefore problematic to feminists. Coates, however, pointed to the creative use and constructive function of gossip among women friends. For example, she found that chatter is used to elaborate on the rhythm of conversation and that gossip is used to include rather than exclude participants not present (Coates, 1996).

Jane Pilkington (1998) conducted one of the few comparative studies on female and male friendships and in-group conversation. Her work both supported and contradicted Coates's findings. Pilkington's study took place in New Zealand and involved two groups of women friends and two groups of male friends (White, lower to middle class, from the 20–40 age group). She confirmed that both women and men gossip but claimed that they do so in different ways and for different purposes. Pilkington found that both genders enjoy and value gossip, though it is usually regarded as trivial, but that it is integrated in gender-specific conversational styles. The female style is characterized by few and short pauses, short turns, minimal responses, supporting questions, repetitions, mutual extension of topics, disagreement countered by politeness, and so on. The male style, on the other hand, is characterized by silences, longer pauses, sudden changes of subject, lack of response, marked disagreement in terms of either questioning or negating the other's proposition or making an opposing statement, criticism going into abuse, and ritual abuse framed as fun. Pilkington (1998) reasoned that the two types seem to correspond to the established notion of cooperation versus competition, but she also expressed doubts, in particular when it came to the presumed male mode (p. 267). She reported that her male informants often valued their own abusive behaviors positively, while considering polite behavior to be women's conversational mode and devaluing it. Pilkington's conclusion was that the competitive style is part of a male culture that is built on challenge, risk, and power and it is also seen in a range of male leisure activities. She openly declared her own prejudices against such a communicative style but admitted that her informants themselves found it reassuring and considered it a sign of comradeship. Thus, both women and men were aware of and preferred their own in-group style and considered it a part of identity and community building.

In-depth research in male speech communities and male in-group communication has been carried out by Coates (2003). We briefly describe the study and then elaborate below. The study was conducted over several years and in different contexts, and it reports not only on talk among groups of male friends of different ages and professions in Britain but also on talk in mixed-gender groups (couples), focusing in particular on storytelling. Coates confirmed the central thesis of the two-culture model and maintained that the assumptions shared both by scholars and the public at large, namely, that "men either don't talk much [strong and silent] or talk compulsively and competitively about sport, cars and drinking exploits" (Coates, 2003, p. 1), still holds empirically, even though they must be challenged. Thus, Coates found that such talk is still relevant even if it is mixed with other topics, formats, and renegotiations of current masculinities and is now to be understood as a means of "in-grouping" and thus as a particular kind of sociability and joint enterprise.

During the 1990s, research in gendered stylistics tended to become even more sophisticated and reflective, questioning its own premises. A good example is the above-mentioned discussion of who gossips, how, and for which purposes, which was taken a step further by Deborah Cameron. Cameron (1997a) agreed with Pilkington that boys and men both chatter and gossip but also found that gossip among men can be constructive and even cooperative. Reverse examples were given in documentations of competitive strategies in women's talk, such as conflict management (Sheldon, 1990/1993), teasing (Eder, 1993), disagreement and independence (Eckert, 1990/1993), and tactical uses of stories (Goodwin, 1990/1993). In a study on the use of politeness among Mayan Indian women in Tenejapa, Mexico, Penelope Brown (1990/1993) even found that politeness in this particular speech community and within particular speech situations created a "patina of agreement" that emphasized disagreement, revealing sarcasm and competition. Such studies contributed to the questioning of standpoint theory.

### Mixed Interaction

During the 1980 to 1990s, the second main focus of feminist communication research from the perspective of standpoint theory was cross-gender communication. In this type of research, the dominance and deficit approach was once again abandoned in favor of the gendered stylistics approach. Even though the question of power was still in focus when it came to how imbalances are created in and through the structuring of discourse, cross-gender communication was now primarily understood in terms of cross-cultural communication, and hence neglect or conflict were understood as miscommunication.

One of the most significant documented variables in cross-gender communication was the private/public distinction. The most frequently reiterated finding was that women talk less in public settings and more in private settings (Crawford 1995; Tannen, 1990). Most scholars further agreed that women talk less than men in public settings, whereas it was highly debated whether they talk more than men in private settings (James & Drakich, 1993; Tannen, 1993b). Research using the difference and identity approach has further documented how women tend to follow the procedures of the situation, the etiquette of the setting, and the roles of their position, whereas male participants challenge such schemes (Holmes, 1995). The overall pattern is completed by the following features: In public, women tend to speak only when it is expected of them, in accordance with the format, or when asked; they tend to keep their contributions short, often ask for others' opinions, and express support of others' contributions (Crawford, 1995; Talbot, 1998). In short, they carry out what is understood in the paradigm of dominance and deficit as the "shitwork" of interpersonal communication. Difference and identity scholars understand women's ways of handling cross-gender communication in terms of co-optation and as valuable competencies for adjustment—keeping things going and people working together, for example, within educational or organizational contexts (Crawford, 1995; Talbot, 1998). Moreover, conflict is understood more as an example of miscommunication than of dominance, even though dominance is still a central issue. The findings in private settings are similar, except that in this context, women seem to play a more initiating role, for example, when introducing topics.

Deborah Tannen (1986, 1990) has delivered some of the most elaborate research on interaction in intimate heterosexual relationships. Her main thesis is that miscommunication between the sexes occurs because of different approaches to communication, which she equated with two different languages or, in the context of intimate communication, two different conversations running on parallel tracks. Thus, women do "rapport" talk (about internal affairs, such as home, close relationships, and intimacy), whereas men do "report" talk (about external affairs, such as sports, politics, and women/sex) (Tannen, 1986, 1990). According to Tannen, one of the driving forces behind the miscommunication between rapport and report talkers is that women tend to see intimate communication as a mirror of the relationship and also want to discuss intimate affairs, whereas men tend to see even intimate communication as means of factual exchange and want to keep it there. Therefore, women look for the more subtle meanings of men's words, the "subtext," whereas men do not look for the implied statement and tend to take women's contributions at face value.

One of the main questions within this overall framework has been whether the supplementary discourses of power and solidarity, found in much classic ethnomethodological work, may be seen as gendered articulations. Several feminist researchers from the 1980s argued that this is reasonable. Tannen (1993b) has also addressed this question and directed attention to social interaction analyses that have documented the ambiguity of communicative strategies and, in particular, the polysemy of power and solidarity. On this ground, she claimed that the ambition of consensus in women's talk may be a way to gain power, for example, by not allowing disagreement, and vice versa (Tannen, 1993b, p. 169). She went on to underscore that the final evaluation depends on the total picture and may be related to other central sociolinguistic topics, such as the control of floor, management of turn-taking, length of turns, interruptions, and topic raising.

Carole Edelsky (1981/1993) has done research in cross-gender interaction and has critiqued underlying assumptions, such as the implicit schema for the "right" conversation: the norm of turn-taking, the rules for facilitating shifts of turns by circulating the right to speak, the standards of sequencing and adjusting, and the dynamics of face-keeping. Whereas the schematics have been considered universal within ethnomethodology, feminist researchers from a standpoint of view have seen it as characteristic of the collaborative style—and undermined by the competitive style. Edelsky, however, questioned whether particular discursive practices can or should be seen as elevated or understood as univocal. In her own study, she demonstrated how "taking a turn" and "having the floor" cannot be equated, because several floors often coexist, not least in cross-gender conversations. In the cross-gender interaction in a standing committee meeting, she identified two distinct floors, a collaborative (collective) floor and a single floor, that were continuously interacting and striving for legitimacy. She found that women dominated the first floor and were dominated on the second, both relatively and quantitatively, but she made a point of not claiming greater legitimacy for one than the other. Furthermore, she underscored the importance of context, task, and format, for example, the fact that the context is a formal meeting and that the task and format are given (Edelsky, 1981/1993, p. 219).

Deborah James and Sandra Clarke (1993) have investigated interruptions in cross-gender interaction. They have stressed the multifunctionality of interruptions and claimed that these may function to prevent others from completing their talk and allow the interrupter to take over the floor, but that this is only one of various functions (see also Greenwood, 1996). According to James and Clarke, a central problem is that there is no simple, objective way of determining function; on the contrary, it is necessary to consider a range of contextual aspects and ways of embedding speech. Along these lines, James and Clarke (1993) maintained that the use of interruptions in mixed-gender interaction seems equally complex and that the results do not indicate the stable pattern that has often been put forward—that men interrupt women more than the reverse (pp. 246–247). However, they admitted that there seem to be different types of interruptions that can to some extent be related to gender: The competitive (often abrupt) interruption aims to take over the floor, while the cooperative interruption (often in the form of back-channel responses and simultaneous speech) functions to signal solidarity and joint discourse. They further underscored that the function of the interruption depends on embedding, for example, whether conflict or competition prevails, as well as context, for instance, whether the communicators' status is even. If that is the case, the competitive way of interrupting can also be used to collaborate and may serve to promote community building, whether the group in question is all male or all female.

Much like research on same-sex settings, research on mixed interaction has increasingly questioned the initial assumptions of a gendered stylistics by differentiating between situations, participants, contexts, and so on. Thus, researchers have also argued for a reformulation of the relatively simple model of communication, which much communication scholarship, also from a feminist standpoint, has drawn on. This model implies that you can identify a speaker (or writer), who encodes her ideas and feelings into messages (combinations of words); a hearer (or reader), who decodes the message/text and understands the ideas/feeling; and a message/text, to be en- and decoded without "noise" (mimesis) or, rather, without noise that cannot easily be traced and treated as miscommunication (Mills, 1995a, p. 27). Mills is one of the feminist communication scholars who has both provided a critique of the model and elaborated on it in different ways, specifying parameters such as the genre of the message (e.g., poetry or irony); the channel of the message (e.g., conversation in real life, TV, or on the Internet); the background of speaker/hearer (e.g., personal history, education, social conditions, political conviction); and the material as well as immaterial circumstances of the communicative event in question. Mills has stressed that it is particularly important to feminist standpoint communication scholarship to maintain *the dialectics of text and context;* in fact, according to Mills, this is what feminist standpoint communication scholarship is about.

## Differences Within and Among Women

During the 1990s, two perspectives became of particular importance to standpoint communication scholarship: (a) the study of differences between women (and men) according to either more steady social categories, such as class, ethnicity, and sexuality, or more flexible categories, such as taste and lifestyle and different intersections hereof and (b) the study of differences within every single woman (or man) in terms of the multiplicity of identity itself, along the above-mentioned distinctions but also due to unique personal experiences or the uniqueness of the situation in question. However, these new perspectives also tended to lead to a questioning of the difference and identity concept (Bergvall, Bing, & Freed, 1996; Mills, 1995a; Wodak, 1997). "Femininity takes different forms, so we should really use it in the plural and speak of femininities," said Mary Talbot (1998, p. 188), and stressed the plurality of differences between women, whereas Jennifer Coates talked about "the construction of differing femininities" (1996, p. 232) and "competing discourses of femininity" (1997a, p. 285) and asserted the range of femininities at hand for every single woman.

Jennifer Coates (1996) has most explicitly dealt with the topic of differences within individuals and pointed out that women (and men) participate in a range of contexts in a lifetime or even daily and change their performances accordingly, just as they are able to manage multiple identities during a conversation. Analyzing her informants' talk, she spotted quite a range of femininities (p. 239). She also claimed that her informants not only expressed their authentic experiences through their communication styles but also used available discourses to explore and express different types of femininity: "The talk we do in our everyday lives gives us access to these different modes of being, these different versions of femininity" (p. 239). Deborah Cameron (1997b) went even further, suggesting that instead of looking for how women and men express themselves in and by language, we should look for how we construct gender in and through discourse. Such considerations, however, indicate that we are now on the verge of poststructuralism and the performance turn, which we discuss in detail in the next chapter.

The critique of the difference approach from within has been found especially in scholarship on differences *among* women according to class, race/ethnicity, sexuality, and other significant social categories. During the 1980s and 1990s, working-class, Black, and lesbian feminist scholars challenged the interests and results of "classist," "Whitist," and "heteronormative" feminism. In her landmark essay *Talking Back* (1989), bell hooks directed our attention to the importance of language and communication to Black feminism (and to her, this term includes women of color):

> Moving from silence into speech is for the oppressed, the colonized, the exploited . . . a gesture of defiance that heals, that makes new life and new growth possible. It is the act of speech, of "talking back," that is no mere gesture of empty words, that is the expression of our movement from object to subject—the liberated voice. (hooks, in Houston & Davis, 2002, p. 15)

In Black feminist communication studies, the basic power of voice and speech has been a key subject, together with struggle, sisterhood, and community among Black women (Houston & Davis, 2002). Mary Bucholtz (1995, 1996a) and Karla D. Scott (2002) have argued for Black feminist scholarship in communication and have emphasized the importance of language to ethnic research since William Labov's studies during the 1960s and 1970s on African American vernacular English. Labov has been criticized for excluding women or considering them less authentic, more middle class, and Whitist ("indirect speech") than young, male, working-class Blacks ("counter-language"). However, Bucholtz and Scott have both claimed that it is necessary to rethink his findings in a Black feminist context. Historically, characterizations of language use in the Black community have focused on the inability of this group to speak or use language correctly. Quite often, differences in language use have been attributed to the inherent inferiority of Africans and their descendants. One exception was Geneva Smitherman's (1977) work on the language of "Black America," where she made reference to Labov and contended that "Black English" (or "Ebonics") is not a kind of "anti-language" or "counter-language," but rather a legitimate form of speech with a distinct history and origin. Smitherman identified uniqueness in three areas: grammar and pronunciation, specialized vocabulary or lexicon, and the use of oral tradition. Whereas proficiency in standard English (SE) had hitherto been considered an important mark of credibility, she suggested that Blacks may choose not to speak SE in order to mark their Black identity and to serve certain purposes. Both Bucholtz and Scott further hypothesized that due to the "double consciousness" that follows from their position as "other Others" in terms of both gender and race/ethnicity, Black women can be skilled in both language styles and may switch freely between language style or code as a means of asserting their position in-between or across cultural worlds (Buchholz, 1996a, pp. 271–272; Scott, 2002, p. 58).

Furthermore, Bucholtz (1996a) studied a radio panel discussion convened in response to the nationwide uprisings in the United States in 1992. She found that the two Black women, who were both university professors, carried out what she called a "creative adaptation" to the particular context and format. Thus, they did not directly hinder the discussion, but rather took it over by subverting the role of the moderator (asking questions themselves), creating political alliances with listeners (using features of African American vernacular—phonological, morphemic, or lexical—in an emblematic way), and by supporting each other (back channeling, minimal responses, and so on). Instead of concluding whether or not these findings testify to a certain identity/community/politics and discussing which elements should be ascribed to gender and which to race, Bucholtz (1996a) chose to argue that "the result of such strategies is to challenge the power differences that inhere in institutional and social subject positions—that is . . . the strategies are designed as a challenge to hegemonic discourse" (p. 284). This study is an example of how women's identities are constituted in intersections of differences and how this affects their ways and means of communication in terms of multilayered communicative practices and even ambiguous messages.

Scott (2002) did focus group interviews with young Black women (students at a midwestern university) and focused on the informants' rhetorical use of, on one hand, "girl," and on the other, "look." She found that both techniques contributed to creating a self-conscious rhythmical stress placement and marked intonation pattern during the talk, and simultaneously served as contextualization cues, which, again, allowed the person doing the switching to embed an in-group message and signal ethnic identity. Thus, Scott's case serves as an example of how women, in this case Black women, rework their identities in and through communication and thereby also challenge more fixed communication models. To understand the way these students communicate, you need a very dynamic communication model that accounts for the play with identity, message/text, and context.

Bucholtz (1995, 1996a) has emphasized that the intention of Black feminist scholars to indicate Black women's unique language and their position as the "other Others" may easily slip right back into stereotyping. This is the paradox of the difference approach, be it in terms of gender or of gender and class, race/ethnicity, sexuality, and so on. It has, for instance, been expressed in assumptions that working-class women are more conservative, correct, polite, and underachieving or that they use slang and resistant language in particular settings much the same way as working-class men (Foster, 1995). Thus, making class, race, or women's ethnic culture the central organizing concept remains an ambiguous project. However, such a project does acknowledge that gender is both racialized and classist and that race and class are both gendered and sexualized. Moreover, it makes it necessary to realize that women are enculturated to a gendered communication ideal within specific ethnic/social groups and that they learn how to communicate as women in the context of particular ethnic/social experiences (Scott, 2002, p. 56). In the next chapter, we focus on the complications that arise in the case of multiethnic backgrounds and identities and on the phenomena of passing, "verbal cross-dressing," and "cross-expressing."

Scholars of color such as Trinh T. Minh-ha (1989) and bell hooks (1981, 1989) have initiated the development of colored/third-world (Minh-ha) and Black/African American (hooks) feminist standpoints. However, they have also maintained that they see this only as a necessary step toward a more advanced theory of multiplicity. They have challenged the very notion of difference and underscored the conceptual ambiguity of identity politics. In continuation of the work done by Minh-ha and hooks, American linguists Victoria Bergvall and Janet M. Bing (1996) have introduced the term *diversity* to feminist communication studies as a possible alternative to the concept of difference, in order to denote differences both *within* and *among* women and to multiply the axes of differentiation (pp. 17–18).

## The Masculine Mode?

Far less research has been carried out on male communication strategies, partly because, as discussed in Chapter 4, "male" has been the genderless norm, whereas "female" has been the deviance in need of explanation. Feminist research in the 1980s and 1990s created a reverse story of the opposition of the communicative styles of co-optation and competition, in which the former is positively invested, the latter negatively.

Jennifer Coates's study in *Men Talk* (2003) focused on male narratives in different settings, but within an all-White, middle-class, and adult (British) context. As mentioned above, it confirms some of the central themes from the difference paradigm, such as men's in-group positioning according to hegemonic/heterosexual masculinity and the avoidance of intimate/emotional topics. However, it also documents new findings, such as collaborative storytelling among heterosexual couples and some men's way of handling in-group conversation by introducing more openness and vulnerability.

Deborah Cameron (1997a) elaborated on empirical research undertaken by one of her students in the United States in a group of five young men (White, middle-class, American suburbanites in their early 20s). The student titled his report "Wine, Women, and Sports" in order to relate his findings to other research on men's talk in all-male groups. He documented typical male topics, roughly dividing them into, on one hand, "serious" matters, such as sports and politics and, on the other, women and sex. The point of Cameron's revision is that this may not be a false interpretation of data. However, it is an interpretation that is very much in accordance with cultural assumptions and that therefore overlooks any data that point in other directions, as well as the complex embedding and multifunctionality of linguistics features. First, she estimated that the young men also talk a lot about daily life and domestic arrangements. Second, she found that they do gossip in the sense that they have a discussion of several persons not present but known to the participants, with a strong focus on critically examining these individuals' appearance, dress, social behavior and sexual mores. Lending yet another twist to this interpretation, she noticed that the individuals talked about were all suspected or known to be gay and that the whole conversation could be reinterpreted as coping with this issue. In that case, the in-group talking functioned as a mechanism for coping with sexual and gender deviance and thus constitutes an excellent example of jointly produced discourse, hitherto exclusively reserved for the co-optation style. However, Cameron also found examples of face-threatening interruptions, put-downs, the use of jokes and witty remarks to "capture" a turn, and so on, that have been attributed to all-male groups and the competitive genderlect. Her conclusion was that some of the participants did occasionally dominate the conversation, compete, and try to establish a hierarchy in the group. Thus, their exchange cannot be said to be egalitarian. Nevertheless, there are also collaborative moments and "sidetalks" that mark another intention and drive (Cameron, 1997a).

Although this was only a rather small study, Cameron (1997a) used it to warn against oversimplification in communication research, identifying cooperative versus competitive conversational styles and applying them to gender. She suggested that most conversations in most contexts may be said to contain elements of both co-optation and competition and that the different features that have been ascribed to these two conversational styles can have different meanings in different contexts. Ascribing them in any simple way to gender is problematic because of the danger of binary reductiveness, which indicates multiplicity and complexity. There are diverse repertoires and a range of different approaches available to women and men (whose boundaries qualify as legitimately gendered), as well as heterosexual subjects in a given context. Thus, Cameron ended up agreeing with Coates, that "being a man" in Western culture still is "not being a woman" and that men are still under pressure to constitute themselves as masculine linguistically by avoiding forms of talk that associate primarily with women/femininity. Moreover, in the young men's talk, "being a man" was defined using "the antithesis of man," that is, being homosexual. "What is being established as 'shared' here is a view of gays as alien" (Cameron, 1997a, p. 51). She hypothesized that both men and women tend to construct differentiation through discourse more than they express differences in discourse, once again mirroring Coates (1996) and introducing the performance turn, the focus of Chapter 6.

The relational construction of gender identity through discourse is discussed in all the contributions to *Language and Masculinity* (Johnson & Meinhof, 1997) and also highlighted in a range of primarily British studies of boys' interaction during the 1980s and 1990s, now often framed as "boy-centered research" (Frosh, Phoenix, & Pattman, 2002). Most of these studies were conducted in cross-ethnic, educational settings and demonstrate how gender identity is constructed among boys in a complex mixture of sexuality, class, and ethnicity. Frosh, Phoenix, and Pattman have studied young White and Black men from different social backgrounds regarding school, friends, families, and so on. They have argued that among White boys from the working or lower classes, masculinity is constructed in opposition to femininity, which is attributed to "other Others" such as homosexuals, upper-class boys ("the real Englishmen"), school-achieving middle-class boys, or Asian boys. "The real Englishmen," however, differentiate themselves from the "macho lads" because of their "macho" attitudes toward and ways of talking about girls and women. The "macho lads," finally, differentiate among themselves according to, for instance, age, and reportedly develop different types of masculinity by means of diverse heterosexual performances, such as "fashionable heterosexuals" versus "explicit heterosexuals" (Frosh et al., 2002, p. 54).

When it came to Black boys, Frosh et al. (2002) drew on a series of studies by other researchers, who reported that Black boys locate themselves in "a phallocentric framework," much like White boys, except that they position themselves as superior to both White and Asian students in terms of their "sexual attractiveness, style, creativity and hardness" (p. 55). Furthermore, Black boys reportedly refer to White boys as "pussies" (female) or "batty man" (homosexuals) and speak of White boys' fears of explicit performance (p. 55). Again, this approach may take different forms. The most radical is that of the so-called rebels who cultivate machismo styles, listen to "hard" rap, boast about their heterosexual prowess, develop specific body language, and so on. These rebels seem to resist racism, while playing with, or even reinforcing, White racist stereotypes. Conversely, young, White, working-class men are reported to construct the African Caribbean man in terms of "the fear and desire couplet" and in contrast to, for example, Vietnamese men (p. 55).

The research on young masculinities challenges not only the concept of the dual stylistics but also the scope of standpoint theory by reflecting on the premises and purposes of the approach and situating the research as well as the researchers themselves. Studies like these illustrate how the difference and identity approach needs greater nuance in order to adequately describe and theorize multicultural societies and hybrid identities that put gender on the agenda in new ways and in obvious intersection with class, ethnicity, sexuality, and age.

## Settings of Difference

Standpoint research in gender and communication has been undertaken within various settings during the 1980s and 1990s, not least in media and organization. In those days, focus shifted radically in both contexts. Feminist media studies moved from an interest in the sphere of male production/ producers, the questions of access, and the (mis)representation of women in media and mediated texts to an interest in women's own traditions, productions, media and texts, and women's agency as audience and users. A similar shift took place within the field of feminist organization studies, where women's values, competencies, enterprises, and leadership became central themes.

## Mediated Differences

Researchers in gender and media have used a difference and identity approach to identify an alliance among mass communications, popular culture, and female audiences. On this basis, they have confronted the distinctions between "Enlightenment and Entertainment," and "Highbrow and Lowbrow," and also explored the meanings and pleasures involved in women's media reception (Ang, 1985; Modleski, 1982; Radway, 1984). In particular, they have reclaimed undervalued "women's media," such as gothic novels, magazines, film romances, soaps, sitcoms, and talk shows. And they have reinterpreted the genre of melodrama, which runs through them all, representing a domestic and emotional stand that is also a woman's perspective—albeit not unambiguously and uncritically so.

Ien Ang (1985) analyzed *Dallas*, one of the first big soap operas ("soaps") that peaked in the United States as well as in Europe during the 1980s. Ang defined the genre as a late-modern version of melodrama that is exclusively related to the gendered conventions of consumption, visual culture, and the TV serial. The genre thus derives its generic enterprise from the contract it is able to make with (segments of) the female audiences, for instance, in terms of particular (daytime) sending hours. From her analysis of *Dallas*, Ang further introduced a distinction between the thematic realism of the production, of which there is very little, and the emotional realism of the reception, which is rich, at least according to the (Dutch) informants who reported a lack of emotional support and social acknowledgment and an underlying sense of tragedy. That said, Ang (1985) also emphasized that the success of *Dallas* simultaneously derived from the visual effect of stylistic glamor (p. 47). Between these two extremes, she identified a range of minor pleasures attached to the serial repetition, extended suspense, and endless variation of the dramas of everyday life.

According to Ang (1985), the features of 20th-century melodrama are narrative excess and the continuous crossings between the trivial and the extraordinary in women's everyday lives: incest, rape, wife assault, child abuse, and so on. The so-called postmodern soap is concerned with social issues such as the feminization of poverty and even takes up feminist issues such as sexual harassment, abortion, pornography, and discrimination. However, the purpose is merely to convince the audience that somebody else is worse off, to legitimate life's misfortunes, and to highlight the soap itself as the only real and secure source of pleasure in life.

During the 1980s, the soap format was differentiated and turned into, for instance, the situation comedy ("sitcom"). Although the soap is rooted in tragedy, the sitcom represented a revival and often direct citation of comedy. One of the most popular American shows from the 1980s in the sitcom format was *Roseanne*, which Roseanne Barr wrote, coproduced, and starred in. Jewish, working class, and overweight, she became the "mother goddess" of the multicultural United States of the 1980s (Lee, 1995). According to Janet Lee, Roseanne embodied late-modern female independence, universal maternity, and feminist consciousness, while also representing differences in and among women. Under the cover of humor and self-irony, she introduced a whole range of controversial issues to the American public. Nevertheless, there were limits to the issues that could be broached, not least in terms of racial and sexual questions. That the same goes for the British context is documented in an analysis of the concurrent show *Cagney and Lacey*, on female partnership and lesbian relations, which was revised several times and eventually turned down by British networks (D'Acci, 1995). Nevertheless, "queer sitcoms" became a success during the 1980s and 1990s, and they have since multiplied due to the segmentation of powerful audiences in the wake of modern satellite TV and electronic media technology (Gross, 1995).

During the 1980s and 1990s, Black women writers not only became fashionable in the United States, there was an almost aggressive commercial move toward adapting Black women's literature for film and television, a controversial example of which was *The Color Purple*, written by Alice Walker, in 1982, and produced by Steven Spielberg, in 1985. To Black feminist media scholars, this represents a highly ambiguous trend, as demonstrated in an analysis of the TV show *The Women of Brewster Place* (1989) (Bobo, 1995; Bobo & Seiter, 1997). *The Women of Brewster Place* is the television version of a novel by the African American writer Gloria Naylor, directed by independent White director Donna Deitch and starring the famous talk show hostess Oprah Winfrey. The show does remain true to the cultural history of Black women in that it emphasizes the sense of community among Black women rather than focusing on sexism, racism, and homophobia. It confronts issues of incest, rape, child abuse, and violence against Black women by Black men, as well as stereotypes such as the sexual Black woman, the domestic servant, and the dominating Black mother (Bobo & Seiter, 1997, p. 175). However, feminist criticism of *The Women of Brewster Place* has centered on the show's melodramatic "Black soap" character. Bobo and Seiter opposed this criticism, maintaining that melodrama, soap, and glamor were the basic conditions of mainstream TV in the 1990s and preferring to study how the genre was used to rework such visual schemata. Thus, they investigated how the show gratifies the Black woman audience, and they highlighted the emphasis on survival and grief, on family bonds beyond biology, and on women's lifelong friendships. Furthermore, they claimed that *The Women of Brewster Place* plays with the soap framework, especially the expectations of a Black soap, in subtle ways (Bobo & Seiter, 1997, p. 181).

The conventions of melodrama are further explored in an analysis of the controversial *Oprah Winfrey Show* (Squire, 1997). In the 1990s, around 20 million Americans watched the *Oprah Winfrey Show* on weekdays, making it the most-watched daytime talk show. Like others of its kind, it aims to entertain, inform, and encourage communication about difficult issues. The guests are often ordinary people telling their own stories, and the host and star, Winfrey herself, often mingles with the audience in the studio and involves them in the discussion. According to Squire, Winfrey's "brand" is identifying with Black women, which is evident in the fact that Winfrey often invokes the work of Black women such as Gloria Naylor, Toni Morrison, and especially Maya Angelou. She calls Angelou her mentor and claims that the author's account of growing up in the Black South describes her own life. The show can thus be said to "signify" on the texts of African American women writers, rewriting them in a different medium and for a larger, more racially diverse audience (Squire, 1997, p. 105).

The *Oprah Winfrey Show* has been criticized for neglecting or superficially representing both gender and race, for alleviating White guilt by presenting a rags-to-riches, unthreatening Black woman, and for "dissing" African American men. Squire (1997) contradicted such criticism, highlighting Winfrey's consistent involvement in Black women's causes and the difficult balance between having the courage to confront the problems of Black masculinity and giving voice to alternative Black male identities (p. 99). Squire admitted, however, that there is a continuous tension between the sensational and the Black/feminist project, making the show "an odd mélange" of "growth psychology, religious devotion, political analysis, and personal hubris" (p. 108).

The *Winfrey* show represents an extreme example of the common perception of television as the mass medium closest to interpersonal communication, especially of the talk show as the genre closest to personal, intimate conversation, or even a feminine conversational style. Squire (1997) hypothesized that the excess of emotion and empiricism disrupts the genre format and that the paradox of super-real excess (also known from "reality TV" and exposed in the clash between the powerful emotions and the quick shift of commercial breaks) functions to make the talk show "a pastiche of a pastiche." Thus, television culture and the interconnections between genre and gender are said to be reworked and "signified on" in an endlessly repeated suspension between fluff and gravity; psychology, social analysis and emotions; and realism and super-realism (Squire, 1997, pp. 109–110).

## Gender at Work

The theory of dual spheres and voices and many of the distinguishing features of what has been considered female-versus-male communicative styles have been researched in work settings as well. According to Janet Holmes and Maria Stubbe (2003), the literature on gender and communication in organizations during the 1980s and 1990s documents a "feminine" versus a "masculine" mode, distinguished by the features shown in Table 5.2.

**Table 5.2**    Gender and Working Styles

| Feminine | Masculine |
|---|---|
| Indirect | Direct |
| Conciliatory | Confrontational |
| Facilitative | Competitive |
| Collaborative | Autonomous |
| Minor contribution (in public) | Dominates (public) talking time |
| Supportive feedback | Aggressive interruptions |
| Person/process oriented | Task/outcome oriented |
| Affectively oriented | Referentially oriented |

SOURCE: Adapted from Holmes and Stubbe (2003, p. 574).

These features reappear in research on a range of organizations, institutions, and work places, and the so-called masculine style of interaction is usually considered to be in line with the workplace norm. However, as Holmes and Stubbe (2003) have also pointed out, the list does not take into account the variations, the communicative embedding, and the contextual framing of the communicative events in question and the nuances in many of the reported studies. Thus, the list may actually obscure more than it reveals. Holmes and Stubbe have emphasized that when they speak of "feminine" and "masculine" communicative strategies or workplaces, they do so in terms of cultural perceptions and dimensions that are a matter of degree.

Thus, different communication strategies or workplaces may be considered more or less feminine or masculine in different respects. In their own research, Holmes and Stubbe (2003) have investigated the common prejudice that women as well as "feminine" discourses and workplaces are less humorous. They found that "in a number of ways, then, women played a proactive positive role in contributing to the humor" (p. 578) and, moreover, that "'feminine' workplaces do not lack humor and that women's contributions to workplace humor are typically frequent and collegial in orientation" (p. 578).

Shari Kendall and Deborah Tannen (1997) have taken a similar journey through the literature on gender, professions, and workplaces from the difference and identity approach and have reached rather similar conclusions. They have found that men are more inclined to claim attention and seek credit for their contributions, use an oppositional format to accomplish a range of interactional goals, and view challenge and debate as a kind of ritual opposition. Women, on the other hand, often begin with a disclaimer, try to be succinct so as not to take up more speaking time than necessary, and find it impossible to do their best in what they perceive as a competitive environment (Kendall & Tannen, 1997, p. 84). The consequence is that when women and men interact in work settings, a stylistic mismatch is likely to produce unbalanced participation, so that men end up having proportionately more influence. However, the authors also drew attention to the many missed nuances in the reported studies and called for caution in terms of conclusions. Kendall and Tannen have suggested yet another (structuralist) model that provides a scale of evaluation in terms of gender, workplaces, and communication strategies along the lines of hierarchy/equality and closeness/distance. The model suggests a sliding scale along two sets of parameters, instead of a fixed set of categorizations (Kendall & Tannen, 2003, p. 98). The model can be outlined as shown in Figure 5.2.

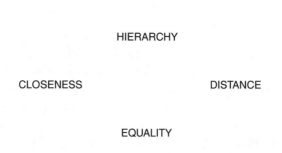

Figure 5.2    Gender and Work Mode

In commenting on the model, Kendall and Tannen (1997) referred to a growing bulk of literature on women's organizational skills and leadership during the 1980s and 1990s (see also Acker, 1992; Mills & Tancred, 1992). The point here is to highlight what is now understood as women's facilitative style and the way it matches the competencies that are required in new public and private management, since it fosters a type of power that involves the ability to accomplish one's own goals and to help others achieve theirs while doing so.

To nuance the picture, research on gender in different professions shows that women manage in intricate ways to conform to the usual (male-generated) norms, while succeeding in projecting new standards. For example, in one study on women police officers, women employees were found to substitute the traditional, authoritarian and patriarchal image for a more middle-class image of police work as professional and efficient (McElhinny, 1998). Several studies on women health care professionals and doctors have found that women seem better equipped to establish an evenly balanced relationship with patients and to minimize status and authority by using fewer directives and more appreciative inquiry, which is much more in accordance with the demands of information-oriented public service (Coates, 1995; West, 1998).

As Marta B. Calás (1992) and Calás and Linda Smircich (1992) have pointed out, research on gender and organization has been relatively sparse, but there is even less research on race/ethnicity and organization, not to mention on the intersections of gender and race/ethnicity and other differences on various levels in institutions and workplaces. However, as general demographics and certain organizational conditions in Europe and the United States in the new millennium render the discourses of globalization and diversity pivotal to innovation, change is afoot (see, for instance, Buzzanell, 2000). We return to this important discussion in Chapter 6.

---

# Case Study: Feminist Critical Discourse Analysis (FCDA)

As discussed in Chapter 2, feminist critical discourse analysis (FCDA) aims to reveal connections between language, power, ideology, and gender and to describe the ways in which power is produced and transformed in engendering discursive practices (Holmes & Meyerhoff, 2003, p. 13). FCDA is especially concerned with mapping this process: "Different identities are discursively constructed according to context, that is according to the audience to which they are addressed, the setting of the discursive act, the topic being discussed, and so on" (Wodak, 2003, p. 678). Wodak (2003) pointed to attention given to the relation between discourse, situation, and context and the complex interactions of producers and receivers of discourses through practice. Although she did not herself explicitly mention feminist critical discourse analysis, she did talk about combining theories of gender, feminist theory, and methodology with critical discourse analysis. According to Wodak, this combination is distinguished by a circular process of (a) empirical and theoretical elaboration, (b) macro- and microlevel investigation, and (c) multidisciplinary approaches and "toolboxes."

We have chosen a relatively recent case study by Ruth Wodak (2003) about the constitution of identities through discourse in the context of "the multinational, multilingual, and multicultural" European Union (EU) (p. 674). The study is part of a bigger research project on the EU and its institutions and organizations (including the European Parliament, the European Commission, and the European Council of Ministers, etc.). The purpose of the study is to examine how national, organizational, and individual identities are invoked and addressed in this context and how gender identities in particular are displayed and enacted in the midst of this complexity. The public domain in question is seen as particularly complex and characterized by inter-cultural, ideological, ethnic, national, and gender conflicts. The aim of the study, therefore, is to ask what strategies women employ to present and promote themselves and to guarantee that they are taken seriously (Wodak, 2003, p. 673). The part of the study referred to here is based on qualitative interviews conducted in Brussels with 14 delegates to the European Parliament (EP), and it concentrates on the interviews with the 5 women members (MEPs). The interviews focus on the issue of unemploy-ment, the purpose of the primary organizational bodies of EU, day-to-day working life, and the personal history of the interviewees.

The context of the study is that equal rights are now anchored in laws of equal opportunity in most Western European countries and also in the legislative framework of the EU and its institutions. Moreover, the European Commission has introduced a strategy of "gender mainstreaming" to promote long-lasting changes in family struc-ture, institutional practice, and organizational work and to establish a balanced dis-tribution of resources and positions between women and men. However, there is a dearth of social structures and political institutions behind all the fine words, partic-ularly in the EU. Even if women constitute 47.5% of the employees of the European Commission, only 5.9% are found at the highest level of the hierarchy. When it comes to the European Parliament, the 27% of the members who are women are unequally distributed among the member states. The Scandinavian countries and Luxembourg take the lead in terms of highest percentages of the total number of employees.

To clarify the premises of her critical discourse analysis, Wodak (2003) takes a quick tour of the different approaches to identity inherent in the tradition of critical theory and their later applications. These approaches correspond to the theoretical concepts of identity outlined in Chapter 2 under the heading of structuralism, but they are further inspired by poststructuralism and in particular positioning theory and analysis (see Chapter 6). Wodak emphasizes the fact that she draws on the tools of critical linguistics and social semiotics, but she focuses particularly on storytelling as a means to approach the discursive construction of identity in interaction (p. 682).

In the following, we examine interviews with two Swedish MEPs and follow part of Wodak's (2003) analysis. Sweden and Finland were among the last three member states to join the EU at the time of the survey (1997), and in Sweden, only a small majority of the population voted yes. Furthermore, Sweden and Finland have a long tradition of Scandinavian-based political associations, for instance, in the Nordic Council (together with Denmark, Norway, Iceland, and the Faroe Islands). This means that the Swedish people have very complex regional and national affiliations to refer to. Wodak does not seem to know that for historical reasons, Finland does not belong to Scandinavia. Scandinavia consists of Sweden, Norway, and Denmark, whereas the Nordic countries comprise Scandinavia, Iceland, and Finland. However, this is not crucial to her analysis.

According to Wodak, it is characteristic of the two Swedish informants that they draw on quite a range of identities, such as woman, Green/left, Swedish/Scandinavian/ Nordic, European Unionist/(North) European, mother, political outsider, and so on. But when is one identity highlighted on behalf of the others, and how do the informants themselves relate these different identities? In the transcript below, a colon indicates extension of sound, a dash indicates abrupt cutoff, emphasized syllables/words are underlined, words in single parentheses were difficult to understand and transcribe, and double parentheses indicate paralinguistic features:

[1]   it/ it's quite *simple*. - why we have this - high - unemployment rate no

[2]   and it's because we are changing soti/ society

[3]   I mean we had a - highly in/ industrial society and now we are *changing*

[4]   so. - so: eh - this is completely *new* for us

[5]   and-/ and then we are trying - to *amend that*

[6]   and try to - eh: help that up

[7]   with-/ with - kind of *old* -/ old *structures:* and - *old* - *answers.* -

[8]   eh: and - we don't want to *face* that we really *have* to -

[9]   adjust a *lot* of - *thinking*

[10]   I mean that/ that's-/ what it is *about.* - and -/ and -

[11]   we have to - *reconsider* -

[12]   eh what is full employment and what is

[13]   what is eh: -/ to have a eh/ eh - a *work* for *salary:* -

[14]   and a lot of that so/ sort of things. -

[15]  because I don't think that - we will *ever* -

[16]  ever *have* what called -

[17]  usually in Sweden

[18]  and -/ and -/ and *my* solution to that and/ and

[19]  *the Green group* is of course that

[20]  for the *first* you have to *see:* -

[21]  *we* have a/ had a -/ eh have another - eh eh another eh: - *approach*

[22]  and another - *view:* of - full employment. -

[23]  just to say that - akay. - this is - nineteen ninety. - *seven*

[24]  and h -/ we have had so many f/ people in -/ unemployed.

[25]  so the *first* thing we should *do:* - is of course to *reduce:* - the *working time.* -

[26]  because - eh forty hours:

[27]  a week *as we are working in Sweden* now

[28]  it was not - eh institution of *god.* -

[29]  it/ it was - decided of with/ us ((*laughs*))/

[30]  the/ the time when we -/ when we *needed* a lot of people to *work*

[31]  so - re-/ reduction of working time of course

[32]  and *also* - to change the attitudes in society against

[33]  the people that *have* work and *don't* have work

[34]  . . .

[35]  *and* eh: -/ and *then* also of course we have to - *support* and/

[36]  and say that *flexibility* in that sense

[37]  you could work the hour that you *like*

[38]  and you could have a half-time *jo:b* and so on

[39]  and have a small company in size

[40]  so all these *taxations*

[41]  and all - the regulations

[42]  has to be: - sh -/ *changed*

[43]  and *altered also.* - to make this *possible*

[44]  eh: and of course - the *taxation* or the/ the: -

[45]  you don't say taxation you say - eh: -

[46]  the tax on *labor* -/ on *labor.* -

[47]  *it's* it's quite *high*

[48]  I s:uppose it's - eh: - all the same in the European Union

[49]  but *in Sweden* - eh which I/ know most of course ((*laughs*))/

[50]  in the North West

[51]  there eh -/ there we have - *really high*

[52]  percentage of tax *on* - labor. -

[53]  and that should be *s:witched* and *changed*

[54]  of course so you put it on - *as I'm a Green* -

[55]  *eh MEP* - on energy:

[56]  and non resourceable -

[57]  eh: eh:m - ninedren/ non

[58]  *renewable resources* and energy and so on

[59]  so - *this:* should be *switched* of course.

---

SOURCE: Wodak, R., Multiple personalities: the role of female parliamentarians in the EU parliament, in J. Holmes & M. Meyerhoff (Eds.), *The handbook of language and gender.* Copyright © 2003. Reprinted with permission of Blackwell Publishing, Ltd.

In this first extract from MEP10, concerning the issue of unemployment, the national (Swedish) and political (Green) identities are foregrounded and used as contextual markers. However, Wodak claims that whereas it is not quite clear why MEP10 refers to national identity in lines 17 and 27, it is explained in line 49, where it is clarified that she estimates unemployment to be worse in Sweden than in the rest of the EU due to the extraordinarily high taxes on labor. Or rather, MEP10 estimates that this is the case in the "North West" (line 50). Unlike Wodak, we understand this phrase not as reference to a Swedish region (as regional differences in taxes in Sweden are only very small and regional taxes only a minor part of state taxes), but as a reference to Sweden as part of "North Western" Europe and this again as distinct from the EU. Wodak herself later on refers to the fact that a relatively large number of Scandinavian MEPs in the study distinguished between being European and being a European Unionist. In contrast to her national self-identification, MEP10's reference to her membership of the Green Party is unambiguous and immediately made relevant in terms of delivering a politics of full employment by reducing the standard number of hours worked per week (19–26) and a shift in taxes from labor to energy (53–59).

In another excerpt, MEP3 says that her fellow citizens are stubbornly bound to thinking of themselves as opponents of the EU even if they are now members, which is illustrated in the following anecdote:

[1]  I know that *we* are a very stubborn country

[2]  Most of the people ah: are now: ah well

[3]  A ha./ mo/ most of the people

[4]  At least when was it fifty-one point four percent or something like that

[5]  Voted in the referendum for entering the European Union

[6]  But today *we* - almost never meet anyone who did -

[7]  I don't know what they did

[8]  Yeah because everybody said - do/ they said "no: I voted no:" and

[9]  Ye said "well I really do I re - I really do regret" ((*laughs*))

[10]  Aha:. - so it (happened) ((*laughs*)) okay

[11]  So I mean it's make/ it doesn't make the whole ah - /

[12]  The whole billing - easier.

SOURCE: Wodak, R., Multiple personalities: The role of female parliamentarians in the EU parliament, in J. Holmes & M. Meyerhoff (Eds.), *The handbook of language and gender.* Copyright © 2003. Reprinted with permission of Blackwell Publishing, Ltd.

MEP3 tells this story in terms of a national "we"; however, she also tells it to *distinguish* herself from her fellow countrymen, and in so doing, she puts herself on the Unionist side. According to Wodak, this is an example of the highly complex identity *bricolage* in which different identities are either fore- or backgrounded depending on situation and context. In both cases, however, gender identity is overrun not only by (supra)national but also by political identity. Wodak directs our attention to the finding that both MEP10 (Green) and MEP3 (left wing) highlight both their national and their political identities. Furthermore, both seem to understand their identities as distinctly different from the mainstream of MEPs of continental Europe and from the political center. In their narratives, they construct themselves as belonging to distinct groups, and MEP3 further extends this format both to her professional role as a social worker and to her gender. Or rather, you may say that the semantics of being "a very special bird . . . everything's wrong" (Wodak, 2003, p. 689) builds up to a climax that culminates with a reference to her gender. From there on, it is possible to understand the row of deviations backward, now illuminated by this "prime" marker of difference:

[1]  I figure here the most common - eh civil - job. - for an MEP

[2]  is eh to be a lawyer.

[3]  me myself *I'm far from that*

[4]  the job I had doesn't even exist outside *Scandinavia.*

[5]  so: - it's a sort of a social teacher - so

[6]  so I'm/ I'm very in/ an:/ a very special bird in this a:

[7]  If mhm mhm so now you don't feel like you - fit into sort of a *typical* MEP eh

[8]   Me *no. no: no: I'm not. I'm left I'm a woman I'm Swedish* and I'm also

[9]   everything -/ everything's wrong. ((*laughs*))

SOURCE: Wodak, R., Multiple personalities: The role of female parliamentarians in the EU parliament, in J. Holmes & M. Meyerhoff (Eds.), *The handbook of language and gender*. Copyright © 2003. Reprinted with permission of Blackwell Publishing, Ltd.

In Wodak's analysis, MEP3 here points out many of the identities (social teacher, left, female, Swedish) that she associates herself with and that in her own perception mark her as different from the norm, by traditional/conservative/patriarchal European standards. Wodak considers the sequence a good illustration of how a successful woman has managed to come to terms with all her differences, which have served to marginalize her, and now emphasizes them on her own terms. She "turns the tables," in a manner of speaking, and strategically redefines the negative connotations into positive attributes: "a very special bird." In this way, she appears to solve conflicting ideological problems and dilemmas through self-irony, self-reflection—and, we might add, circumvention. To emphasize Wodak's analytical procedure and push it to its logical conclusion, we highlight the way it pinpoints the climax of the interview that is also the climax of suspense in MEP3's self-narration in lines 8 and 9. This is the turn of the screw of self-interpretation that makes MEP3 able to redefine her activity as politician:

[1]   I mean I know that - even on/ on a: national level

[2]   I mean there are very many politicians all sorts in all parties -

[3]   that *prefer* to/ to meet the/ the - eh/ the citizens through - media.

[4]   eh -/ so *I know that I'm not that sort.*

[5]   so I prefer to meet people. -

[6]   it/ it could be hard but it's more interesting . . .

[7]   and that's the way *I* learn at the same time - a lot.

[8]   . . . and a (xx) of -/ I met so very many politicians - during my - living 45 years

[9]   ((*laughs*)) so: - and it's the -/

[10]   I mean do you really - when you've seen them in action

[11]   when you were a child or

[12]   all through the years - you say oh - how disgusting and -

[13]   what behaviour they've done and instead I -/

[14]   *for sure I will not be that sort of person that I always despised!*

[15]   that means that if you go to a meeting

[16]   you just don't go there. -

[17]  and you just don't talk for forty-five minutes

[18]  telling everybody how the situation really is

[19]  and then you leave *off.* -

[20]  mostly with the plane first a limo and then a plane and

[21]  that's - not a boring life.

SOURCE: Wodak, R., Multiple personalities: The role of female parliamentarians in the EU parliament, in J. Holmes & M. Meyerhoff (Eds.), *The handbook of language and gender.* Copyright © 2003. Reprinted with permission of Blackwell Publishing, Ltd.

Through irony and overt criticism, she again marks her difference from other MEPs and constructs her own unique identity as a responsible and visionary MEP who listens and is in close contact with the people she represents. In both lines 4 and 14, she explicitly dissociates herself from being "that sort," implicitly referring to the typical dominant male politician who is in fact uninterested in people and politics and aspires only to power.

Wodak concludes that she has identified three types of female gender role constructions, which seem to be successful in this context and at this level of politics: There is the assertive activist, the expert, and the positive difference (the "special bird"). These are very different from the roles often maintained in other contexts, at least in Austria. For example, there are woman principals in schools (where one prototype is the mother) or "big business" (where there is the new prototype of the female co-opter). One of the questions Wodak raises is whether the role of "special bird" may be compared with former articulations that make strong women leaders the exception.

From our view, the standpoint view, the significance of Wodak's (2003) contribution lies in her application of the difference and identity approach and her focus on women's multiple identities, on one hand, and the pertinence of a critical discourse analysis methodology, on the other. Of particular interest is her focus on the communicative practice of the informants and the way they storytell their multiple identities, thereby forming a coherent discourse of radical and productive otherness. It is important to note, however, in terms of Wodak's initial setting and the demands of FCDA, that she does not to any great extent consider the interaction taking place in the interview setup. What is going on in this particular situation, and how do the informants use it in terms of storytelling their own identities? Wodak could have more accurately analyzed the interview as a communicative event by studying the rhetorical strategies involved. However, we do not know whether she in fact does so in the extended study. To learn from the case, we would suggest the following list of items to consider when planning research from the perspective of FCDA:

1.  What is the particular problem that you want to address?

2.  Where do you ground your theoretically based thesis and core terminology?

3. How do you define the social practice in question and frame it as discourse in context?

4. Where and how do you locate gender and see it related to power?

5. What are your particular tools for collecting and analyzing data?

6. How do you relate your own research to FCDA?

# 6

# Gender and Performance

Considering gender in terms of performance has radically changed the agenda of gender and communication. The "performance turn" not only denotes a new intellectual framework, it alters communication policies by attending to situated performances. Since this book is intended to sharpen analytic skills, we shall focus on how the performance turn in feminist communication scholarship is generated from a new poststructuralist basis. In this chapter, we start by presenting significant studies from the performance and positioning perspectives, move on to examine research in a media and organization context, and conclude with a case and a sample analysis illustrating the methodology of feminist poststructuralist discourse analysis.

## Gender, Performance, and Communication

Kristin M. Langellier is one of the researchers who has explored the possibilities of adding performativity to feminist communication studies (Langellier 1989, 1999; Langellier, Carter, & Hantzis, 1993; Langellier & Peterson, 2004). She has been inspired by the work of Judith Butler (1990) but has also researched the field of classic performance studies, linking the embodied practice of performance art to the recent performance turn. She has also elaborated on the distinction between performance and performativity: Whereas performance designates a type of imperfection that implies a transgressive desire for agency and action, performativity articulates a display of differences that challenges the forces of discourses and institutionalized networks of power (Langellier, 1999, p. 129). This distinction clarifies the differences between some of the attempts to effectuate the performance turn. In light of Butler's and Langellier's work, we consider this turn to be a long struggle, perhaps not yet fully affected. Thus, we have come to think of it in terms of two phases: an early phase, to be described in this chapter, and a later phase, to be tentatively outlined in Chapter 7.

## Queer Communication

*Madonna announced to her screaming fans: "I want you all to know that there are only three real men on this stage—me and my two backup girls!"*

— Liz Smith, quoted in Garber (1997, p. 164)

We begin by examining studies that demonstrate how gender is displayed through communication in ways that question the coherence between gender and sexuality, which is assumed in the heterosexual imperative and which has been put forward in a kind of "coat-rack theory." Such studies must perform a double task: (a) to determine what to call people whose sexual and gendered practices or identities fall beyond normative heterosexuality and (b) to identify and describe their ways of speaking (Cameron & Kulick, 2003; Kulick 2000).

We shall start with what has been called the "lavender" part of the project: the naming of different types of sexual practices and identities. In *Queerly Phrased: Language, Gender, and Sexuality,* from 1997, Arnold M. Zwicky suggested distinguishing between category labels used within the sexual minority communities (as sexual category labels) and those used among the sexual mainstream community (as social category labels). However, Zwicky (1997) also pointed out that the lexical items used by "insiders" vary according to time and place and that it is almost impossible to refer to, for instance, lesbians, gays, and bisexuals or "LGB" people in any consensual way (p. 23). Thus, some would prefer *homosexual* to *gay,* and vice versa, and they see a distinction with reference to behavior, identity, sensibility, or speech. For similar reasons, some would use gay as an adjective, but not a noun. And some would see gay as an exclusive term for men only, while others would see it as an inclusive term, referring to both homosexual women and homosexual men and sometimes bisexuals. Some would see it as a superior term, others as ambiguous or even derogative. Similar complexities apply to alternate terms such as *fag* or *faggot* or in the case of lesbians, the term *dyke,* which has been reclaimed recently by North American lesbians (Zwicky, 1997).

To strengthen the criticism of so-called heteronormativity and highlight queer practices, parts of the "LGB" community have chosen the word *queer* as their new common label. However, while some use the term exclusively as a common denominator for what was earlier called "LGB" people, others include all nonheterosexual practices and identities. Thus, it has turned out to be almost as problematic as earlier terms. This is so partly since it may, once again, silence particular sexualities and minorities and partly because it blurs the distinctions between a growing variety of "queer queers," such as those who favor certain sexual practices like bondage, sadism, and masochism and, on the other hand, all who have ever had same-sex sexual experiences: "Gay, lesbian, hetero or undefined, all the anarchists were queer in their own way" (*Love & Rage,* an anarchist magazine, quoted in Murphy, 1997, p. 48). Today, "queer" has come to represent just one more identity to be tacked on to the end of an ever-expanding and thus meaningless list. Thereby, it seems to collapse into a nonsignifying and therefore nonsignificant term (Kulick, 2000). The linguistic sensibility resulting from identity politics has culminated in an offer to every self-identifying individual or group to signal not only different genders and sexualities but also various intersections hereof, including those related to class and ethnicity.

The other part of the project involves the notion of a particular speech style, related to both a particular identity claim and a particular speech community. Whether known as "lesbian and gay" language or "lesbian, gay, and bisexual" (LGB) language or "lesbian, gay, bisexual, transsexual, and transvestite" (LGBTT) language or even "lesbian, gay, bisexual, transgendered, two-spirit, queer, or questioning" (LGBTTSQ) or just "queerspeak," there are numerous possibilities (Kulick, 2000, p. 244). The naming of the research field and the increasing complexity of the suggested acronyms reflects the challenges presented by the subject. Kulick has drawn on a range of scholars when confronting the conceptual difficulties bound to the notion of a particular communication style (Harvey & Shalom, 1997; Queen & Schimel, 1997). Such assumptions are, in the end, he says, based on what is known as Darsey's theorem (after the critic J. Darsey). The fact that gays (or lesbians) do X does not make X gay (or lesbian). To be able to make the argument that gays and lesbians speak in a gay/lesbian manner, you must first prove the phenomenon empirically; second, you must prove this manner of speaking to be unique to gays or lesbians; and finally, you must define gay and lesbian. Attempts in this direction will inevitably raise the issue: If gayspeak is defined as English spoken by gay men, then its "gayness" is defined by its users, whose speech, paradoxically, is also explained through their sexuality. Such an argument is not only circular but also collapses the distinction between the social and the symbolic because it views communication as a mere mirror of the social. As pointed out by Kulick, this mistake has already been reproduced in different contexts and in different speech communities (women, Blacks, homosexuals, Black homosexuals, Black female homosexuals, etc.). This, again, leads us to question the whole concept of a speech community:

> The concept is especially unhelpful when it comes to thinking about the language of gays and lesbians, because racial and ethnic diversity, being "in" or "out" of the closet, and the overlap between, for example, middle class white gayspeak and the speech patterns of members of other groups (such as heterosexual women, or African Americans) make the idea of a homogeneous gay, lesbian, or transgendered community untenable. (Kulick, 2000, p. 266)

Kulick (2000) suggested that the phrase *queerspeak* should be used exclusively to identify a range of sexual positionings, such as the signaling of lesbianism through nonspecific gender references or the gay argot "faglish," characterized by female names, pronouns, and address and effeminate grammatical forms that signal not only gayness, but a position as faggot (p. 258). Kulick here drew on Susan Sontag's now classic essay on camp, from 1964, in which she defined the communication style as a means of signaling a(n)/other sexual orientation. In our view, Kulick here has suggested a distinction between the indexical quality of queerspeak as a means of performing sexual orientation, of which he approves, and the symbolic quality of queerspeak as a claim of identity and community, of which he disapproves. As pointed out by Kira Hall (2003), this distinction appears rather arbitrary. It also seems to have been abandoned in favor of focusing on the subtle and often ambiguous workings of desire in language and establishing an alternate research field of communication and desire (Cameron & Kulick, 2003).

## Linguistics of Contact

To handle the dilemma outlined by Kulick and others, another North American scholar of sexuality and communication, Rusty Barrett, again reminded us of Benedict Anderson's concept of "imagined communities," underscoring his assertion that they "are to be distinguished not by their falsity/genuineness, but in the style in which they are imagined" (Anderson, in Barrett, 1997, p. 189). Barrett proposed an adaptation of this basic definition in terms of a "homo-genius speech community," a queer-speech community in which the very notion of community cannot be taken for granted: "While all communities are imagined in some sense, queer communities recognize that they are imagined and knowingly and openly question the membership status of a variety of potential members" (Barrett, 1997, p. 189). However, this also means that analysis centers on the ways in which features of queer speech overlap with those of other groups, hence requiring an alternative to the phrase "intersectionality." Barrett suggested a term developed by the British literary critic Mary Louise Pratt in 1987, "linguistics of contact":

> Imagine, then, a linguistics that decentered community, that placed at its centre the operation of language *across* lines of social differentiation, a linguistics that focused on modes and zones of contact between dominant and dominated groups, between persons of different and multiple identities, speakers of different languages, that focused on how such speakers constitute each other relationally and in difference, how they interact difference in language. Let us call this enterprise a *linguistics of contact*. (Pratt, 1987, p. 60, in Barrett, 1997, pp. 191–192)

Barrett (1997) used this notion of a "linguistics of contact" in a specific linguistic sense as well as in a broader sense as a metaphor for communication. He referred to specific types of "contact languages" and the way people can imitate styles that reflect a group with whom they wish to be associated, for example, in the case of the interesting overlap between gay-male speech and African American vernacular English. Barrett (1999) also drew attention to his own research on African American drag queens and the finding that they index queerness by switching between a number of styles that stereotypically denote other identities, such as those of either White women or African American men, and that such types of linguistic incongruence may be understood both as ambiguous and as a means of solidarity and resistance in much the same way as maintained by Susan Sontag in the context of camp (Barrett, 1999).

The North American media researcher Robin M. Queen (1997) has developed these ideas in relation to lesbian language in her research on lesbian comics. She called on Roman Jacobsen and his poetics of speech (speech genre and style) and Paul Friedrich's work on the trope, among others, to argue that the lesbian comic style can be perceived as a unique creation of various paradigms of social meanings, indexed through linguistic forms and put together in a polyphonic mimicry of conventions and stereotypes. Her primary claim is that "by combining the stereotypes of non-lesbian communities with the stereotypes that lesbians hold about themselves, lesbians create an indexical relationship between language use and a lesbian 'identity'" (Queen, 1997, p. 239).

Queen proposed four generic tropes that are used to construct a lesbian style:

1. Stereotypical women's language: tag questions and rising intonation at the end of statements, hedges, hypercorrect grammar, super-polite terms, empty adjectives, etc.

2. Stereotyped nonstandard varieties, often associated with working-class, urban males: cursing; nonnormative consonant cluster simplification; contracted forms such as "gonna," "oughta," "I dunna"; ethnically marked linguistic forms such as "kapeesh," "yo'mama"; vowel quality changes depending on the region; postvocalic "r" deletion likewise often regionally marked; "in'" versus "ing," etc.

3. Stereotyped gay-male language: use of wider pitch range for intonation variety; hypercorrection: the presence of phonological nonreduced forms; the use of hyperextended vowels, etc.

4. Stereotyped lesbian language: use of narrow pitch range and "flat" intonation patterns; cursing; male-related expressions such as "bite me" and "suck my dick"; lack of humor and joking, especially irony and sarcasm.

Like Barrett, Queen (1997) emphasized the significance of the "linguistics of contact" as a model for discussing lesbian communication and the way that lesbians make stylistic choices on the basis of any number of individual and/or contextual factors that may or may not overlap. The style or mode can, for instance, be used according to the "butch-femme" distinction, but not in any simple way. It is not that butches talk like men and vice versa, rather, they appropriate particular elements of these stereotyped styles and construct their respective identities through the interaction of some of these elements (Queen, 1997, p. 241).

Both Barrett and Queen have tried to reformulate the project of queer communication by displacing the focus of research from identity categories to signifying practices. However, they can both be criticized for, in the end, upholding the idea of an authentic "homo-genius" speech community. It is not easy to see how they distinguish their chosen terms from gay and lesbian, while at the same time distinguishing between speakers and speech. Thus, the dilemmas of the dominance, especially the difference approach, seem to "sneak in" on the performance approach (see Chapters 4 and 5).

Are there any alternatives? What do our fellow critics Deborah Cameron and Don Kulick say? They emphasize the importance of the shift in focus from being queer to performatively becoming queer and define this as materializing oneself as queer through particular ways of communicating (Cameron & Kulick, 2003). They also spot the missing theory of sexuality that has caused scholars to see "gay" and "lesbian" as identity categories—along the same lines as, for instance, "woman," "African American," or

"Black"—and call for a new conceptual outline of desire and discourse. They further emphasize (agreeing with Butler and the tenets of speech act theory) that sexual desire is conveyed through a range of semiotic codes, which we may or may not be conscious of but which are recognizable as conveying desire, for example, of a man for a woman. Exactly because it relies on the force of iterability for its expression (see Chapter 2), desire is, however, also subject to both appropriation and forgery, which is again a mechanism behind sexual insults, rape, and so on. Cameron and Kulick (2003) concluded by suggesting that the scope of inquiry be expanded to explore the role of fantasy, repression, and unconscious motivations in interaction. At the same time, they open up to a critical perspective by referring to what was labeled "silence" by Derrida and "foreclosures" by Butler; these are terms that indicate the subtle workings of culture and power and the complex webs of the social and the individual, the material and the symbolic, by rendering some experiences unspoken and some even unspeakable. With this particular perspective, a whole new and exciting research agenda opens up to scholars of communication studies.

## Mimicry and Symbolic Reversals

In *This Sex Which Is Not One* (1977/1985b), French feminist philosopher Luce Irigaray suggested that mimicry is a way for women to recover a voice in communication (see Chapters 1 and 2). The technique of mimicry implies that women assume the feminine role, outlined for them, without being entirely engulfed by it, playing with it and thereby positioning themselves someplace else:

> To play with mimesis is thus, for a woman, to try to recover the place of her exploitation through discourse, without allowing herself to be simply reduced to it. It means to resubmit herself—inasmuch as she is on the side of the "perceptible," of "matter" to "ideas," in particular to ideas about herself, that are elaborated in/by a masculine logic, but so as to make "visible," by an effect of playful repetition, what was supposed to remain invisible: the cover-up of a possible operation of the feminine in language. It also means to "unveil" the fact that, if women are such good mimics, it is because they are not simply resorbed in this function. (Irigaray, 1977/1985b, p. 76)

Women, then, may use mimicry of patriarchal discourses as a playful repetition for their own purposes. By making this claim, Irigaray took inspiration from psychoanalyst Joan Rivière. In her now classic essay, "Womanliness as a Masquerade," from 1929, Rivière claimed that the border between what could be considered real as opposed to virtual womanliness is in fact nonexistent. To Rivière, womanliness *is* mimicry and womanliness is masquerade. She claimed this to be a long-established fact that was only exposed by the emergence of the "new" woman at the beginning of the 20th century who aspired to economical and political independency and a career of her own—and was therefore considered to suffer from a masculinity complex. Confronted with this, Rivière suggested that women should consciously use mimicry to suit their own ends. Interestingly, the reverse debate of "true" masculinity took place a generation later, in the midst of the 20th century, as a result of women's "liberation." A range of male performers such as Liberace and Elvis Presley at this time impersonated womanliness and thereby caused the notion of mimicry to be extended to masculinity (Garber, 1997).

Butler's preferred example of mimicry is the drag show. The central claim in Butler's essay on this, "Critically Queer" (in *Bodies That Matter*, 1993), is that in imitating social gender while simultaneously expressing the desire *to pass* as a woman and exposing the knowledge of the tragedy of this socially marked desire, the drag figure implicitly reveals the imitative structure of gender itself, thereby questioning what can be seen as original and imitation, respectively. According to Butler, the drag figure is a parody whose chief quality is its ambiguous character. Such gender mimicry is not so much about original and imitation but about the very idea of such a notion. The drag show thus exposes us to the fact that we must all *pass* as belonging to a certain gender and sexual identity within a given community and culture and that we attempt to do so by engaging in conventional formats. But the drag figure does not itself really engage in passing. On the contrary, it *cross-dresses* in order to direct our attention to the fragility of desire and the non-self-identical subject. Whereas "passing" enacts the illusion of identity, cross-dressing enacts the deferral of identity. Together, they embody the ambiguous rhetoric of mimicry.

Rhetorician Anne Teresa Demo (2000) provided us with another example of mimicry. She showed how the New York-based Guerrilla Girl group uses mimicry visually, thereby inventively revising history, and how they use strategic juxtaposition to highlight the absence of women in the art world (see Chapter 1). From their inception in 1985, the Guerrilla Girls have creatively appropriated patriarchal discourses through their Web site, posters, books, and actions. One early example is the 1989 poster titled: "Do Women Have to Be Naked to Get Into the Met Museum?" illustrated by Auguste Dominique Ingres's 1814 painting of the Grand Odalisque with the head of a roaring gorilla. The text answers the question: "Less than 5% of the artists in the Modern Art Sections are women, but 85% of the nudes are female" (Demo, 2000, p. 148). In her analysis, Demo maintained that "the text/image juxtaposition and implied contrast between Ingres's odalisque and that of the Guerrilla Girls create an argument by incongruity that challenges art world claims of gender equality" (p. 148). She concluded that the Guerrilla Girls use mimicry and strategic juxtaposition in ways that both inform and persuade.

Karlyn Kohrs Campbell has also highlighted symbolic reversal by using "the master's tools" to undermine patriarchal power. Not only are these the only tools we have, she says, they become "parasitic," when they "reframe," "juxtapose," "satirize," "reverse," and "ridicule" dominant discourse (Campbell, 1998, p. 112). An example of successful symbolic reversal is Queen Elizabeth I, who avoided marriage by strategically referring to England as her husband, thereby manipulating the language of family and marriage. According to Campbell, such a rhetorical move at once acknowledges and mocks gendered expectations, thereby raising our awareness of social constructions of gender (Campbell, 1998). Like Irigaray, Campbell has maintained that marginalized groups can use such techniques to gain power and create new symbolic spaces.

We shall now take a closer look at mimicry as it is exemplified in "passing" and "cross-expressing" and as it relates to issues of gender, sexuality, and race/ethnicity. We shall also discuss its effects in terms of subversion and the social constructionist point of view implied therein.

## Passing and Cross-Expressing

To Mary Bucholtz (1995), the act of "passing" refers to the ability to be taken for a member of a social category other than one's "own" "real" one (p. 351). Whereas feminist queer communication scholars have lauded passing and connected it with supposedly subverting concepts such as theatre and masquerade, feminist communication scholars in the field of ethnic studies have criticized the term. Bucholtz maintained that while poststructural feminists have been eager to declare the end of identity and the destruction of social categories, scholars of color are hesitant. To the latter, "passing" and the related technique of "cross-expressing" may be seen as an evasion of racism, an escape that few would consider available or desirable. We, therefore, wish to discuss the issue of passing and cross-expressing from the perspective of feminist queer communication, while taking to heart the issues brought to our attention by Bucholtz.

We begin with Kira Hall's interesting study of telephone sex workers and so-called fantasy lines. Her findings support the general points in Judith

Butler's performance theory and also, as we shall demonstrate, Butler's theory of stereotyping and hate speech (Hall, 1995). The operators in San Francisco primarily serve a White heterosexual clientele, and they report how they, in order to have a "successful" conversation, must mimic the inequality between the sexes, perform submissiveness, and give "lip service" to the male customers. In this way, they draw on the stereotypes of women's language that are part of (White, heterosexual) conventional wisdom and expectations, or rather, "To sell to a male market, women's pre-recorded messages and live conversational exchange must cater to hegemonic male perceptions of the ideal woman" (Hall, 1995, p. 324). In Hall's case, the ideal woman's communication style is astonishingly reminiscent of Pamela Fishman's "maintenance work" (see Chapter 4), now performed in an exaggerated, stereotyped manner that the women sex workers themselves term "sweet talk."

This type of communication is a performed ritual of male dominance and female submission that usually characterizes pornographic regimes of representation. So, how can we evaluate such types of representation? According to Hall (1995), this particular setup is made possible by the advancement of telecommunications. First, the dramatic technological developments have caused an explosive increase in not only the quantity but also the quality of personal, intimate communications that have benefited adult message services in general and the 900 lines in particular. Second, because of the lack of visual cues afforded by telephone communication, customers must engage in fantasy, enhanced partly by anonymity and partly by the unique mixture of public and intimate discourse. Third, and most important, Hall has maintained that though the women telephone workers partake in a pornographic performance, it is not necessarily the same as being exposed to sexual assault. Thus, the operators report that they are most often completely in control. They initiate and dominate each conversation, they are the creators of the storyline, and they refuse to be seen as victims. The operators themselves do not appear interested in the feminist debate on pornography. They are more concerned with issues such as social flexibility, economic freedom, better working environments, and so on. Furthermore, many of the so-called adult message services are woman owned and operated, and a large percentage of employees identify themselves as feminists and participate actively in feminist organizations. Many are working freelance, living simultaneously, for example, as graduate students, fashion designers, and writers. Only a few report situations in which they have felt harassed and exposed to male violence. Those who do, speak of being reduced to a submissive role and feeling involved on a personal and bodily level. In such cases, the particular contract of this ritual (setup and script) has been broken. Hall's conclusion is a manifestation of Butler's theory that performances are multifaceted, bodily actions.

Hall's study illustrates the mechanics of passing. The operators are reported to be of different sexuality, ethnicity, age, and even gender, aimed at matching clients' sexual preferences, without necessarily representing any correspondence between "real" and "virtual" identity. While some customers associate sexiness with images of Black or lesbian women, the most common request is for a stereotype best performed by a White, heterosexual woman. But, the best woman performer of "sweet talk" may be bisexual, and the best "White" performer may be African American. Thus, on the fantasy lines, cross-expressing in order to pass as a certain category is a very common phenomenon, and the creativity that is mobilized in order to develop different characters can, according to Hall, be every bit as artistic as in theatre. So according to Hall, the performance of a telephone fantasy artist may just as well be compared to improvisational erotic theatre as to pornography.

The multiple discourses of desire and the refinements of cross-expressing have been explored in a range of other studies focusing on the interplay of markers of sexuality and gender. Of particular interest is, for instance, Joanna Channell's (1997) humorous analysis of the famous phone conversation between the Prince of Wales and Camilla Parker-Bowles, during which he expressed a fantasy of being a Tampax and thereby becoming a part of his (illegitimate) lover, or Wendy Langford's (1997) analysis of Valentine Day's personal messages in *The Guardian*. They each in their way demonstrate the mechanism of deferral in the sexual context of cross-expressing, creating an ambiguity that evokes desire and perhaps distinguishes eroticism from pornography.

On the basis of the studies and reflections mentioned above, we would suggest that it is possible to cross-express in order to pass and that this type of mimicry constitutes a form of pastiche, by citing a social convention without any distance. It is however, also possible to cross-express in order *not* to pass, thereby destabilizing the very same mechanism of categorization and identity claiming. This is exactly the point that Butler (1993) made in her analysis of the drag figure and the drag show, and she furthermore equated it to the genre of parody by which social conventions are cited *and* simultaneously both desired and distanced. Contrasting with both pastiche and parody, we have irony, the mocking of convention, as we shall see below. We hence propose the following model of the opposing dynamics of passing and cross-expressing (see Table 6.1). It illustrates the communication strategies extrapolated from the studies in the crossings of gender, sexuality, and race/ethnicity from a performance perspective.

**Table 6.1**    Figures of Mimicry

| Passing | Cross-Expressing |
| --- | --- |
| Pretending to be (desiring to be recognized as) something which she/he "is" not | Demonstrating that she/he is not what she/he pretends to be (recognized as) |
| Pastiche | Parody |
| Difference as identity | Identity as difference |

## Mediation and Confrontation

The ambiguities associated with passing and cross-expressing that we have explained so far can be used consciously and critically and transformed into strategies of mediation or confrontation. In this section, we shall introduce partly the strategy of mediation, as dialogue and an attempt to compromise in a kind of collage, and partly the strategy of confrontation, as an exposition of the very impossibility of compromise, drawing up the lines of conflict with an ironic twist.

However, to discuss the scope of these tools, let us return for a moment to Mary Bucholtz's reformulation of the concept of passing. She argued that the idea of passing is founded on the same premises as the claim of authenticity in the reformulation of race as ethnicity, and she was out to criticize both. She has reserved the term *passing* for cases in which individuals are of ambiguous or mixed ethnic background:

> Authenticity—that is, the legitimacy of one's claim to ethnicity—underlies the traditional definition of passing given above, which posits a re-categorization of the passing individual from her "own" ethnic group to another that is not her "own." The framework of authenticity is especially difficult to sustain, however, in the case of individuals of ambiguous or mixed ethnic background, for when multiple identities are available it is not at all clear which identity takes precedence. As I use the term for the remainder of this chapter, then, *passing is the active construction of how the self is perceived when one's ethnicity is ambiguous to others.* (Bucholtz, 1995, p. 352)

Bucholtz (1995) widened her redefinition to include individuals of ambiguous gender and sexuality, with a reference to Garfinkel's case study from 1967 of Agnes, who was born with male genitals but self-identified as a female and managed to "cheat" the medical establishment, developing female secondary-sex attributes by ingesting hormones that had been prescribed for her mother. On the basis of this case, Garfinkel argued as early as 1967 that passing is the continuous process of achieving a position in a recognized social category.

Passing, in Butler's poststructuralist theory, is a communication performance, and language, therefore, is a crucial resource in moving from one category to another (Bucholtz, 1995). In her own illuminating study, Bucholtz (1995) focused on how young women of mixed race, coming from complex ethnic backgrounds, use communication strategies and speech styles in particular contexts. She referred to other studies of mixed-race Americans in which passing has been seen as a subversive exercise of selection and agency, finding this to be the case in her own interviews as well, although these also reveal experiences of being assigned a particular identity or positioned on the margins of a given speech community. She demonstrated how her informants used communication to challenge external perceptions and lay claim to their own, for example, through vernacular English or standard English, nonstandard "slang" Spanish, or English only. Most important, she documented how gender and sexuality interlock with class and race/ethnicity in both the assignments of others and in the self-declarations of these young women. Thus, Bucholtz demonstrated how gender and sexuality are highly racialized and imbued with class, as is apparent in classifications such as "Cholas" for a traditional female Mexican American or Chicana identity. In the case of one of her informants, Claudia, ethnicity, class, gender, and sexuality are all mixed up in others' positioning of her, as well as in her own self-positioning.

> I think it has a lot to do with how you present yourself. And if I don't have an accent, if I don't use slang a lot, if I don't dress a certain (way), they tend to think, "You know, she could be something else." Because if I had a perm, if I had, like, a plaid shirt with jeans . . . they would know right off [that I was Mexican]. (Bucholtz, 1995, p. 364)

According to Bucholtz, Claudia's badges of ethnicity are also badges of gender: specific hairstyles, distinctive clothing, pronunciation, and so on. Ethnicity and gender/sexuality are inextricably linked in the contingent practices and emergent selves of her informants. We agree, but we also suggest that Claudia's performances are neither examples of passing nor of cross-dressing—instead, she performs an embodied linguistics of contact, surfing in and out of identity markers to suit her ends in a given situation!

Other possible strategies have been pointed out by Michèle Foster (1995) and Maria D. G. Vélasquez (1995), who elaborated on the discussion of code switching that we introduced in Chapter 3. Foster documented how middle-class African American women in the teaching profession carefully use African American vernacular to index social identity, communicate a particular cognitive or emotional stance, or express solidarity with their listeners. They use code switching freely—albeit not always consciously—in particular situations and for particular ends (Foster, 1995). We would suggest that what this refers to is a strategy of mediation. Vélasquez found that Chicana women from the outskirts of the New Mexican town of Cordova have adapted to the general shift from Spanish to English and that they can be said to mediate between the native speech community and the English-speaking community. At the same time, they use code switching as a means of resisting absolute linguistic assimilation, thus managing to cross cultural and linguistic borders without succumbing to "linguistic terrorism" (Vélasquez, 1995). We suggest that Vélasquez has documented the alternate strategies of mediation and confrontation, which can each be used to criticize the complex realities of identity and power.

The use of race/ethnicity and gender markers is approached differently in Birch Moonwomon's (1995) case study of interracial rape. She analyzed graffiti in the women's restroom at a college where an Asian American student had been raped by African American members of the local football team. Her point was that the female costudents shifted in ambiguous ways between a racial and a gender point of view in order to find a stance from which to approach the incident and that they illustrate the intricate borderline cases of race/ethnicity and gender in double-bind situations. She thereby highlighted the equally complex rhetoric uses of "difference carts" (race/ethnicity, gender, sexuality, etc.) under different circumstances and for different purposes.

The model illustrating different types of communication strategies from a performance perspective can now be expanded as shown in Table 6.2.

Table 6.2    Figures of Mimicry

| Passing/Cross-Expressing | Contact | Mediation/Confrontation |
|---|---|---|
| Pretending to be what one is not *or* demonstrating that one is not what one pretends to be | Surfing between possible points of identification and self-representation | Representing oneself as a mix of identifications or confronting different expectations and categorizations |
| Pastiche or parody | "Contact" | Mixture or irony |
| Difference as identity or identity as difference | Identity as a complex and contingent process | Identity as mediated or conflicting |

# Situated Performances

As demonstrated above, the performance turn has had a considerable impact on feminist communication research. It is also relevant in the context of mediated and organizational communication research, which consequentially focuses on the intricate interplay of gender, power, and discourse. In accordance with third-wave feminism, the topic of investigation now becomes the manner in which women partake in and aspire to areas formerly dominated by men and the ways in which they engage in multiple and diverging voices. In this section, we shall showcase performance work in two mediated contexts, rap and CMC (computer-mediated communication), as well as in the context of organizational communication.

## Rapping Gender

> Some think we can't flow (can't flow)
>
> Stereotypes they got to go (got to go)
>
> I'm gonna mess around and flip the scene into reverse
>
> With what?
>
> With a little touch of ladies first

SOURCE: Ladies First, performed by Queen Latifah. Written by Faber Shane Harbin, James Mark, Howard Johnson, Simone Antoinette, Peaks Anthony, and Queen Latifah. Copyright © 1989. Warner Chappell Music Group. Reprinted with permission.

Rap has been, and still is, highly contested in feminist communication scholarship, because the genre itself questions the meaning of words while confronting hate speech—sexism, racism, and so on—in complex and not easily "readable" ways, simultaneously miming Black culture in ways that both signal and disguise. You may say that Black rap is the proper heir to the technique of "signifying" (by insiders, called "signifyin'") and the inherent aesthetics of ambiguity. It reflects upon the underlying belief that "the Black man" can imbue things with life and gain dominion over them by the force of his words and the rhythm of naming. One example of this is the way in which slavery is coded in a way that is comprehensible only to (particular) Black communities, thus indicating a spiritual heritage (Davis, 1998). Only in certain special circumstances have Black women been granted this particular power—or rather, having seized it, they are often neglected or trivialized. Black female rappers, however, provocatively challenge this, thus reclaiming a Black female tradition (Rose, 1995, 1997).

According to Tricia Rose (1997), the musical tradition taken up by young Black women rappers goes back to Harriet Tubman and the "Underground Railroad" (1851 to 1865) and its constitutive myth of leading the masses of the South to the North. This musical tradition also involves the recontextualization of songs of slavery such as "Old Chariot" and "Go Down Moses," which were introduced by Sojourner Truth. Finally, it includes the new realities of discrimination recounted by the blues during the 20th century. One honored foremother of women's rap is Gertrude "Ma" Rainey, known as the "Mother of Blues." Another is Billie Holliday, who coded the language of love/personal relationships in a manner that expressed the social circumstances of Black people and created a collective southern experience. Yet another is Bessie Smith, who crossed into Black lesbianism (see also Davis, 1998). To sum up, Rose (1997) found that Black female rap creates a Black women's tradition of foremothers, solidarity, and self-reliance: "Trust no man" is one of the "signified" refrains.

New trends in rap music during the 1990s changed it from a subculture into a corporate media industry, which caused a reinscription of the authenticity of Black community as Black, working-class, urban, male youth. Still, Rose (1997) chose to focus on the increase of women rappers, as well as other, new forms of lyrical dialogue, between past and present, men and women, Black and White, and so on. Latifah and other rappers, such as MC Lyte and Salt-N-Pepa (a female rap duo), were said to have an ongoing dialogue with both their audiences and male rappers about sexual promiscuity, emotional commitment, infidelity, drugs, racial politics, and Black cultural history. Latifah's "Ladies First," for instance, was emphasized because of the ways this track acknowledges political activists such as Sojourner Truth, Angela Davis, and Winnie Mandela. Rose has not overlooked the problem of sexist rap expressing a fear of female sexuality and acting as a kind of symbolic control (Ice Cube, for example) but argued that young Black women rappers engage with young Black male rappers on this subject. By expressing their sexuality openly in their own language while distinguishing themselves from the "poisonous" and "insincere" women figures of Black male rap, they challenge their Black male colleagues to take women seriously. They also express their own anxieties of Black men's betrayal and the tension between trust and savvy, vulnerability and control, in ways that further challenge the depictions of women in male rap.

In the 21st century, Black women rappers seem to be widely acknowledged as representatives of hip-hop and rap, openly concerned with female bonding and self-reliance, while at the same time able to engage in female-male relationships. It is precisely this cocktail of dialogue and criticism and witty and sometimes aggressive communication that has challenged feminist critics. Their videos and body language have been accused of exposing traditionally female positions, but following Rose's (1997) argument, they can just as well be said to reclaim Black women's sexuality by "dirty dancing," mocking both the tradition of celebrating (or ridiculing) "the Black butt" and the slim, White ideal. When understood in this way, the performance of young women rappers is a challenging resignification of Black women's sexuality, which has hitherto been silenced and caught in the nexus between gender and race as "the black hole(s)" (Hammonds, 1997, p. 144). According to Hammonds, the cost of this struggle has long been a politics of silence among Black feminists, concerning, for example, lesbianism. This has, again, caused young women rappers to be skeptical of both feminism and the Black tradition of womanism, even if they prefer to speak of themselves as womanists.

Although young Black women rappers are able to keep a critical distance from both feminism and womanism, they are simultaneously contributing to the third-wave feminist agenda. Discussing this phenomenon requires a sophisticated perspective. For example, while third-wave feminists seek to reclaim the word *bitch,* this is a highly ambiguous strategy to Black women rappers because of issues related to Black female sexuality in the context of rap. Nevertheless, we see some common ground between young Black women rappers and the concept of "signifying" and the way young "grrls" use "grrl rhetoric" as means of inversion and thereby subversion. We already discussed the grrl movement at some length (see Chapter 1). So, let us for now simply recall how grrl rhetoric is particularly expressed within the context of new information technologies and the Internet. According to grrl Carla Sinclair (1996) (who, indeed, spells the word "grrl"), the Net is flooded with the energies of sharp "Net Chicks." Grrls approach the Net with an attitude, reclaiming the formerly derogatory word *girl,* transforming it into *grrl,* giving it growl and bite, and thereby transgressing the connotations of "girl"—much the same way that Niggers With Attitude reclaim the term *nigga* or Queer Nation the term *queer.* Grrls appropriate the word girl by changing the spelling of the word as well as the sound; grrls are "girls" who growl and bite. Calling on the tradition of Gates and his work on "signifying," Jacobs (2002) called this a "loop of semantic inversion." (See Figure 6.1.)

"Grrl" cannot be separated from "girl," because it involves a criticism of the other term ("girls" are weak, emotional, immature, etc.) but also an identification that again implicates a generational and philosophical distancing to "woman" ("women" are mature, second-wave feminists, older, etc.). This doubled identification and opposition gives rise to a new term with an

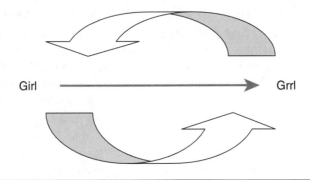

Girl ──────────────────────▶ Grrl

**Figure 6.1**    Semantic Loop

entirely different meaning ("grrls" are strong, assertive, feminine, empowered, etc.). Thus, the use of the word *grrl,* we would say, articulates a performative desire of agency and action, while at the same time performatively delivering a criticism of both sexism and feminism. Taking inspiration from Gates (1987) and Jacobs (2002), who in their discussions of "signifying" both pointed out that the appropriation of the word *nigga* is not aimed at the oppressor, we would further suggest that the use of *grrl* is not aggressively turned against boys, men, or even second-wave feminists, but rather it serves to create an empowered teenage-girl identity.

Jacobs (2002) further posed that "signifyin(g)" is a distinct example of what others in other contexts have seen as reverse discourse (Foucault), back-talk (Butler), or double-voiced discourse (Bakhtin). In our work, we have emphasized the same connections, drawing also on Patricia H. Collins and her work on the double-voiced discourse. A double-voiced word signals a least two points of view. It becomes a kind of palimpsest in which the uppermost inscription is a commentary on the one beneath it. The latter can become known to others only if they examine the contextual clues. However, double-voiced rhetoric also demonstrates that the context is never completely secure since it reclaims communication that has not been formerly validated, setting it in new contexts. "Grrl," then, is both a repetition and a reversal of "girl," and it thereby aspires to move "girl" from being in an object position to a subject position ("grrl"). At the same time, it signals the fact that rhetorical strategy does not put an end to the idea "signified upon"—it does *not* put an end to sexism (Jacobs, 2002). From the perspective of communication agency and third-wave rhetoric, "signifying" opens up new spaces for feminist agency. We agree and suggest that girl/woman gains new meanings insofar as "grrl'ing" succeeds in transgressing the underlying gender schemes.

# Gender Mimicry in
## Computer-Mediated Communication (CMC)

Both the performance turn and the concept of mimicry and its diverse manifestations have been well covered by cyberfeminist communication scholarship. An early example can be found in the work of North American sociologist and psychologist Sherry Turkle, who first conceptualized the computer as a mirror, a second self, and in *Life on the Screen: Identity in the Age of the Internet* (1995), discussed issues of identity in light of new computer technology such as chat rooms and multi-user domains (MUDs). Turkle's thesis is that gender cross-expressing in online environments helps destabilize our conventional notions of gender, and she pursued this idea through a range of cases. One of her informants, "Garrett," a 28-year-old computer programmer who had played a female frog in a MUD, said that gender cross-expressing enabled him to move outside the competitive masculine communication environment that he was continuously faced with in his offline relationships (Turkle, 1995, p. 216). Another informant told the story of how he simultaneously played at least three different characters in three different MUDs: a seductive woman, a macho cowboy, and a gender-nonspecific rabbit. Turkle used these cases to point out that the absence of verbal (intonation, pitch, etc.) and nonverbal (facial features, body, dress, gestures, posture, etc.) communication cues not only permits cross-dressing, but also allows for new conceptualizations of gender to emerge.

Other feminist scholars have pursued the discussion of gender-bending on the Internet in different ways. Shannon McRae (1997) agreed on the basic idea of cross-expressing, but she further made the point that the techniques provided by the Internet give the participants the opportunity to experience the "other" only to find that the "other" is not outside us, but inside us (p. 253). The potential she sees in this lies in deconstructing "masculine" and "feminine" communication styles and reconfiguring them as communication resources available to anyone. Jewish American Brenda Danet (1998) sees the liberating capacity of the Internet in its long-term potential for destabilizing the ways we do gender, but unlike Turkle, she does not think of offline gender identities as "original" or "true" identities. MUD participants, for instance, are required to create a persona that may be read by others, marking gender, age, and sometimes race/ethnicity. In meeting these rather conventional demands, "mudders" have found creative and even transgressive solutions by inventing up to 11 genders by playing with pronouns: female (she), male (he), neuter (it), either (s/he), spivak (E), splat (*e), plural (they), egotistical (I), royal (We), 2nd (You), person (per) (see Chapter 4).

Kira Hall (1996) dove further into online communication exchanges to explore this new "in-between" and the way it is practiced in CMC (p. 150). She drew on what we discuss in this chapter as mimicry and denote as a linguistics of contact, exemplifying it in a case where a supposedly female participant performs a male homosexual in the following way: "Hi hon. How are you today? I saw so-and-so and sister did he look *bad*. A *serious* fashion no-no. Throw that boy *back* to the straights . . ." (Hall, 1996, p. 153). Hall pointed out that the author used a number of terms that are associated with a gay conversational style, such as the use of "hon," "sister," "fashion no-no," "the straights," decorating the adjectives to suggest the greater pitch variation and flamboyancy stereotypically associated with gay men's communication. The example seems to illustrate gender-bending, while reinforcing existing stereotypes of gay male speech. Hall suggested that both interpretations can be valid due to the inherent ambiguity of CMC in general and the techniques of cross-expressing and the linguistics of contact in particular. In this manner, performance-oriented cyberfeminists suggest that virtual environments allow participants to play with gender as well as sex and sexuality to an extent impossible in offline environments, though not unambiguously so. In this case, the evaluation is complicated by the fact that the person in question seems to belong both to a majority group (sexuality) and a minority group (gender). But then again, the really intriguing thing about CMC is that you really do not know, and hence, as a critic, you must be very careful about the analytical tools you use in your analysis.

Nicola Döring (2000) also argued that text-based virtual interactions like MUDs allow participants an exceptional freedom of expression. However, she also stated that each community embodies its own set of possibilities, risks, and restrictions through the way MUD participants textually co-construct and co-opt their reality. She demonstrated this through a case of MUD rape, in a domain called "TinyMUD." Her claim is that even something as upsetting as virtual rape can be both textually executed and textually challenged, depending on the way participants understand and handle their mutual "contract": "Rape is first and foremost an issue of violated consent. When a man in Minnesota types 'tears your skirt' or some other intense or graphic obscenity, you can reasonably feel disgust or offense. But TinyMUDs are only as real as you want them to be. At any moment you can stop believing in what's happening around you, and it loses its reality" (Döring, 2000, p. 23). Döring brought forth the possibility of either ignorance or back-talking, for instance, by asserting "skirt too tough to tear," thereby establishing agency and an alternate reality. Her point is that what is really violated here is the very consensus of the digital community. Keeping in mind Butler's work on hate speech and back-talking, we would agree to some extent, but we also wish to emphasize that every incident of male-to-female rape activates a history of violence against women.

A range of scholars have explored the relation between on- and offline bodies, and some have described it as a "slip" that often surprises participants in CMC (Nyboe, 2003). Online participants tend, for instance, to be angry or amused when others misread, doubt, or otherwise question their online representations of their offline bodies. On the other hand, the offline body interferes with online textual representation in complicated ways, related to the premise of typing and the role as typist. Lotte Nyboe has approached this difficult discussion through an analysis of *The Turing Game* (http://www.cc.gatech.edu/elc/turing/), developed by Amy Bruckman and Josh Berman from the Georgia Institute of Technology in 1999. Participants are asked by the moderator to perform as either a man or a woman in order to be graded by an audience and partake in a discussion at the end of the game. During the game the "fe/malers" (a term used generically by Nyboe to describe participants) are asked questions aimed at revealing their "true" gender identities. Nyboe pointed out that the answers and the discussions expose how stereotypes work in computer-mediated interactions, both on the part of the participants and also the audience when they claim "proper" gender performances. Even when participants play "themselves," they are frequently challenged, which shows both the importance of gender to people and its fragility. Performances of gender in *The Turing Game* may therefore be seen not only as replications of conventional gender stereotypes but also as replications of our fantasies of what gender is supposed to be like. Nyboe (2003) concluded,

> Individuals parody an idea of an original within the framework of the heterosexual matrix, but the natural and the original do not exist as such. In *The Turing Game,* the interlocutors plunge into a loop of reversing or producing copies of copies, parodically repeating an original which proves to be nothing other than a parody of a fantasy. (p. 226)

In Nyboe's analysis, gender becomes a "slippery affair" (p. 232), and because fe/malers frequently experience an "in-between" or a "neither-nor-position" as a result of their unconvincing performances, Nyboe has chosen to see them as cyborgs: "The fe/malers are caught in a production, which not only points to gender as a technology, a skill, competency, technology, and acquisition, but also points to slips between enacting and represented bodies in the cybernetic circuit" (p. 233).

## Organizational Diversity

Whereas feminist perspectives in institutional and organizational literature expanded in the 1990s, interest in the intersections of gender, ethnicity, and sexuality has been sparse. However, as mentioned in the previous chapter, the general demographics of the United States and Europe have caused a move toward discourses of diversity management. Until now, these discourses were mostly found in writings on human resource, which tended to emphasize the benefits of multiple forms of employee expertise, while still bound to a "realist" paradigm that presupposes competencies to correspond to social categories. However, rethinking organizational and managerial communication from a feminist perspective today means challenging the notions of both gender and organization (Buzzanell, 2000), and it means challenging the very language of organization (Westwood & Linstead, 2001). Within "avant-garde" organizational studies, the perspective of difference and "Othering" is now integrated (Westwood, 2001) and the theoretical consequences of the performance turn are discussed (Chia & King, 2001), as is the question of gendered performances (Brewis, 2001). In our opinion, this sample of studies is the long-overdue result of inspiration from poststructuralism and discourse theory, and it constitutes a new framework for future work in the field.

Westwood (2001) examined the dilemma of representing difference and otherness that is evident in much of early, highly normative literature on diversity management. His point of departure is the work of Calás (1992) and Calás and Smircich (1992) (see Chapter 5). They identified universalism as the central problem in the current Western episteme of organization, the consequence of which is the notion of a generic organizational subject against which any gendered or ethnic-other existence is made "the Other" and "whose only possible mode of existence depends on its mimetic characteristics, on its homogenization into a 'normal cultural subject'" (Calás, 1992, p. 205). Under such circumstances "the Other" can be appropriated only in a discourse of cultural difference, that is, a discourse of essentialism and exoticism, the consequence of which is, on one hand, lack of authenticity and authoritarianism on behalf of the organization, and on the other hand, that the ethnic or gendered subject must in a paradoxical manner deny her own specificity and suppress any drive to contribute to diverse organizational knowledge.

Westwood (2001) claimed that diversity management, in order to move beyond this, must be fundamentally anchored in the postcolonial project concerned with criticizing both the universalism inherent in Western imperialism and the very notion of colonialism as a monolithic and homogeneous project: a zero-sum game in which the colonizer has had all the power and the colonized have been mere "passive objects and disempowered dupes"

(Westwood, 2001, p. 273). According to Westwood, only such a move away from the old conceptions of unidirectional, colonial imposition and determinacy can lead to recognition of the agency of the colonized, in the past as well as in the future. It further requires an alternate conceptualization of the multiple layers of present-day neocolonialism in terms of motives, goals, practices, and effects. Furthermore, it requires a thesis of the postcolonial condition as a fragmentation into metropolitan power centers and peripheral administrations, engaged in multidirectional power relations. Accordingly, strategies of mirroring, imitation, and crossing should be exposed, along with the ways in which the West itself has been constituted in and through the process. Westwood is strongly influenced by British Indian postcolonial theorist Homi K. Bhabha, who, in the tradition of Franz Fanon and his critique of Hegel (see Chapter 2), has pursued the idea that colonial practices create a mimetic response among the colonized, termed "Black skin/White masks." Bhabha finds in the notion of hybridity a mutual creation of the positions of both colonizer and colonized in which there is no direct correspondence and no perfect reproduction; each category remains different, and no one position can claim authenticity. According to Westwood, it is necessary to pursue such postcolonial critique if the proclamation of diversity management is to be more than just another trendy slogan and is to supply fertile ground for a truly new agenda of multiplicity within organizations.

To question the conceptual construction of the categories of gender and management/organization, respectively, and the possible consequences hereof, Joanna Brewis (2001) has taken a slightly different direction. She maintains that difference feminism can be understood as yet another truth regime, imposed on gender and organizational studies. However, she has also explored how understandings of gender and organization are normally, in a modern, Western context, presented as mutually exclusive: emotional females versus scientific modernism. Her aim is to trace how women, in certain organizational situations, are discursively positioned in ways that ensure their degradation and denigration, or at the very least different treatment, and how particular ways of knowing inevitably operate in exclusive and inclusive ways (Brewis, 2001, p. 293). Her empirical study consisted of qualitative interviews in a British university and a British financial services institution. She documented a range of sexist discourses on and by both women and men, which she explores in relation to class, ethnicity, and sexuality and in relation to the particular organizational complex in which they occur. She concluded that gender can be identified as a significant variable but not as a monolithic force. Thus, women's constitution as women seems, to some extent, to result in their derogation in these organizations, thereby emphasizing the dual effects of the discourses of scientific modernism and of gender difference for both women and men (Brewis, 2001, p. 301).

Patrice M. Buzzanell (2000) arrived at roughly the same conclusions in her case study of career management by critically examining the rhetoric of new enterprises among stakeholders and in organizations in terms of what she calls "new career" and "new social contract." According to her analysis, this rhetoric is closely related to new trends within human resource management that refer to self-management and self-leadership, thereby indicating a self-regulating adaptation of a technical rationale (like demanding employees' identification with their jobs and the organization). This again privileges groups who are traditionally comfortable with this rationale and thus already have the advantage—it certainly does not benefit (groups of) women and ethnic minorities. Buzzanell has suggested another enterprise, grounded in mutual responsibility, democratic involvement, and appreciation of diverse contributions.

The classroom setting is of continued interest to feminist communication scholarship. Joan Swann (2003) and Judith Baxter (2003a, 2003c) have both examined the classroom from a poststructuralist perspective. Swann is critical of this turn insofar as it leads to a set focus on language and thereby, in her opinion, to a kind of servility toward educational policies. Baxter has worked chiefly with recent trends in British educational settings, which seem to be based on a neoliberalist conceptualization of schooling and pedagogy, introducing a more individualistic and competitive approach among teachers and students. Baxter is critical of this new approach, but she also emphasizes that it has had effects that cannot be easily assessed, such as new examination criteria for effective speech in public contexts. To her, the new criteria seem to multiply the number of discourses by which both boys and girls are positioned and position themselves and which work in intricate ways to empower and disempower both genders. Thus, scholastically high-achieving girls seem to benefit from the new demands even if the general finding is that "girls are nonetheless subject to a powerful web of institutionalized discourses that constitute boys more readily as speakers in public settings and girls more readily as an appreciative and supportive audience" (Baxter, 2003c, p. 126). Let us now examine another case from Baxter concerning organization.

---

## Case Study: Feminist Poststructuralist Discourse Analysis (FPDA)

Feminist poststructuralist discourse analysis (FPDA) springs from various different sources and has also assumed slightly different directions (see Chapters 2 and 3). Inspired by both performance and positioning theory (Butler and Davies, respectively),

Judith Baxter has been one of its main proponents. Outlining these inspirations in a concise methodology, she prefers the broader term *poststructuralist discourse analysis* (PDA). She has explicitly expounded on FPDA as a variation of PDA, grounded in a critique of conversation analysis (CA) (see Chapter 4) and critical discourse analysis (CDA) (see Chapter 5) or, rather, a further development of discourse analysis from CA and CDA to PDA (Baxter, 2002). She has also carried out two major studies, presented in *Feminist Poststructuralist Discourse Analysis: From Theory to Practice* (2003a), and has introduced the methodology in the course book *Positioning Gender in Discourse: a Feminist Methodology* (2003c). We have therefore opted to borrow our case from her work. However, in the title of the course book, Baxter signals she considers FPDA closely related to positioning theory and analysis. In Chapters 2 and 3, we introduced readers to this particular theoretical and methodological "package," which we related to, among others, the work of feminist poststructuralist Bronwyn Davies and sociologist Rom Harré. Whereas Davies has a background in discursive psychology and narrative analysis, Baxter's is in linguistics and CA. In some respects, we consider Davies to be more sophisticated in her theoretical approach, but Baxter is far more explicit in her outline of the methodological part. In the following, we elaborate on what she terms an "FPDA approach," commenting on one of her case studies, the Management Team Study. First, let us cite her definition of the approach:

I highlight a central concern of the FPDA approach: namely to examine the ways in which speakers negotiate their identities, relationships and positions in the world according to the ways in which they are *multiply* located by different discourses. (Baxter, 2003c, p. 10)

This basic concern is very much in accordance with both performance and positioning theory. However, Baxter has contributed to the poststructuralist approach a few principles borrowed from Russian formalist Mikhail Bakhtin: polyphony and heteroglossia. *Polyphony* in Baxter's (2003c) interpretation denotes the multiplying of methodological techniques and the process of working with competing interpretations of the same act, thereby emphasizing process over product. *Heteroglossia* denotes the reinforcement of polyphony by focusing differently on participants and perspectives or by presenting the analysis to the involved participants with an eye to subsequently reworking it.

Baxter (2003c) introduced us to the context of her Management Team Study (MTS). It is carried out in Hook3 (pseudonym), a small but successful 4-year-old British dotcom company that markets and sells houses, cars, and jobs on its Web site. The company is owned by major shareholders in the British media industry and has over 100 employees, with approximately equal gender representation in its different sections. However, the management consists of a team of seven senior managers: one woman and six men. The key questions of the research have been: What constitutes power, and how is power negotiated through spoken interactions in the organization, particularly in the context of leadership and the situation of a business meeting?

The study focuses on the management team (MT), and the research consists of a range of ethnographic data, gleaned from meetings, daily work situations (observations, interviews), and so on. However, the readers of *Positioning Gender in Discourse* (2003c) get just a brief glimpse of the main study through transcriptions of the spoken interaction during two meetings. To frame the selected case, Baxter presented four central and competing discourses, identified in the main study. These constitute the matrix of the company in general and the MT in particular: historical legacy (explicit value, linked to people's various levels of experience as well as implicit value, related particularly to "the pioneers"); competing areas of expertise (explicit value, based on the need of specialized competencies); open dialogue (explicit value, aimed at both acknowledging and openly confronting the competing specialisms); masculinization (implicit value, generated as an upgrading of a "boysy culture" of directness and playful confrontation).

The MT consists of *Keith,* the chief executive officer (CEO) who chairs the meetings; *Sarah,* who started the company, initially performing all functions and now operation manager and Web site designer; *Jack,* sales and marketing manager; *Pete,* finance director; *Richard,* manager of the car sites; *Cliff,* manager of the home sites; and *Don,* manager of the job sites. Keith, Sarah, and Jack have been in the company longer than Pete, Richard, Cliff, and Don. Whereas Don is not present at either of the selected meetings, Cliff does not speak in the featured excerpts. Regular meetings such as these usually start with each member making a report and proceed to a discussion of selected themes and issues. Baxter (2003c) highlighted what she perceived as key moments, in which members position themselves and others according to the four constituting discourses of the team. Our focus lies on the first meeting; the two following excerpts showcase confrontations between Jack and Richard, and Jack and Sarah, respectively.

[211]    **Richard**: . . . and that's just about it.

[212]    **Jack**: Going back to cars, do you have any clarity yet on the launch date?

[213]    **Richard:** No we don't. Kirsten is the person who is pulling together the project plan. She's

[214]    desperately uncomfortable with pulling together a date at this stage. It's not the work isn't

[215]    moving ahead very quickly. She understands the value of the final date, but she just doesn't have

[216]    enough information because there's a bottleneck with the analysts to understand the scale of some of

[217]    the developments that are being done, so if pushed, it would be the same date as we had before . . .

[218] **Jack**: (INTERRUPTING) What's that, what's that? April (APPEARS TO BE SPEAKING OVER

[219] RICHARD FROM "She understands . . .")

[220] **Richard**: I think April is what we are talking about. Beginning of April, end of April. The

[221] same date as we had before. April is the time they're looking at . . .

[222] **Jack**: (OVERLAPPING FROM "April is the time . . .") We've launched two sites haven't we?

[223] We have, yes.

[224] **Keith**: You've got to be careful you don't end up at the sharp end of not being able to deliver cars.

[225] **Jack**: No, no, this is quite amazing because we've launched two sites.

[226] **Richard**: Yes.

[227] **Jack**: So we know what to do.

[228] **Richard**: They're just not top level sexy sites, so they're not something we've been

[229] shouting about quite as much, is it . . .

[230] **Jack**: (SHOWING INCREASING FRUSTRATION BECAUSE RICHARD APPEARS TO BE

[231] MISSING THE POINT.) No, no, we've launched jobs and we've launched homes

[232] **Richard**: Oh right, we're talking about the latest launches now?

[233] **Jack**: No, no, no, we've launched jobs and we've launched homes.

[234] **Richard**: (VERY LONG PAUSE) Yes. Yes.

[235] **Jack**: We know what to do, hopefully.

[236] **Richard**: (LAUGHS BUT SOUNDS HESITANT) Yes. The site was down. We had this

[237] conversation before the site was down yesterday.

*Example 1*

SOURCE: Baxter, Judith. Positioning Gender in Discourse: A Feminist Methodology. Copyright © 2003. Palgrave. Reprinted with permission of Palgrave Macmillan.

In this excerpt, Jack is confronting Richard just after his report, because there is a delay in the launch of the car site. Richard responds directly in the beginning but gradually becomes defensive and starts to justify (220–221), repeat (220–221), and explain himself (228–229), and even goes from speaking fluently and persistently to becoming less vocal and almost monosyllabic (223, 226, 234). Jack, on the other hand, is getting still more offensive, indicated by interruptions (218, 222), eruptions (225, 230, 233), and marked repetitions (227, 230, 233). He also speaks on behalf of the whole team ("we") and assumes the authority of wrapping up the session (235). Richard is dismissed by Jack when he attempts to get back into the dialogue (233, "No, no, no . . .").

[532]  **Jack:** Does everyone in the company know that the system was down?

[533]  **Sarah:** Yes.

[534]  **Jack:** And single node was what it was on yesterday which meant that . . .

[535]  **Sarah:** No, it was . . . it's really, really complex. I'm sorry, I can't explain it simpler . . .

[536]  **Jack:** Ok, then, the question really is . . .

[537]  **Sarah:** (OVERLAPPING) No, no . . . I really can't explain it.

[538]  **Jack:** Is . . . is the way that it comes up going to mean that performances is less than . . .

[539]  **Sarah:** (INTERRUPTING) The way . . . no.

[540]  **Jack:** So yesterday was . . .

[541]  **Sarah:** (INTERRUPTING) We are aiming . . . we are aiming that it will come up on the

[542]  database server with 12 CPUs on it, rather than the standard 6 anyway.

[543]  **Jack:** Right, so it won't mean that . . .

[544]  **Sarah:** (INTERRUPTING) Last night, it was screaming, it was screaming through.

[545]  **Jack:** So when it really does come up, it won't be performance issues,

[545]  it's just like that it's going to be . . .

[546]  **Sarah:** (INTERRUPTING) We had different issues yesterday afternoon as I said, in that we had,

[547]  one, a database issue which shouldn't have affected performance at all.

[547]  But we had a problem with the

[548]  networks falling over, and it's hard to correlate the two. I can't guarantee . . .

[549]  **Jack:** (INTERRUPTING) No, no, no . . . all I'm concerned about is that, when an email is sent out

[550]  that says, "Hurrah, it's back up" that if necessary we say, "It's back up but at the same time there will

[551]  be some performance issues, so if you're talking to customers and you are taking people through the

[552]  site, that they may well experience difficulties.

[553]  **Keith**: There's a sort of user interpretation of "back up" and a technical interpretation.

[554]  Yesterday afternoon I thought it was down because I couldn't get to it but there was a

[555]  different reason, I understand that.

[556]  **Sarah**: I didn't understand you were having those experiences, and I sit next to you

[557]  (LAUGHS) I knew what we were doing, I knew we were having issues, but I did not

[558]  understand that user issues were absolutely appalling. (WITH EMPHASIS) Nobody told me.

[559]  (SILENCE AMONG WHOLE MEETING FOR SEVERAL SECONDS.)

[560]  **Jack**: Well, I just thought the site was down all day you see . . .

[561]  **Sarah**: (INTERRUPTING) We did communicate to everybody when it was back up.

[562]  **Keith**: Could we have some way of making sure when the site is back up . . .

[563]  **Sarah**: Yeah, well, the guys upstairs would have been aware, but I'm just saying that I

[564]  wasn't. It isn't as if they would get it back up and ignore it. You know, get it back up and just walk

[565]  away, it doesn't work that way.

[566]  **Jack**: That's why I just assumed that if the guys upstairs, if they were having problems with it,

[567]  they . . .

[568]  **Sarah**: (INTERRUPTING AND OVERLAPPING) The guys upstairs understand it but you're

[569]  asking (CONTINUING TO TALK OVER THE OTHERS) you're asking for a different

[570]  interpretation to different people, which is fine, but I just need to be aware of that and this

[571]   discussion is absolutely fine. (SILENCE AMONG WHOLE MEETING
FOR SEVERAL

[572]   SECONDS).

*Example 2* (p. 156)

SOURCE: Baxter, Judith. *Positioning Gender in Discourse: A Feminist Methodology.* Copyright ©
2003. Palgrave. Reprinted with permission of Palgrave Macmillan.

This excerpt follows Sarah's report, which has been concerned with the fact that
the network the day before had been temporarily down. Again, Jack takes on an inter-
rogative stance by subjecting Sarah to a series of questions. In this case, he is out to
question Sarah's dispositions, but he is also very careful to testify that he is able to
match Sarah technically (534) and is therefore in a position to question her (538, 540,
545) and make suggestions to her (549–552). Sarah responds rather offensively, partly
by refusing to explain (535) or even apologize and partly by repeatedly interrupting
Jack (538, 540, 543, 545). Instead of focusing on what went wrong, she emphasizes
what she has done to put it right (541–542, 544), and she even returns the implied
criticism and redirects it to her colleagues (556–558). Unlike Richard in the previous
excerpt, she does not let herself be silenced—on the contrary, it is she who causes the
meeting to fall silent on two occasions (559, 571).

In comparing the two excerpts, Baxter (2003c) drew on the main discourses of
the company and the MT that she had identified: historical legacy, competing fields
of expertise, open dialogue, and masculinization. She found that Sarah was more
successful because she scored higher in terms of historical legacy than Richard did
(signaled by Jack in his initial motivations), and consequently she was more skilled
at maneuvering between the other interpretative repertoires. She exposed her special competencies to open dialogue, simultaneously balancing the explicit norm of
open dialogue and the implicit norm of masculinization through the pursuit of individual goals, in this case by using interruptions, lengthy turns, talking over others,
blocking statements, refusal to comply, and bald assertions (Baxter, 2003c, p. 164).
Compared with Jack, Sarah drew explicitly on her competence as the IT expert and
furthermore on her insight into the skills of the others; thereby, she implicitly also
drew on her legacy as founder of the company and the one who once performed all
job functions. Because the two discourses of historical legacy and competing expertise are simultaneous in her case, Baxter asserted that they also encouraged Sarah to
upgrade the discourse of masculinization and correspondingly to downgrade the discourse of open dialogue. Whereas this strategy of power and "effective speech" can
in itself be ambiguous, it was made even more complicated in Sarah's case by her
position as the only woman on the board and the director. Thus, the silence she met
on two occasions, according to Baxter, might have signaled agreement from the
other team members, but it might just as well have signaled embarrassment and

withdrawal in response to "the hysterical woman." This interpretation seems further supported by Sarah's own attempt to counteract it in her final and only positive response to the criticism (570–572). At first glance, then, Sarah seems to be assimilated very well within the "boysy culture" of the team; however, the unease with her performance at certain moments and her own need to meta-analyze the situation are both conducive to the interpretation that she is also separated from it.

Baxter (2003c) brought in two excerpts from another meeting to validate her analysis of the complex interrelationships of discourses and interlocutors. In this case, Keith and Pete are active, too. To maintain her own principles of multiple approaches, Baxter this time focused on Keith and his function as CEO. The topics of the two excerpts are what to do about Christmas Eve and Christmas cards, respectively. Keith appears out to highlight the value of open dialogue by asking the team members for their opinion and not wanting to have the final word. Jack, Sarah, and Pete, however, want him to make the decision when it becomes apparent that there is no immediate consensus. According to Baxter, Keith's performance belongs to what is usually considered a feminized communication culture; he seeks to provoke his team into making a decision they want him to make. In so doing, he also risks his authority as CEO. Baxter suggested that breaking the discourse of masculinization thus has consequences for him, not only in the present situation but also in the long run.

Baxter (2003c) concluded that there was no evidence that the communicative styles often classified as (fe)male should be bound to either (biological) sex or (social) gender. On the other hand, they still appear relevant, partly as a cognitive landscape, partly as a means of stylization. This may seem contradictory. However, it is similar to the question of camp or "homo-genius" speech style (discussed above), that is, a style that is conscious of itself as a style, in this case "hetero-genius" style. Baxter, however, did not take up that thread and thus did not fully explain the dilemma. We find that her initial construction of the discourse of masculinization is problematic and might contribute to the problem. But then again, we wish to emphasize that she pursued her initial methodological points by concluding that there were no winners and losers in terms of power and authority in the management team, although she also concluded that team members with high scores in most of the high-priority discourses had a better chance of asserting themselves. She further emphasized the tensions between the four main discourses and the explicit and implicit values of both the organization and the management team, which contributed to the impossibility of establishing a perfect communication strategy. Nevertheless, Baxter found that the discourses of competing fields of expertise and masculinization tended to overrun the discourse of open dialogue, thereby signaling a trend within organization and communication, which may be attributed to the current success of a new liberalism in management theory and practice. Thus, she highlighted the complexity of research questions, preferring to underscore methodological complications and analytical tensions in order to avoid neat patterns and simple conclusions. This is very much in accordance with the implied criteria of the performance turn.

We think that Baxter's study illustrates very well the strengths as well as the weaknesses of an FPDA or FPA approach. We see new gains in multilayered address and the readiness to keep the analysis dynamic. There are, however, still weaknesses to be found when it comes to determining the premises of the research and formulating research questions. The initial categories and questions are crucial to the outcome. Furthermore, Darsey's theorem (described earlier in this chapter) still presents a potential pitfall. In order to heighten awareness of this problem, we suggest the following list of questions to consider when planning research with FPDA:

1. What is the particular phenomenon that you want to address? How would you describe the purpose of the project?

2. What are the theoretical foundations of your thesis and core terminology? How do you stay open to new ideas?

3. How will you situate and contextualize the phenomenon as communication, and how do you frame it as performance and/or positioning?

4. How do you describe and understand the ways gender and power are displayed as discursive practices?

5. What specific tools will you use when collecting and analyzing data? How do you remain sensitive?

6. How do you relate your own research to FPDA?

# 7

# Conclusion

By now, gender communication scholarship is an established discipline in communication studies. As we have demonstrated, it draws on inter-disciplinary connections to linguistics, cultural studies, anthropology, and sociology, to name a few, thus subjecting disciplinary boundaries to negotiation. We have sought to demonstrate the wealth of theoretical as well as methodological principles upon which gender communication scholars build, and the influence it has had on more established disciplines. Although gender communication scholarship is not necessarily feminist, we have chosen to focus on examples that share a feminist epistemology questioning the "nature" of gender and how we come to know about it, thereby approaching the interplay of gender and communication. As a consequence, we have also chosen to focus on scholars who have aspired to generate new perspectives on gender and communication, and have challenged not only traditional approaches to communication but also confronted feminist canon building.

In light of the plurality of voices, we want to sum up the different theoretical and methodological approaches we have presented and conclude by addressing visions for the future, focusing specifically on our own idea of "transversity."

## From Silence to Performance

In this book, we have taken you through various perspectives on gender and communication and demonstrated the relationship that each perspective articulates between theory, methodology, and analysis. The following central questions are raised: Does communication constitute identity, community, and society? Does communication mark a previously extant identity or an established community or society? Or is it perhaps more appropriately seen as a performative gesture that brings about identity, community, and society? We have linked these different questions to the notion of a performance turn, during which structural communication scholarship (dominance and difference approaches) is abandoned in favor of poststructural communication scholarship (the performance and transversal/transgender approaches). Furthermore, we have linked this significant turn with the breakthrough of third-wave feminism that challenges the political and theoretical issues and strands of both first- and second-wave feminism. However, we have also asserted that these academic and political perspectives are continuously renewed. It is our hope that you are now equipped to recognize the tenets of each when you meet them. For the sake of clarity, we summarize some of the key points of each approach.

We began our journey with a description of gender communication theories inspired by dominance and deficit perspectives. Communication scholars such as Cheris Kramarae, Julia Penelope, and Dale Spender have pointed to the struggles that women continually engage in when trying to define and create their reality. Building upon the work of Shirley Ardener and on muted group theory, these scholars pose that in patriarchal cultures, men's experiences override those of women; they become the norm of society, and women's voices are accordingly muted, meaning that they are rendered deviant, suppressed, and eventually forgotten. Women are thus forced to struggle to uncover their own voices through layers of mutedness and to translate them into the male norm in ways that can expose the underlying voice and open up alternatives. This work has been pivotal in helping us understand the importance of language and communication in shaping gendered lives and the influence of patriarchy on our available means of communication. They have challenged the communication discipline to include and revise communication concepts, and they have also impacted the development of communication models and standards, for instance, generating an academic discussion of the inherent norms of sociolinguistics and ethnomethodology or a political discussion of appropriate language at campuses. Therefore, these early examples are still central to researching gender and communication.

While we acknowledged the importance and continued relevance of this work, we saw weaknesses in the approach as well. Difference feminists have argued that early feminist communication scholarship in fact presents a simplified perspective—paradoxically continuing to devalue women's communicative competencies—and holds on to a liberal concept of equal opportunities, thus maintaining the status quo. Early feminist communication scholarship has been challenged by scholars such as Marsha Houston, Jennifer Coates, and Deborah Cameron, who have pointed to women's "double vision," "dual standpoints," and unique communication styles. Inspired by standpoint theorists such as Patricia Hill Collins and the difference and identity perspective, these communication scholars have reassessed women's communication and pointed to new ways of understanding it. That which was referred to as women's "shitwork" of communication in the dominance perspective, they see as a distinguished communicative intelligence that discloses not only an alternate aesthetics but also an alternate ethics and a rhetoric of invitation and cooperation. Difference scholars have further highlighted differences among women according to intersections of class, race/ethnicity, sexuality, and so on. Within difference theory, women of color not only hold dual standpoints as women and as women of color; in the words of Vietnamese American Trinh Minh-ha, "inappropriated others" are individuals who cannot be either "self" or "other" and who are therefore forced into not only dual, but multiple visions and developing ambiguous strategies. Thus, the difference and identity approach has critically examined the intersections of power, identity, discourse, and knowledge and developed ways of using multiple voices and visions to create alternate modes and models of communication. This implies that power can be located and subverted, and hints at a utopia without gender and other types of oppression. This has been the starting point of poststructuralist critique.

Dominance and difference scholars also tend to see gender as a social construct in a dialectic exchange between identity and society. Within this approach, sex is distinguished from gender as a biological and usually unquestioned entity. This idea is also challenged by the performance turn, which gives rise to a critique of the implied essentialism in difference and identity feminism and of the paradoxical claim of both universalism and particularism of women's values and interests. The performance turn is represented by performance theory (e.g., Judith Butler), cyborg theory (e.g., Donna Haraway), and transgender theory (e.g., Judith Halberstam). Although these scholars may not necessarily see themselves as communication scholars, their work has influenced the development of feminist communication scholarship and has inspired some of the authors that we have included in Chapter 6: Don Kulick, Kira Hall, Mary Bucholtz, and Kristin Langellier. Inspired by the poststructural strand of these theories, they see gender/sex as a complex set of discursive practices—or in the words of Haraway, material-semiotic practices—that produce the effects that they are said to name. These are still seen to be imbued with power and interlocked with sexuality, race/ethnicity, class, and so forth, but not in any easily detected or deterministic way. The introduction of the discursive perspective has opened to communicative agency, but again not in any simple way. Unlike the difference and identity approach, the performance approach operates neither with the notion of identity nor with the notion of a truth or reality outside discourse and power. Thus, change occurs only through a continued struggle to open up to new perspectives and horizons. We saw that Butler's preferred example of such transgression is the drag figure, because it challenges the norms of heterosexual society and the ways it links gender and sexuality. The drag figure exposes how we all have to pass as gendered/legitimate beings and that identity is to be understood as a kind of pastiche—not of a reality, but of an established norm. Furthermore, we saw examples in Kira Hall's work with telephone sex workers and Brenda Danet's work with multi-user domains, in which gender and sex become a matter of discourse and, as such, a performative gesture. Mimicry, irony, and parody now serve to open up spaces of feminist empowerment, and we pointed to the rhetoric of the Guerrilla Girls as a particularly clever way in which women can subvert dominant culture and open to other ways of acting and thinking.

# From Conversation Analysis to Poststructuralist Discourse Analysis

The diversity of methods evident in feminist communication scholarship reflects the larger diversity in methodology that the field of communication studies has historically employed. There is no single feminist method, but feminist communication researchers have incorporated and transformed different methodologies. As we see it, this transdisciplinary approach is a strength of feminist scholarship. What the feminist-informed methods share is that they put gender and gender-related concerns at the center of analysis and highlight notions of power in different ways. On the other hand, we have also claimed that it is possible and important to identify different approaches and that there is a clear coherence in the choices that are made in terms of theory and methodology. At this point, we would like to pay a final visit to the analytical toolboxes.

We began our methodological exploration with feminist conversation analysis. Inspired by, on one hand, structuralism and muted group theory and, on the other, by ethnomethodologists such as Harold Garfinkel, Harvey Sacks, and Del Hymes, feminist conversation analysts (Pamela Fishman, Susan Herring, Candace West, and Don Zimmerman, among others) study talk-as-action, and they choose to focus on ways in which gender is involved in conversational ordering of turn-taking, turn allocation, sequence organization, repair work, and turn-constructional units. Feminist conversation analysts maintain gender as a pivotal category of analysis in understanding talk-as-action, and, as such, they depart from a pure conversation-analytic point of view. We also indicated that in recent years, feminist conversation analysis has adopted poststructuralist elements and that the mutual orientation toward action and practice makes this a productive alliance. Significant to feminist conversation analysis is the notion of talk as gendered and talk as both reflective and constitutive of larger societal discrepancies. For instance, within a patriarchal framework, silence is a significant practice of submission and domination, respectively: When women fall silent, it is both a sign of their oppression and the creation of it, and when men fall silent, it is both a mark and form of domination. Thus, feminist conversation analysis reads communication as a gendered societal pattern, and within this pattern, women are more readily muted and men engage in muting.

We next introduced feminist critical discourse analysis. Inspired by feminist critical theory in terms of standpoint theory, on one hand, and by critical discourse analysis, on the other, feminist critical discourse analysis was developed by scholars such as Ruth Wodak. They focus on the interplay of text and context and discursive as well as nondiscursive elements in order to highlight relations of power, discourse, and identity. They also study written and monologic communication, such as political speeches and advertising, but as illustrated in our case study, the more contemporary branch of feminist critical discourse analysis now also examines interpersonal and oral communication practices. In contrast to feminist conversation analysts, who focus on shorter extracts of communication and the single communicative act or practice, feminist critical discourse analysis moves from the micro- to the macrolevel of discourse to foreground the ways in which gender and communication work dialectically with institutions and organizations and the larger relations, structures, and symbolic orders of society. These scholars share a critical societal perspective, hoping that change can take place.

We ended our survey of feminist communication methods with an introduction to feminist poststructuralist discourse analysis. Poststructuralist theories of performance and positioning are central to the approach, as are cyborg and transgender theories, and they have largely been elaborated by feminist scholars and closely connected to methodologies such as speech act theory (Judith Butler, Kristin Langellier) and positioning analysis (Bronwyn Davies, Margaret Wetherell, Judith Baxter). Poststructuralist discourse analysis is used to demonstrate the dynamics of social encounters in terms of a performative engagement and a mutual positioning on behalf of what are now considered agents. The focus is on situated practices and the ways they both confirm and resist being "formatted" by hegemonic norms of gender, sexuality, ethnicity, and so on. Such resistance is explored in terms of symbolic reversals and different types of mimicry. As demonstrated in Judith Baxter's work, the methodology clarifies how individuals shift between different positions made available to them in the process of communication, often in contradictory but also creative ways. Thus, Baxter's study of management communication practices combines a microanalysis of communication with a poststructural view on gender to illustrate the ways in which managers—of both genders—negotiate shifting subject positions and power relations during a board meeting and thereby also negotiate the meaning of gender.

Methodological differences are to some extent minimized when poststructuralism functions as a shared theoretical platform. As we have seen, feminist poststructuralist discourse analysis is easily aligned with the poststructural strand of feminist conversation analysis. Poststructural feminist conversation analysis examines the ways in which communication not only affects, but *effects* gender as well as other social distinctions, moving from the notion of talk as gendered to the idea that it is through talk that we perform gender. The focus now comes to rest on ways in which talk is "producing speakers as males or females" (Kitzinger, 2002, p. 56). Paul McIlvenny (2002a) offered a general guide for research questions inspired by poststructural feminist conversation analysis:

> Ask not "How do lesbians talk?" but "How do participants talk such that their lesbianness is made salient and consequential for their activities?" Ask not "How does a bisexual woman pass as 'half straight, half lesbian'?" but "How does an interlocutor actively construct (or resist) how a 'split self' is perceived when their gender/sexuality is ambiguous to others?" (p. 141)

Within this poststructuralist perspective on feminist conversation analysis, McIlvenny and Kitzinger suggest that researchers attend to the ways in which the local management of conversation produces identities, rather than to the ways in which identities produce particular ways of talking. In short, we see the performance turn as a move away from gender as a precommunicative category to something that develops in communication.

The ongoing exchange between poststructuralism and feminist communication methods extends, as Ruth Wodak's work demonstrates, to feminist critical discourse analysis as well. Wodak adopts the poststructuralist critique of identity and society and has chosen to work with increasingly complex intersectional patterns and webs of material and immaterial phenomena. However, she still devotes herself to the critical project of identifying who has the power. Conversely, we also see how poststructuralist work still makes evident the difficulty in integrating the performance turn. Judith Baxter, who advocates feminist poststructuralist discourse analysis, focuses on identity making and power in much the same way as Wodak. They both address a rather traditional "woman question" in a rather traditional way by asking—with the new vocabulary, though—how the woman leader/MEP performs and thereby positions herself. Thus, they focus on "woman" as constitutive of a gendered and still rather naturalized perspective.

Nevertheless, these new combinations demonstrate the ways in which poststructuralism and the performance turn have given rise to methodological reconfigurations. While the key analytical tools related to discourse analysis are upheld, the method is revised to encompass more contemporary feminist theory work.

## Toward Transversity: What Does the Future Hold?

In the wake of an increasingly complex world, the performance turn has, in our view, been a constructive response to the sophisticated demands of intersectionality in questioning gender in relation to the multiplying list of social markers, such as, but not limited to, class, sexuality, race/ethnicity, age, and ability. All of these markers are continually subject to differentiation and multiplication. We obviously enjoy the work of Judith Butler, Donna Haraway, and Judith Halberstam, because they suggest ways to rethink these markers but also widen the discussion to include intersections of discourse and practice, discourse and body, categorization and subversion. Whereas Butler suggests possibilities of agency in speech, she also points to the notion of performativity as a conceptualization of the constant tension between performances and the underlying conventions and the ways words and bodies are involved in both. Haraway refines the new framework by speculating as to whether the notion of "affinity" might be a more useful resource than "identity" for rethinking identity claims. It may help us build an awareness that affinities (such as gender, race/ethnicity, and class) do matter but that they are multiple and continually shifting in importance (Haraway, 1987/1991). In this way, Haraway draws on the work done by Halberstam and others on transgenderism and mixing and recombining methodologies, as well as on Nira Yuval Davis's work on transversal politics and the communication strategy of "pivoting," which we also have seen as a possible academic method.

The concepts of transversal politics and transgenderism question the very foundation of feminism, exposing a transfeminist perspective that may serve as a theoretical and methodological point of constant academic trouble and thereby creativity. We have chosen to let the concept "transversal politics" converge with "diversity" into what we call "transversity," and we have presented it as a framework for developing transversal discourse analysis. This particular methodology encourages us to critically interrogate essentialist terms and feminist canons and develop ways in which to rethink and reuse former toolboxes. We believe that *trans* here should be viewed as a metaphor for a plethora of approaches, based on the view that gender is always situated and dynamic. It directs our attention, for example, to young women's resignification of the word *girl* to *grrl* as a really transformative action that reveals the layers of meanings and methods that must be continuously examined and challenged.

We have been particularly intrigued by the possibilities that we see opening up in digital environments. Digital environments make available not only notions of communication play but also the view that gender is textually created and managed by participants themselves. Computer-mediated communication provides a rare look into the workshop of gender and challenges us to elaborate on the distinction between performance and performativity. Can it be made? Or is it only a dream, symptomatic criticism, deeply rooted in structuralism and second-wave feminism? It must by now be considered a premise to feminists, as transgender theorists put it, that the two-tiered sex-and-gender system does not adequately convey the lives of individuals who do not fit neatly into these categories. However, although we may be tempted to deconstruct "sex" and "gender" altogether, normative gender constructions continue to manifest and make a difference in people's lives. Thus, as long as these categories continue to affect us, we do need to operate with them to some extent, at least on an analytical level. However, we do not need to succumb to simplistic gender dichotomous analyses, as exemplified by many digital environments.

But let us direct your attention back to our own situatedness in Scandinavia and the case that we presented in the introduction: Fadime, who was killed by her father in 2002. You may recall that her only crime, in our Westernized eyes, was her love for a young non-Muslim Swedish man. But in the eyes of the Turkish-Muslim community in Sweden, she brought shame and dishonor on her family. And when she took the internal dispute into the public eye, she deepened that shame. She engaged in a very specific type of communication agency, and she gained an assertive and thus provocative voice in the Swedish media and in the minds of the Swedish public. In sharp contrast to her positive public image, her family was seen as locked into their old patriarchal practices. She became a prime symbol of contemporary young, outspoken Turkish-Swedish women. However, she also sadly came to illustrate the limitations that in this case were so unfairly attached to communication agency: the harsh repercussions for venturing outside of her prescribed roles, repercussions about which the Turkish-Swedish community kept silent, and repercussions that took her agency—her voice—away. Fadime's case serves to show the complexities that the field of gender communication is faced with. It demonstrates the tension that continually exists between agency and underlying societal norms.

We have now come to the end of our story on gender and communication. Third-wave feminists wake up in the context of increased complexity—globalization and diversity—a transversity of sorts. How do we now make sense of identity markers? The old slogan "Sisterhood is global" turned out to be an imperialist assertion of Western gender ideals. What can—or should anything—take its place? Third-wave feminists cannot be entirely separated from the politics of the 20th and 21st century. The fall of the Berlin Wall in 1989, the destruction of the World Trade Center in 2001, the contemporary exportation of democracy that parts of the Western world are engaged in, threats of terrorism and terrorist acts, as well as a range of civil wars, show how difficult but also vital it is for third-wave feminists to build new alliances and webs of understanding. We believe in the creative recombination of old and new. And we hope that this book has demonstrated the delicate interplay between theory, methods, and politics, while we also hope that you have achieved a sophisticated analytical understanding that the way in which we examine questions of gender and communication is vital.

# References

Acker, J. (1992). Gendering organizational theory. In A. J. Mills & P. Tancred (Eds.), *Gendering organizational analysis* (pp. 248–260). Newbury Park, CA: Sage.

Ang, I. (1985). *Watching Dallas: Soap opera and the melodramatic imagination*. London, New York: Methuen.

Ardener, S. (1975). *Perceiving women*. New York: Wiley.

Austin, J. L. (1962). *How to do things with words*. Cambridge, MA: Harvard University Press.

Baken, R. (1987). *Clinical measurement of speech and voice*. London: Taylor, Francis.

Bamberg, M. (2000). Critical personalism, language, and development. *Theory and Psychology 10*, 749–767.

Bamberg, M. (2004). "We are young, responsible, and male": Form and function of "slut-bashing" in the identity constructions in 15-year-old males. *Human Development, 47*, 331–353.

Barrett, R. (1997). The "homo-genius" speech community. In A. Livia & K. Hall (Eds.), *Queerly phrased: Language, gender, and sexuality* (pp. 181–201). New York, Oxford: Oxford University Press.

Barrett, R. (1999). Indexing polyphonous identity in the speech of African American drag queens. In M. Bucholtz, A. C. Liang, & L. A. Sutton (Eds.), *Reinventing identities: The gendered self in discourse* (pp. 313–331). New York, Oxford: Oxford University Press.

Baumgardner, A., & Richards, J. (2000). *Manifesta: Young women, feminism, and the future*. New York: Farrar, Straus, Giroux.

Baxter, J. (2002). Competing discourses in the classroom: A post-structuralist discourse analysis of girls' and boys' speech in public contexts. *Discourse & Society, 13*, 827–842.

Baxter, J. (2003a). *Feminist post-structuralist discourse analysis. From theory to practice*. London: Palgrave.

Baxter, J. (2003b). Is PDA really an alternative? A reply to West. *Discourse & Society, 13*, 853–860.

Baxter, J. (2003c). *Positioning gender in discourse: A feminist methodology*. London: Palgrave.

Bergvall, V. L., Bing, J. M., & Freed, A. F. (Eds.). (1996). *Rethinking language and gender. Research: Theory and practice.* London, New York: Longman.

Bing, J. M., & Bergvall, V. L. (1996). The question of questions: Beyond binary thinking. In V. L. Bergvall, J. M. Bing, & A. F. Freed (Eds.), *Rethinking language and gender. Research: Theory and practice* (pp. 1–30). London, New York: Longman.

Bloom, L., Coburn, K., & Pearlman, J. (1975). *The new assertive woman.* New York: Delacorte Press.

Bobo, J. (1995). The color purple: Black women as cultural readers. In G. Dines & J. M. Humez (Eds.), *Gender, race, and class in media* (pp. 52–60). Thousand Oaks, CA: Sage.

Bobo, J., & Seiter, E. (1997). The women of Brewster Place. In C. Brunsdon, J. D'Acci, & S. Lynn (Eds.), *Feminist television criticism: A reader* (pp. 167–183). Oxford: Clarendon Press.

Bodine, A. (1990). Androcentrism in prescriptive grammar: Singular "they," sex-indefinite "he," and "he or she." In D. Cameron (Ed.), *The feminist critique of language: A reader* (pp. 166–186). New York: Routledge.

Braidotti, R. (1996). *Cyberfeminism with a difference.* Retrieved September 2002, from http://www.let.uu.nl/womens_studies/rosi/cyberfem.htm

Brewis, J. (2001). Telling it like it is? Gender, language, and organizational theory. In R. M. Westwood & S. Linstead (Eds.), *The language of organization* (pp. 283–309). Thousand Oaks, CA: Sage.

Brown, P. (1993). Gender, politeness, and confrontation in Tenejapa. In D. Tannen (Ed.), *Gender and conversational interaction* (pp. 283–309). New York, Oxford: Oxford University Press. (First published in 1990)

Brunsdon, C., D'Acci, J., & Lynn, S. (1997). (Eds.). *Feminist television criticism: A reader.* Oxford: Clarendon Press.

Bucholtz, M. (1995). From Mulatta to Mestiza: Passing and the linguistic reshaping of ethnic identity. In K. Hall & M. Bucholtz (Eds.), *Gender articulated: Language and the socially constructed self* (pp. 351–374). New York, London: Routledge.

Bucholtz, M. (1996a). Black feminist theory and African American women's linguistic practice. In V. L. Bergvall, J. M. Bing, & A. F. Freed (Eds.), *Rethinking language and gender. Research: Theory and practice* (pp. 267–290). London, New York: Longman.

Bucholtz, M. (1996b). Theories of discourse as theories of gender: Discourse analysis in language and gender studies. In J. Holmes & M. Meyerhoff (Eds.), *The handbook of language and gender.* Malden, MA; Oxford: Blackwell.

Bucholtz, M. (1999). Purchasing power: The gender and class imaginary on the Shopping Channel. In M. Bucholtz, A. C. Liang, & L. A. Sutton (Eds.), *Reinventing identities: The gendered self in discourse* (pp. 348–368). New York, Oxford: Oxford University Press.

Bucholtz, M. (2003). Theories of discourse as theories of gender: Discourse analysis in language and gender studies. In J. Holmes & M. Meyerhoff (Eds.), *The handbook of language and gender* (pp. 43–68). Oxford: Blackwell.

Bucholtz, M., Liang, A. C., & Sutton, L. A. (Eds.). (1999). *Reinventing identities. The gendered self in discourse.* New York, Oxford: Oxford University Press.

Butler, J. (1990). *Gender trouble.* New York: Routledge.

Butler, J. (1993). *Bodies that matter: On the discursive limits of "sex."* New York: Routledge.

Butler, J. (1997). *Excitable speech: A politics of the performative.* New York: Routledge.

Butler, J. (1999). *Gender trouble. Feminism and the subversion of identity.* New York: Routledge.

Buzzanell, P. M. (2000). *Rethinking organizational and managerial communication from feminist perspectives.* Thousand Oaks, CA: Sage.

Calás, M. B. (1992). An/other silent voice? Representing "Hispanic woman" in organizational texts. In A. J. Mills & P. Tancred (Eds.), *Gendering organizational analysis* (pp. 201–221). Newbury Park, CA: Sage.

Calás, M. B., & Smircich, L. (1992). Using the "F" word: Feminist theories and the social consequences of organizational research. In A. J. Mills & P. Tancred (Eds.), *Gendering organizational analysis* (pp. 222–234). Newbury Park, CA: Sage.

Cameron, D. (Ed.). (1990). *The feminist critique: A reader.* New York: Routledge.

Cameron, D. (1992). *Feminism and linguistic theory* (2nd ed.). London: Macmillan.

Cameron, D. (1995a). Rethinking language and gender studies: Some issues for the 1990s. In S. Mills (Ed.), *Language and gender: Interdisciplinary perspectives* (pp. 31–44). Essex, New York: Longman.

Cameron, D. (1995b). *Verbal hygiene.* New York: Routledge.

Cameron, D. (1996). The language-gender interface: Challenging co-optation. In V. L. Bergvall, J. M. Bing, & A. F. Freed (Eds.), *Rethinking language and gender. Research: Theory and practice* (pp. 31–53). London, New York: Longman.

Cameron, D. (1997a). Performing gender identity: Young men's talk and the construction of heterosexual masculinity. In S. Johnson & H. Meinhof (Eds.), *Language and masculinity* (pp. 47–64). London: Blackwell. (Reprinted in J. Coates, Ed., *Language and gender: A reader,* Malden, MA; Oxford: Blackwell, 1998)

Cameron, D. (1997b). Theoretical debates in feminist linguistics: Questions of sex and gender. In R. Wodak (Ed.), *Gender and discourse* (pp. 21–36). Thousand Oaks, CA: Sage.

Cameron, D. (Ed.). (1998a). *The feminist critique of language: A reader* (2nd rev. ed.). London & New York, Routledge.

Cameron, D. (1998b). Performing gender identity: Young men's talk and the construction of heterosexual masculinity. In D. Cameron (Ed.), *The feminist critique of language* (pp. 270–284). London & New York, Routledge.

Cameron, D. (2000). *Good to talk? Living and working in a communication culture.* Thousand Oaks, CA: Sage.

Cameron, D. (2001). *Working with spoken discourse.* Thousand Oaks, CA: Sage.

Cameron, D., & Coates, J. (1989). Some problems in the sociolinguistic explanation of sex differences. In *Women in their speech communities: New perspectives on language and sex* (pp. 13–26). London & New York, Longman. (3rd ed. published in 1991)

Cameron, D., & Kulick, D. (2003). *Language and sexuality*. Cambridge: Cambridge University Press.

Campbell, K. K. (1989). *Man cannot speak for her* (Vol. 1). Oxford: Praeger.

Campbell, K. K. (1998). Inventing women: From Amaterasu to Virginia Woolf. *Women's Studies in Communication, 21*(2), 111–126.

Channell, J. (1997). Tampax telephone conversation between the Prince of Wales and Camilla Parker-Bowles. In K. Harvey & C. Shalom (Eds.), *Language and desire: Encoding sex, romance, and intimacy* (pp. 143–169). London, New York: Routledge.

Chia, R., & King, I. (2001). The language of organization theory. In S. Linstead & R. Westwood (Eds.), *The language of organization* (pp. 310–328). London: Sage.

Chideya, F., Rossi, M., & Hannah, D. (1992, November 23). Revolution, girl style. *Newsweek, 120,* pp. 84–86.

Cixous, H. (1981a). The laugh of Medusa. In E. Marks & I. de Courtivron (Eds.), *New French feminisms: An anthology* (pp. 245–264). Hemel Hempstead, UK: Harvester Wheatsheaf. (Original work, "Le rire de la Méduse," published in 1975)

Cixous, H. (1981b). Sorties. In E. Marks & I. de Courtivron (Eds.), *New French feminisms: An anthology* (pp. 90–98). Hemel Hempstead, UK: Harvester Wheatsheaf. (Original work, "La jeune née," published in 1975)

Coates, J. (1989). Gossip revisited: Language in all-female group. In J. Coates & D. Cameron (Eds.), *Women in their speech communities: New perspectives on language and sex* (pp. 94–121). London: Longman. (Reprinted in J. Coates, Ed., *Language and gender: A reader,* Malden, MA; Oxford: Blackwell, 1998)

Coates, J. (1993). *Women, men and language. A sociolinguistic account of gender differences in language* (2nd ed.). London, New York: Longman. (First published in 1986)

Coates, J. (1995). Language, gender and career. In S. Mills (Ed.), *Language and gender: Interdisciplinary perspectives* (pp. 13–30). Essex, New York: Longman.

Coates, J. (1996). *Women talk: Conversation between women friends.* Oxford: Blackwell.

Coates, J. (1997a). Competing discourses of femininity. In H. Kotthoff & R. Wodak (Eds.), *Communicating gender in context* (pp. 285–314). Amsterdam/ Philadelphia: John Benjamins.

Coates, J. (1997b). Women's friendships, women's talk. In R. Wodak (Ed.), *Gender and discourse* (pp. 245–262). Thousand Oaks, CA: Sage.

Coates, J. (Ed.). (1998). *Language and gender: A reader.* Malden, MA; Oxford: Blackwell.

Coates, J. (1999). Changing femininities. The talk of teenage girls. In M. Bucholtz, A. C. Liang, & L. A. Sutton (Eds.), *Reinventing identities: The gendered self in discourse* (pp. 123–144). New York, Oxford: Oxford University Press.

Coates, J. (2003). *Men talk: Stories in the making of masculinities*. Malden, MA; Oxford: Blackwell.

Coates, J., & Cameron, D. (Eds.). (1989). *Women in their speech communities: New perspectives on language and sex*. London: Longman. (3rd ed. published in 1991)

Collins, P. H. (1986). Learning from the outsider within: The sociological significance of feminist thought. *Social Problems 33,* 514–532.

Collins, P. H. (1997). Comment on Hekman's "Truth and Method: Feminist Standpoint Theory Revisited." Where's the power? *Signs, 22,* 382–391.

Crawford, M. (1995). *Talking difference. On gender and language*. Thousand Oaks, CA: Sage.

D'Acci, J. (1995). Defining women. The case of *Cagney and Lacey*. In G. Dines & J. M. Humez (Eds.), *Gender, race, and class in media* (pp. 454–468). Thousand Oaks, CA: Sage.

Daly, M. (1978). *Gyn/ecology: The metaethics of radical feminism*. Boston: Beacon Press.

Danet, B. (1998). Text as mask: Gender, play, and performance on the Internet. In S. Jones (Ed.), *Cybersociety 2.0: Revisiting computer-mediated communication and community* (pp. 129–158). Thousand Oaks, CA: Sage.

Davies, B., & Harré, R. (2001). Positioning: The discursive production of selves. In M. Wetherell, S. Taylor, & S. J. Yates (Eds.), *Discourse theory and practice* (pp. 261–271). Thousand Oaks, CA: Sage. (First published in 1990)

Davies, E. (2004). Finding ourselves: Postmodern identities and the transgender movement. In S. Gillis, G. Howie, & R. Munford (Eds.), *Third wave feminism: A critical exploration* (pp. 110–121). Basingstoke, UK: Palgrave.

Davis, A. Y. (1998). *Blues legacies and black feminism: Gertrude "Ma" Rainey, Bessie Smith, and Billie Holliday*. New York: Pantheon Books.

Davis, A. Y. (1981). *Women, race, and class*. New York: Random House.

Demo, A. T. (2000). The Guerilla Girls' comic politics of subversion. *Women's Studies in Communication, 23*(2), 133–157. (Electronic version)

Dickson, A. (1982). *A woman in your own right*. London: Quartet Books.

Dines, G., & Humez, J. M. (Eds.). (1995). *Gender, race, and class in media*. Thousand Oaks, CA: Sage.

Döring, N. (2000). Feminist views on cybersex: Victimization, liberation, and empowerment. *Cyberpsychology & Behavior, 3,* 863–884.

Dow, B. J. (1996). *Prime-time feminism: Television, media culture, and the women's movement since 1970*. Philadelphia: University of Pennsylvania Press.

Eckert, P. (1993). Cooperative competition in adolescent "girl talk." In D. Tannen (Ed.), *Gender and conversational interaction* (pp. 32–61). New York, Oxford: Oxford University Press. (First published in 1990)

Eckert, P., & McConnell-Ginet, S. (1992). Think practically and look locally: Language and gender as community-based practice. *Annual Review of Anthropology, 21,* 461–490.

Eckert, P., & McConnell-Ginet, S. (1995). Constructing meaning, constructing selves: Snapshots of language, gender, and class from Belten High. In K. Hall & M. Bucholtz (Eds.), *Gender articulated: Language and the socially constructed self* (pp. 469–508). New York, London: Routledge.

Eckert, P., & McConnell-Ginet, S. (Eds.). (2003). *Language and gender.* Cambridge: Cambridge University Press

Edelsky, C. (1993). Who's got the floor? In D. Tannen (Ed.), *Gender and conversational interaction* (pp. 189–230). New York, Oxford: Oxford University Press. (First published in 1981)

Eder, D. (1993). "Go get ya a French!" Romantic and sexual teasing among adolescent girls. In D. Tannen (Ed.), *Gender and conversational interaction* (pp. 83–109). New York, Oxford: Oxford University Press.

Eisenstein, Z. (1981). *The radical future of liberal feminism.* London: Longman.

Elgin, S. H. (1984). *Native tongue.* London: Women's Press.

Elgin, S. H. (1990). Extract from *Native Tongue.* In D. Cameron (Ed.), *The feminist critique of language: A reader* (pp. 160–163). New York: Routledge.

Fairclough, N. (1995a). *Critical discourse analysis.* London: Longman.

Fairclough, N. (1995b). *Language and power.* Upper Saddle River, NJ: Pearson Education.

Fairclough, N., & Wodak R. (1998). Critical discourse analysis. In T. A. van Dijk (Ed.), *Discourse as social interaction. Vol. 2: Discourse studies: A multidisciplinary introduction* (pp. 258–284). Thousand Oaks, CA: Sage.

Fenstermaker, S., & West, C. (2002). "Doing difference" revisited: Problems, prospects, and the dialogue in feminist theory. In S. Fenstermaker & C. West (Eds.), *Doing gender, doing difference: Inequality, power, and institutional change* (pp. 205–216). New York: Routledge.

Firestone, S. (1968). The women's rights movement in the U.S.: A new view. In F. Firestone & P. Allen (Eds.), *Notes from the first year.* New York: New York Radical Women. Retrieved August 10, 2004, from http://www.scriptorium.lib .duke.edu/wlm/notes

Firestone, S. (1970). *The dialectic of sex: The case for feminist revolution.* New York: Morrow Quill Paperbacks.

Fishman, P. (1983). Interaction: The work women do. In B. Thorne & N. Henley (Eds.), *Language and sex: Difference and dominance* (pp. 89–101). Rowley, MA: Newbury House.

Fiske, J. (1987). *Television culture.* London: Methuen.

Fitch, K. (2001). The ethnography of speaking: Sapir/Whorf, Hymes, and Moerman. In M. Wetherell, S. Taylor, & S. J. Yates (Eds.), *Discourse theory and practice* (pp. 57–63). Thousand Oaks, CA: Sage.

Foss, K. A., Foss, S. K., & Griffin, C. L. (1999). *Feminist rhetorical theory.* Thousand Oaks, CA: Sage.

Foss, K. A., Foss, S. K., & Griffin, C. L. (2004). *Readings in feminist rhetorical theory.* Thousand Oaks, CA: Sage.

Foss, S. K., & Griffin, C. L. (1995, March). Beyond persuasion: A proposal for invitational rhetoric. *Communication Monographs, 62,* 2–18.

Foss, S. K., Griffin, C. L., & Foss, K. A. (1997). Transforming rhetoric through feminist reconstruction: A response to the gender diversity perspective. *Women's Studies in Communication, 20*(2), 117–135.

Foster, M. (1995). "Are you with me?" Power and solidarity in the discourse of African American women. In K. Hall & M. Bucholtz (Eds.), *Gender articulated: Language and the socially constructed self* (pp. 329–350). New York, London: Routledge.

Fraser, N. (1997). *Justice interruptus: Critical reflections on the "postsocialist condition."* London: Routledge.

Freeman, J. ("Joreen"). (1968). The BITCH manifesto. In F. Firestone & P. Allen (Eds.), *Notes from the first year.* New York: New York Radical Women. Retrieved July 1, 2004, from http://www.scriptorium.lib.duke.edu/wlm/bitch

Freeman, J. (1969). No more Miss America (1968–1969). Retrieved July 1, 2003, from http://www.jofreeman.com/photos/MissAm1969.html

Freeman, J. (1975). *The politics of women's liberation: A case study of emerging social movement and its relation to the policy process.* New York: David McKay.

Frosh, S., Phoenix, A., & Pattman, R. (2002). *Young masculinities. Understanding boys in contemporary society.* Hampshire, NY: Palgrave.

Garber, M. (1997). *Vested interests. Cross-dressing and cultural anxiety.* New York: Routledge Press.

Gates, H. L. (1987). *Figures in Black: Words, signs, and the "racial" self.* New York, Oxford, Oxford University Press.

Gates, H. L. (1988). *The signifying monkey: A theory of Afro-American literary criticism.* Oxford, UK: Oxford University Press.

Gearheart, S. M. (1979). The womanization of rhetoric. *Women's Studies International Quarterly, 2,* 195–201.

Gergen, K. (2002). *An invitation to social construction.* Thousand Oaks, CA: Sage.

Gilligan, C. (1982). *In a different voice: Psychological theory and women's development.* Cambridge, MA: Harvard University Press.

Goffman, E. (1959). *The presentation of self in everyday life.* New York: Doubleday.

Goffman, E. (1979). *Gender advertisements.* Cambridge, MA: Harvard University Press.

Goffman, E. (2001). Footing. In M. Wetherell, S. Taylor, & S. J. Yates (Eds.), *Discourse theory and practice* (pp. 93–110). Thousand Oaks, CA: Sage.

Goodwin, M. H. (1990). *He-said-she-said: Talk as social organization among black children.* Bloomington: Indiana University Press. (From thesis, 1978)

Goodwin, M. H. (1993). Tactical uses of stories: Participation frameworks within boys' and girls' disputes. In D. Tannen (Ed.), *Gender and conversational interaction* (pp. 110–143). New York, Oxford: Oxford University Press. (First published in 1990)

Goodwin, M. H. (1998). Cooperation and competition across girls' play activities. In J. Coates (Ed.), *Language and gender: A reader* (pp. 121–146). Malden, MA; Oxford: Blackwell. (First published in 1988)

Goodwin, M. H. (1999). Constructing opposition within girls' games. In M. Bucholtz, A. C. Liang, & L. A. Sutton (Eds.), *Reinventing identities: The gendered self in discourse* (pp. 388–409). New York, Oxford: Oxford University Press.

Goodwin, M. H. (2003). The relevance of ethnicity, class, and gender in children's peer negotiations. In J. Holmes & M. Meyerhoff (Eds.), *The handbook of language and gender*. Malden, MA; Oxford: Blackwell.

Graddol, D., & Swann, J. (1989). *Gender voices*. Oxford: Blackwell.

Greenwood, A. (1996). Floor management and power strategies in adolescent conversation. In V. L. Bergvall, J. M. Bing, & A. F. Freed (Eds.), *Rethinking language and gender: Research: Theory and practice* (pp. 77–97). London, New York: Longman.

Gross, L. (1995). Out of the mainstream: Sexual minorities and the mass media. In G. Dines & J. M. Humez (Eds.), *Gender, race, and class in media* (pp. 61–70). Thousand Oaks, CA: Sage.

Gumperz, J. J. (1982). *Language and social identity*. Cambridge: Cambridge University Press.

Gumperz, J. J. (2001). Interethnic communication. In M. Wetherell, S. Taylor, & S. J. Yates (Eds.), *Discourse theory and practice* (pp. 138–149). Thousand Oaks, CA: Sage.

Halberstam, J. (1998). *Female masculinity*. Durham, NC; London: Duke University Press.

Hall, K. (1995). Lip service on the fantasy lines. In K. Hall & M. Bucholtz (Eds.), *Gender articulated. Language and the socially constructed self* (pp. 183–216). New York, London: Routledge.

Hall, K. (1996). Cyberfeminism. In S. Herring (Ed.), *Computer-mediated communication: Linguistic, social, and cross-cultural perspectives* (pp. 147–170). Amsterdam: John Benjamins.

Hall, K. (2003). Exceptional speakers: Contested and problematized gender identities. In J. Holmes & M. Meyerhoff (Eds.), *The handbook of language and gender* (pp. 353–380). Malden, MA; Oxford: Blackwell.

Hall, K., & Bucholtz, M. (Eds.). (1995). *Gender articulated: Language and the socially constructed self*. New York, London: Routledge.

Hall, K., Bucholtz, M., & Moonwomon, B. (Eds.). (1992). *Locating power: Proceedings of the second Berkeley women and language conference*. Berkeley, CA: Berkeley Women and Language Group.

Hall, R. M., & Sandler, B. R. (1982). *The classroom climate: A chilly one for women?* Washington, DC: Association of American Colleges, Project of the Status and Education of Women.

Hallstein, D. L. O'Brien (2000). Where standpoint stands now: An introduction and commentary. *Women's Studies in Communication, 23*(1), 1–16 (Electronic version).

Hammonds, E. (1997). Black (w)holes and the geometry of black female sexuality. *A Journal of Feminist Cultural Studies 6.2*(3), 126–145.

Hansen, C. H., & Hansen, R. D. (1988). How rock music videos can change what is seen when boy meets girl: Priming stereotypic appraisal of social interactions. *Sex Roles, 19*, 287–316.

Haraway, D. (1991). *Simians, cyborgs, and women. The reinvention of nature.* London: Free Association Books. (First published in 1987)

Harding, S. (1986). *The science question in feminism.* London: Open University Press.

Harding, S. (1997a). Comment on Hekman's "Truth and Method: Feminist Standpoint Revisited": Whose standpoint needs the regimes of truth and reality? *Signs, 22*, 382–391.

Harding, S. (1997b). *Is science multicultural? Postcolonialisms, feminisms, and epistemologies.* Bloomington: Indiana University Press.

Harding, S. (2004). (Ed.). *The feminist standpoint theory reader: Intellectual and political controversies.* New York: Routledge.

Harré, R., & van Langenhove, L. (1999). *Positioning theory: Moral contexts of intentional action.* London: Blackwell.

Hartsock, N. C. M. (1983). The feminist standpoint: Developing the ground for a specifically feminist historical materialism. In S. Harding & M. B. Hintikka (Eds.), *Discovering reality: Feminist perspectives on epistemology, metaphysics, methodology, and philosophy of science* (pp. 283–310). Boston: Reidel.

Hartsock, N. C. M. (1998). *"The Feminist Standpoint Revisited" and other essays.* Boulder, CO: Westview Press.

Harvey, K., & Shalom, C. (Eds.). (1997). *Language and desire: Encoding sex, romance, and intimacy.* London, New York: Routledge.

Hekman, S. (1997). Truth and method: Feminist standpoint theory revisited. *Signs, 22*, 341–365.

Heritage, J. (2001). Goffman, Garfinkel, and conversation analysis. In M. Wetherell, S. Taylor, & S. J. Yates (Eds.), *Discourse theory and practice* (pp. 47–56). Thousand Oaks, CA: Sage.

Herring, S. (1996). *Computer-mediated communication: Linguistic, social and cross-cultural perspectives.* Amsterdam/Philadelphia: John Benjamins.

Herring, S. (1999). The rhetorical dynamics of gender harassment on-line. *The Information Society, 15*(3), 151–167.

Herring, S., & Panyametheekul, S. (2003). Gender and turn allocation in a Thai chat room. *Journal of Computer Mediated Communication, 9*(1), 1–21.

Hodge, R., & Kress, G. (2001). Social semiotics. In M. Wetherell, S. Taylor, & S. J. Yates (Eds.), *Discourse theory and practice* (pp. 294–299). Thousand Oaks, CA: Sage.

Holmes, J. (1995). *Women, men, and politeness.* London: Longman.

Holmes, J. (1997). Story-telling in New Zealand. Women's and men's talk. In R. Wodak (Ed.), *Gender and discourse* (pp. 263–293). Thousand Oaks, CA: Sage.

Holmes, J., & Meyerhoff, M. (Eds.). (2003). *The handbook of language and gender.* Malden, MA; Oxford: Blackwell.

Holmes, J., & Stubbe, M. (2003). "Feminine" workplaces: Stereotype and reality. In J. Holmes & M. Meyerhoff (Eds.), *The handbook of language and gender* (pp. 573–599). Malden, MA; Oxford: Blackwell.

hooks, b. (1981). *Ain't I a woman? Black woman and feminism*. Cambridge, MA: South End Press.

hooks, b. (1989). *Talking back: Thinking feminist, thinking black*. Cambridge, MA: South End Press.

Houston, M. (1992). The politics of difference: Race, class, and women's communication. In L. F. Rakow (Ed.), *Women making meaning: New feminist directions in communication* (pp. 45–59). New York: Routledge.

Houston, M., & Davis, I. O. (Eds.). (2002). *Centering ourselves. African American feminist and womanist studies of discourse*. Cresskill, NJ: Hampton Press.

Irigaray, L. (1985a). *Speculum of the other woman*. Ithaca, New York: Cornell University Press. (Original work, *Speculum de l'autre femme*, published in 1974.)

Irigaray, L. (1985b). *This sex which is not one*. Ithaca, New York: Cornell University Press. (Original work, *Ce sexe qui n'en est pas un*, published in 1977.)

Jacobs, A. T. (2002). Appropriating a slur: Semantic looping in the African-American usage of nigga. *M/C Journal*. Retrieved August 25, 2004, from http://www.media-culture.org.au/0208/semantic.html

James, D., & Clarke, S. (1993). Women, men and interruptions: A critical review. In D. Tannen (Ed.), *Gender and conversational interaction* (pp. 231–280). New York, Oxford: Oxford University Press.

James, D., & Drakich, J. (1993). Understanding gender differences in amount of talk: A critical review of research. In D. Tannen (Ed.), *Gender and conversational interaction* (pp. 281–313). New York, Oxford: Oxford University Press.

Jefferson, G. (1995). (Ed.). *Lectures on conversation*. Oxford, Cambridge, MA: Blackwell.

Jespersen, O. (1922). *Language: Its nature, development and origin*. New York: Norton.

Johnson, F. L., & Aries, E. J. (1998). The talk of women friends. In J. Coates (Ed.), *Language and gender: A reader* (pp. 215–225). Malden, MA; Oxford. (First published in 1983)

Johnson, S., & Meinhof, H. (Eds.). (1997). *Language and masculinity*. London: Blackwell.

Jones, D. (1990). Gossip: notes on women's oral culture. In D. Cameron (Ed.), *The feminist critique of language* (pp. 242–250). London, Routledge. (First published in 1980)

Kanter, R. (1977). *Men and women of the corporation*. New York: Basic Books.

Kendall, S., & Tannen, D. (1997). Gender and language in the workplace. In R. Wodak (Ed.), *Gender and discourse* (pp. 81–105). Thousand Oaks, CA: Sage.

Kitzinger, C. (2002). Doing feminist conversation analysis. In P. McIllvenny (Ed.), *Talking gender and sexuality* (pp. 49–78). Amsterdam/Philadelphia: John Benjamins.

Kotthoff, H., & Wodak, R. (Eds.). (1997). *Communicating gender in context*. Amsterdam/Philadelphia: John Benjamins.

Koyama, E. (2003). The transfeminist manifesto. In R. Dicker & A. Piepmeier (Eds.), *Catching a wave: Reclaiming feminism for the 21st century* (pp. 244–262). Boston: Northeastern University Press.

Kramarae, C., & Treichler, P. (1990). Words on a feminist dictionary. In D. Cameron (Ed.), *The feminist critique of language: A reader* (pp. 148–159). London: Routledge.

Kress, G. (2001). From Saussure to critical sociolinguistics: The turn towards a social view of language. In M. Wetherell, S. Taylor, & S. J. Yates (Eds.), *Discourse theory and practice* (pp. 29–38). Thousand Oaks, CA: Sage.

Kristeva, J. (1981). Woman can never be defined. In E. Marks & I. de Courtivron (Eds.), *New French feminisms: An anthology* (pp. 137–141). Hemel Hempstead, UK: Harvester Wheatsheaf. (Original work, "La femme, ce n'est jamais ça," published in 1974.)

Kulick, D. (2000). Gay and lesbian language. *Annual Review of Anthropology, 29,* 243–285.

Labov, W., & Gumperz, J. (1972). *Sociolinguistic patterns*. Pennsylvania: University of Pennsylvania Press.

Laclau, E., & Mouffe, C. (2001). *Hegemony and socialist strategy. Towards a radical democratic politics*. London, New York: Verso. (First published in 1985)

Lakoff, R. (1975). *Language and woman's place*. San Francisco: Harper Colophon Books.

Lakoff, R. (2000). *The language war*. Berkeley: University of California Press.

Langellier, K. M. (1989). Personal narratives: Perspectives on theory and research. *Text and Performance Quarterly, 9,* 243–276.

Langellier, K. M. (1999). Personal narrative, performance, performativity: Two or three things I know for sure. *Text and Performance Quarterly, 19,* 125–144.

Langellier, K. M. (2001). "You're marked": Breast cancer, tattoo, and the narrative performance of identity. In J. Brockmeier & D. Carbaugh (Eds.), *Narrative and identity: Studies in autobiography, self, and culture* (pp. 145–184). Amsterdam/ Philadelphia: John Benjamins.

Langellier, K. M., Carter, K., & Hantzis, D. (1993). Performing differences: feminism and performance studies. In S. P. Bowen and N. Wyatt (Eds.), *Transforming visions: Feminist critiques in communication studies* (pp. 87–124). Cresskill, NJ: Hampton Press.

Langellier, K. M., & Peterson, E. E. (2004). *Storytelling in daily life: Performing narrative*. Philadelphia: Temple University Press.

Langer, S. K. (1979). *Philosophy in a new key: A study in the symbolism of reason, rite and art* (3rd ed.). Cambridge, MA: Harvard University Press.

Langford, W. (1997). "Bunnikins, I love you snugly in your warren." Voices from subterranean cultures of love. In K. Harvey & C. Shalom (Eds.), *Language and desire: Encoding sex, romance and intimacy* (pp. 170–185). London, New York: Routledge.

Lee, A., Hewlett, N., & Nairn, M. (1995). Voice and gender in children. In S. Mills (Ed.), *Language and gender: Interdisciplinary perspectives* (pp. 194–204). Essex, New York: Longman.

Lee, J. (1995). Subversive sitcoms: *Roseanne* as inspiration for feminist resistance. In G. Dines & J. M. Humez (Eds.), *Gender, race, and class in media* (pp. 469–475). Thousand Oaks, CA: Sage.

Lee, P. C., & Gropper, N. B. (1974). Sex-role culture and educational practice. *Harvard Educational Review, 44,* 369–407.

Livia, A., & Hall, K. (Eds.). (1997). *Queerly phrased: Language, gender, and sexuality.* New York, Oxford: Oxford University Press.

Maltz, D. N., & Borker, R. A. (1998). A cultural approach to male-female miscommunication. In J. Coates (Ed.), *Language and gender: A reader* (pp. 417–434). Malden, MA; Oxford: Blackwell. (First published in 1982)

Marks, E., & de Courtivron, I. (1981). (Eds.). *New French feminisms: An anthology.* Hemel Hempstead, UK: Harvester Wheatsheaf.

Martyna, W. (1978). What does "he" mean? Use of the generic pronoun. *Journal of Communication, 28,* 131–138.

McElhinny, B. S. (1998). "I don't smile much anymore": Affect, gender and the discourse of Pittsburgh police officers. In J. Coates (Ed.), *Language and gender: A reader* (pp. 309–327). Malden, MA; Oxford: Blackwell.

McIlvenny, P. (2002a). Critical reflections on performativity and the "un/doing" of gender and sexuality in talk. In P. McIlvenny (Ed.), *Talking gender and sexuality* (pp. 111–150). Amsterdam/Philadelphia: John Benjamins.

McIllvenny, P. (Ed.). (2002b). *Talking gender and sexuality.* Amsterdam/ Philadelphia: John Benjamins.

McNaughton, K. (1997). *Internet tour.* Retrieved September 2002, from http://www .tcsys.com/troop250/tour.html

McRae, S. (1997). Flesh made word: Sex, text, and the virtual body. In D. Porter (Ed.), *Internet culture* (pp. 72–85). New York, London: Routledge.

Mills, A. J., & Tancred, P. (Eds.). (1992). *Gendering organizational analysis.* Newbury Park, CA: Sage.

Mills, S. (1995a). *Feminist stylistics.* London, New York, Routledge.

Mills, S. (Ed.). (1995b). *Language and gender: Interdisciplinary perspectives.* Essex, New York: Longman.

Minh-ha, T. T. (1989). *Woman, native, other: Writing post-colonialism and feminism.* Bloomington: Indiana University Press.

Mitchell, J. (1970). *The subjection of women.* Mineola, NY: Dover.

Modleski, T. (1982). *Loving with a vengeance. Mass-produced fantasies for women.* New York, London: Methuen.

Moonwomon, B. (1995). The writing on the wall: A border case of race and gender. In K. Hall & M. Bucholtz (Eds.), *Gender articulated: Language and the socially constructed self* (pp. 447–468). New York, London: Routledge.

Mouffe, C. (1983). The sex/gender system and the discursive construction of women's subordination. In S. Hanninen & L. Paldan (Eds.), *Rethinking ideology: A Marxist debate* (pp. 139–143). New York: International General.

Mulvey, L. (1975). Visual pleasure and narrative cinema. *Screen, 16*(3), 6–18.

Murphy, L. M. (1997). The elusive bisexual: Social categorization and lexico-semantic change. In A. Livia & K. Hall (Eds.), *Queerly phrased: Language, gender, and sexuality* (pp. 35–57). New York, Oxford: Oxford University Press.

Nyboe, L. (2003). *Doing cyberspaces: Performing selves and wor(l)ds through cyborg discourse.* Odense: University of Southern Denmark Press.

Olsen, T. (1990). Extract from *Silences.* In D. Cameron (Ed.), *The feminist critique of language: A reader* (pp. 164–165). New York: Routledge.

Penelope, J. (1990). *Speaking freely: Unlearning the lies of the fathers' tongues.* New York: Pergamon Press.

Pilkington, J. (1998). "Don't try and make out that I'm nice!" The different strategies women and men use when gossiping. In J. Coates (Ed.), *Language and gender: A reader* (pp. 254–269). Malden, MA; Oxford: Blackwell.

Potter, J., & Wetherell, M. (2001). Unfolding discourse analysis. In M. Wetherell, S. Taylor, & S. J. Yates (Eds.), *Discourse theory and practice* (pp. 198–209). Thousand Oaks, CA: Sage.

Purcell, P., & Stewart, L. (1990). Dick and Jane in 1989. *Sex Roles, 22,* 177–185.

Queen, C., & Schimel, L. (Eds.). (1997). *PoMoSexuals: Challenging assumptions about gender and sexuality.* Pittsburgh, PA: Cleis.

Queen, R. M. (1997). "I don't speak spritch": Locating lesbian language. In A. Livia & K. Hall (Eds.), *Queerly phrased: Language, gender, and sexuality* (pp. 233–256). New York, Oxford: Oxford University Press.

Radway, J. (1984). *Reading the romance: Women, patriarchy, and popular literature.* Chapel Hill: North Carolina Press.

Rich, A. (1980). Compulsory heterosexuality and lesbian existence. *Signs, 5,* 631–660.

Rose, T. (1995). "Fear of a black planet": Rap music and black cultural politics in the 1990s. In G. Dines, & J. M. Humez (Eds.), *Gender, race, and class in media* (pp. 531–539). Thousand Oaks, CA: Sage.

Rose, T. (1997). Never trust a big butt and a smile. In C. Brunsdon, J. D'Acci, & S. Lynn. (Eds.). *Feminist television criticism: A reader* (pp. 300–317). Oxford: Clarendon Press.

Sacks, H. (2001). Lecture 1: rules of conversational sequence. In M. Wetherell, S. Taylor, & S. J. Yates (Eds.), *Discourse theory and practice* (pp. 111, 118). Thousand Oaks, CA: Sage.

Schiffrin, D. (1994). *Approaches to discourse.* Oxford: Blackwell.

Schneider, J., & Hacker, S. (1973). Sex role imagery and use of the generic "man" in introductory texts: A case in the sociology of sociology. *American Sociologist, 8*(1), 12–18.

Schultz, M. R. (1990). The semantic derogation of women. In D. Cameron (Ed.), *The feminist critique of language: A reader* (pp. 134–147). New York: Routledge.

Scott, K. D. (2002). Conceiving the language of Black women's everyday talk. In M. Houston & I. O. Davis (Eds.), *Centering ourselves: African American feminist and womanist studies of discourse* (pp. 53–76). Cresskill, NJ: Hampton Press.

Sheldon, A. (1992). Preschool girls' discourse competence: Managing conflict. In K. Hall, M. Bucholtz, & B. Moonwomon (Eds.), *Locating power: proceedings of the second Berkeley women and language conference* (Vol. 2, pp. 528–539). Berkeley, CA: Berkeley Women and Language Group.

Sheldon, A. (1993). Pickle fights: Gendered talk in preschool disputes. In D. Tannen (Ed.), *Gender and conversational interaction* (pp. 83–109). New York, Oxford: Oxford University Press. (First published in 1990)

Sheldon, A. (1997). Talking power, girls, gender enculturation and discourse. In R. Wodak (Ed.), *Gender and discourse* (pp. 225–244). Thousand Oaks, CA: Sage.

Showalter, E. (1977). *A literature of their own: British women novelists from Bronte to Lessing.* Princeton, NJ: Princeton University Press.

Sinclair, C. (1996). *NetChick: A smart girl guide to the wired world.* New York: Henry Holt.

Smith, D. E. (1997). Comment on Hekman's "Truth and Method: Feminist Standpoint Theory Revisited." *Signs, 22,* 392–397.

Smitherman, G. (1977). *Talkin and testifyin: The language of Black America.* Boston: Houghton Mifflin.

Spender, D. (1980). *Man made language.* Boston: Routledge & Kegan Paul.

Spender, D. (1985). *Man made language.* (2nd ed.). Boston: Routledge & Kegan Paul.

Spender, D. (1990). *Nattering on the Net: Women, power and cyberspace.* North Melbourne, Australia: Spinifex Press.

Spivak, G. (1987). *In other worlds: Essays in cultural poetics.* London: Methuen.

Spivak, G. C. (1988). Can the subaltern speak? In C. Nelson & L. Grossberg (Eds.), *Marxism and the interpretation of culture* (pp. 271–313). Urbana: University of Illinois Press.

Squire, E. (1997). The Oprah Winfrey Show. In C. Brunsdon, J. D'Acci, & S. Lynn (Eds.), *Feminist television criticism: A reader* (pp. 98–113). Oxford: Clarendon Press.

Stanley, J. (1977). Paradigmatic woman: The prostitute. In D. L. Shores & C. P. Hines (Eds.), *Papers in language variation* (pp. 303–321). Birmingham: University of Alabama Press. Retrieved February 18, 2005, from http://www.scriptorium.lib.duke.edu/wlm/prostitute/

Stanton, C. S. (1948). *Seneca Falls declaration.* Retrieved August 10, 2004, from http://www.ukans.edu/carrie/docs/texts/seneca.htm

Stone, A. R. (1991). The empire strikes back: A posttranssexual manifesto. In K. Straub & J. Epstein (Eds.), *Body guards: The cultural politics of gender ambiguity* (pp. 280–304). New York: Routledge.

Swann, J. (2003). Schooled language: Language and gender in educational settings. In J. Holmes & M. Meyerhoff (Eds.), *The handbook of language and gender.* Malden, MA; Oxford: Blackwell.

Talbot, M. M. (1998). *Language and gender. An introduction.* Cambridge, Oxford, Malden, MA: Polity Press, Blackwell.

Tannen, D. (1986). *That's not what I meant! How conversational style makes or brakes your relations with others.* New York: Ballantine.

Tannen, D. (1990). *You just don't understand: Women and men in conversation.* New York: Ballantine.

Tannen, D. (Ed.). (1993a). *Gender and conversational interaction.* New York, Oxford: Oxford University Press.

Tannen, D. (1993b). The relativity of linguistic strategies: Rethinking power and solidarity in gender and dominance. In D. Tannen (Ed.), *Gender and conversational interaction* (pp. 165–188). New York, Oxford: Oxford University Press.

ten Have, P. (1999). *Doing conversation analysis: A practical guide.* Thousand Oaks, CA: Sage.

Thorne, B. (1993). *Gender play: Girls and boys in school.* Buckingham, UK: Open University Press.

Turkle, S. (1995). *Life on the screen. Identity in the age of the Internet.* London: Weidenfeld & Nicholson.

van Dijk, T. (2001). Principles of discourse analysis. In M. Wetherell, S. Taylor, & S. J. Yates (Eds.), *Discourse theory and practice* (pp. 294–299). Thousand Oaks, CA: Sage.

van Langenhove, L., & Harré, R. (1999). Introducing positioning theory. In R. Harré & L. van Langenhove (Eds.), *Positioning theory* (pp. 14–31). Cambridge, MA: Blackwell.

Velásquez, M. D. G. (1995). Sometimes Spanish, sometimes English: Language use among rural New Mexican Chicanas. In K. Hall & M. Bucholtz (Eds.), *Gender articulated: Language and the socially constructed self* (pp. 421–446). New York, London: Routledge.

Walker, R. (1995). (Ed.). *To be real: Telling the truth and changing the face of feminism.* New York: Anchor Books.

Walter, N. (1998). *The new feminism.* London and New York: Virago.

Weiss, G., & Wodak, R. (2003). *Critical discourse analysis: Theory and interdisciplinarity.* London: Palgrave/Macmillan.

Werry, C. (1996). Linguistic and interactional features of Internet relay chat. In S. Herring (Ed.), *Computer-mediated communication: Linguistic, social and cross-cultural perspectives* (pp. 47–64). Amsterdam/Philadelphia: John Benjamins.

West, C. (1998). "Not just doctor's orders": Directive-response sequences in patients' visits to women and men physicians. In J. Coates (Ed.), *Language and gender: A reader* (pp. 396–412). Malden, MA; Oxford: Blackwell.

West, C., & Zimmerman, D. H. (1983). Small insults: A study of interruptions in cross-sex conversations between unacquainted persons. In B. Thorne & N. Henley (Eds.), *Language and sex: Difference and dominance* (pp. 102–117). Rowley, MA: Newbury House.

West, C., & Zimmerman, D. H. (1987, June). Doing gender. *Gender and Society,* pp. 127–151. (Reprinted in S. Fenstermaker & C. West, *Doing gender. Doing difference. Inequality, power, and institutional change,* New York, London: Routledge, 2002)

Westwood, R. (2001). Organizing silence. Appropriating the Other in the discourses of comparative management. In R. M. Westwood & S. Linstead (Eds.), *The language of organization* (pp. 241–281). Thousand Oaks, CA: Sage.

Westwood, R. M., & Linstead, S. (Eds.). (2001). *The language of organization.* Thousand Oaks, CA: Sage.

Wetherell, M. (2001). Themes in discourse research: The case of Diana. In M. Wetherell, S. Taylor, & S. J. Yates (Eds.), *Discourse theory and practice* (pp. 14–28). Thousand Oaks, CA: Sage.

Wetherell, M., Taylor, S., & Yates, S. J. (Eds.). (2001). *Discourse theory and practice: A reader.* Thousand Oaks, CA: Sage.

Wodak, R. (1996). *Disorders of discourse.* London, New York: Longman.

Wodak, R. (1997). (Ed.). *Gender and discourse.* Thousand Oaks, CA: Sage.

Wodak, R. (2003). Multiple identities: The roles of female parliamentarians in the EU parliament. In J. Holmes & M. Meyerhoff (Eds.), *The handbook of language and gender* (pp. 671–698). Oxford: Blackwell.

Wodak, R., & Meyer, M. (2001). (Eds.). *Methods of critical discourse analysis.* Thousand Oaks, CA: Sage.

Wood, J. (1994). *Gendered lives: Communication, gender, and culture.* Belmont, CA: Wadsworth.

Wood, J. (1999). *Gendered lives: Communication, gender, and culture* (3rd ed.). Belmont, CA: Wadsworth.

Yuval-Davis, N. (1997). *Gender and nation.* Thousand Oaks, CA: Sage.

Zwicky, A. M. (1997). Two lavender issues for linguistics. In A. Livia & K. Hall (Eds.), *Queerly phrased. Language, gender, and sexuality* (pp. 21–34). New York, Oxford: Oxford University Press.

# Index

# About the Authors

**Charlotte Kr\u00f8l\u00f8kke** (PhD, University of Minnesota, Minneapolis; MA, University of North Dakota, Grand Forks; BA, University of Southern Denmark) is Assistant Professor at the Center for Cultural Studies, Institute of Literature, Culture, and Media at the University of Southern Denmark. She has worked especially within the fields of computer-mediated communication and third-wave feminist rhetoric on the Internet. She is a member of U.S. and Danish gender and communication associations and a board member of the National Danish Gender Studies Library in Copenhagen, Denmark.

**Anne Scott S\u00f8rensen** (PhD, University of Southern Denmark; MA, Aarhus University; BA, Royal School of Library & Information Science) is Associate Professor and head of the Center for Cultural Studies, Institute of Literature, Culture, and Media at the University of Southern Denmark. She has written extensively on gendered speech communities, from the salons in Europe in the 18th to 20th centuries to the online communities of young people in the 21st century. She is head of the Danish Network for Cultural Studies and a board member of the international Association of Cultural Studies (ACS).